INVISIBLE EMPIRES

INVISIBLE EMPIRES

*Multinational Companies
and the Modern World*

BY

LOUIS TURNER

HARCOURT BRACE JOVANOVICH, INC., NEW YORK

First American edition 1971

ISBN 0-15-145301-2

Library of Congress Catalog Card Number: 79-134582

Printed in the United States of America

CONTENTS

PREFACE

This book is for the knowledgeable layman who wants to know about world problems created by a new kind of firm, the multinational. Wherever possible, I have tried not only to argue points in the abstract, but also to illustrate them so that readers not actively concerned with management can get a more concrete idea of the important issues being raised.

Though multinational companies will probably seem in retrospect one of the most important institutional developments of the mid-twentieth century, most writing on the subject has been inadequate. Some is dry and academic; some merely repeats uncritically everything the author has been told by top businessmen; some is too uninformed to contain balanced judgments, though written by those with social consciences. This book is an attempt both to describe the activities of multinational firms and also to analyse the social and political problems they present.

The reader can deduce from the book itself exactly what my political priorities are. Politically, I am moderately left of centre. I believe that private companies have an important role to play in our society, but I also believe that there should be much greater public scrutiny of the decisions they are making. When such scrutiny shows that firms are behaving in an anti-social manner (say, by not spending enough on pollution control, or by failing to invest in depressed regions), then I think governments should pressure them into modifying this behaviour. Basically, this book assumes that companies are important enough to consider as political animals.

This study originated as a pamphlet for the Fabian Society. But the bulk of the work was done in the Department of Sociology at Salford University, which generously granted me the freedom necessary to develop this project. Three people, in

vii

particular, were responsible for this book appearing: Mike Rose showed the way and encouraged me; Stuart Reilly made me think deeply about filing systems; Michael Sissons, my agent, sold it. I am grateful to all three.

The facts in this book have come mainly from printed sources, primarily the *Financial Times*, the *Economist*, *Management Today*, *Fortune*, the *Sunday Times*, *Sunday Telegraph*, the *Observer*, *Business Week*, *Business International* and *Time*. Information gleaned here was balanced by interviews with a number of businessmen, trade-unionists, and a few civil servants. As the text probably shows, I found particularly stimulating my visits to IBM, the International Chemical Workers Federation, the International Chamber of Commerce, and Fiat.

Apart from these sources, ideas came mainly from David Froggatt, who dissected an early draft and showed me its weaknesses. Peter Hovell clarified my thinking about the historical development of multinational companies. A different kind of help came from Kevin Connolly, who insistently pushed muckraking articles on to me—some of which proved highly illuminating.

Most of the typing was done by Anne Ellis, with some last-minute assistance from Barbara Evans, Maureen Knapkin and Lynda Green.

This book was written fast, so I was therefore tempted to become anti-social and hermit-like. A number of people tried to distract and civilise me. My thanks to: the other denizens of the research room, Pat Hanlon, Roger Lister, Bill Jones, for tolerating the confusion; the girls from Acton Square, Jenny, Sue, Fran and Ray for tea and general sympathy; John Pilgrim, through whom I got much vicarious amusement; and Roz. Finally, my thanks to Paul Neville who acted as research assistant and compiled the index; without his help, this book could not have been finished on time and would have suffered in a number of ways.

December 1969.

CHAPTER I

Introduction

Long before the creation of the Harvard Business School, popes and emperors ran organisations as international as General Motors. In the 1760's, such wide-reaching companies as the East India Company or the Massachusetts Bay Colony were licensed by the British crown to make profits. The nineteenth century saw international companies formed to exploit Central America's banana republics or Africa's copper belt. And again, in the early parts of this century, American companies like National Cash Register, Eastman Kodak, Singer, Coca-Cola, Quaker Oats, and Woolworth were all active outside the United States. If one drives through small villages in Europe it is possible to find metal signs which have been advertising Singer sewing machines for forty years or more.

Granting all these precedents, however, it is still true that the multinational corporation seeking profits world-wide has been largely a mid-twentieth-century development. This book will discuss the sophisticated successors of so many early ventures, and the ways in which they operate in developed and underdeveloped economies. It will define the multinational company, discuss its organisation and motivation, and finally indicate its impact on the politics and culture of industrial nations.

The best known attack on the American-owned international companies is Jean-Jacques Servan-Schreiber's *The American Challenge* (1968), but one should state initially that more nations than the United States have spawned such organizations. It has sometimes been suggested that *Le Défi Américain* is more a case of *Les Statistiques Américaines*, since U.S. official statistics and business journalism are sources of information which have no compare in Europe. Despite this, figures for Europe which are available show that European firms have invested as large a percentage of their countries' Gross National Products outside their home countries as American firms. The two Anglo-Dutch firms, Royal Dutch-Shell and Unilever, have been international from their beginnings in both the scope of their activities and in their management. Other internationally oriented European firms would include Saint-Gobain (French: glass and chemicals), Volkswagen (German: automobiles), Ericsson (Swedish: electronics), Brown Boveri (Swiss: electrical engineering), Olivetti (Italian: office machinery, small computers, etc.), A.K.U. (Dutch: fibres and chemicals), Philips Lamps n.v. (Dutch: electrical and electronic goods), Hoffman-La Roche (Swiss: pharmaceuticals), British American Tobacco (British: tobacco), and Imperial Chemical Industries (British: chemicals). In fact, few American firms are likely to match the internationality of Nestlé, the Swiss food and confectionery firm: 97·5% of its sales are made outside Switzerland. When considering the widespread fear of American firms like Du Pont, Ford or International Business Machines (I.B.M.), one must also remember that such an American industry as oil is worried by the part-British-government-owned British Petroleum. At the time of this writing, British Petroleum was sitting on territory in Alaska whose proved reserves of oil roughly equal the total historical output of the Texas oil fields, up to now, the United States' chief source of domestic oil.

What is a multinational company?

As the number of companies with an international organisation grew, jargon was developed for describing them. If you follow Professor Richard Robinson,[1] you will describe firms as inter-, multi-, trans-, and supranational. Professor Perlmutter[2] prefers to talk in terms of firms being ethnocentric, polycentric or geocentric. Within this book, however, we will use the term *multinational* to mean any firm which has a number of directly controlled operations in different countries and which tends towards a global perspective ('geocentric', if we used Professor Perlmutter's terms).

[1] Robinson, Richard D. *International Management.* Holt, Rinehart & Winston, New York/London, 1967.
[2] Perlmutter, H. V. 'L'Entreprise Internationale—trois conceptions.' *Revue économique et sociale*, Vol. 23, No. 2, May 1965, pp. 151–65.

Historically, most firms first moved outside their home markets by exporting, or by arranging licensing agreements with foreign firms. Because of tariff barriers and transport costs, some foreign markets were available only if the product were manufactured within the country in which it was to be sold. This arrangement might at first work through a joint venture in which the expanding firm would link forces with another established firm in the export market. If the market was small, the manufacturing operation might consist only of assembling parts manufactured in another country. But if the market expanded, a firm might decide to increase profits by manufacturing specific variants of its product to meet the different needs of the foreigners. At this point, a firm would find itself with coordination problems, since the foreign-based subsidiary might well demand a greater say in deciding what should be manufactured or sold in its own market. The company headquarters would then have to decide how to allocate resources between the foreign subsidiary and the parent company. Ideally, at this point the parent company's headquarters become so internationalised that its decisions are global in vision, in spite of the company's historical ties to a specific nation.

The basic trends

We shall argue in this book that the typical transaction in international commerce is no longer simply exporting or importing. Instead, it is increasingly the creation of manufacturing facilities owned by multinational companies. Moreover, the nature of these companies is changing. In the past they were typically oil or mining companies. Today they are firms manufacturing products like cars, computers and other machinery. Consequently such firms are less dependent on underdeveloped nations and more involved with the most advanced world markets such as Canada, Europe, the United States. In size, these companies rival small-to-medium national economies; moreover, their heavy involvement in science-based industries gives them high political importance. Finally, these companies are controlled by managers increasingly sophisticated at running world-wide operations which maximise the returns to the whole firm.

Servan-Schreiber was not wholly misleading when he proclaimed "In fifteen years the third industrial power, after the United States and the U.S.S.R., could well be not Europe but American industry in Europe."[1] One gains some idea of this statement's truth from figures produced by Mr Judd Polk for the U.S. Council of the International Chamber of Commerce. In 1966, the total book value of U.S. direct foreign investment was $55 billion. Mr Polk estimated that for every dollar thus invested in foreign plants, the resultant annual foreign-based output was roughly double in value. He thus suggests that the foreign-based subsidiaries of U.S. corporations produced goods worth about $120 billion in 1966—a sum slightly larger than the Gross National Products of such nations as West Germany and Japan, which are struggling for the position of third largest industrialised nation. Similarly, calculating the direct investment coming from the rest of the world (estimated at $35 billion in 1966) one estimates conservatively that the value of output resulting from such direct foreign investment was probably around $180–200 billion. Since total exports of the 10 leading capital exporting countries were only $130 billion in 1967, then one can see that exports are considerably less important than the output from the foreign subsidiaries of multinational companies.

A good example of what has been happening appears in the First National City Bank's Monthly Economic Letter of June 1969. This statement showed that both in the machinery and the automobile fields, during the years 1960–65, the sale of U.S. subsidiaries abroad expanded twice as fast as did exports by their U.S. parents. Thus, to take the automobile figures, in 1960 sales by U.S. subsidiaries abroad were running at three times the value of U.S. exports in this field; by 1965, this proportion had risen to three and a half ($10·8 billion to $3 billion respectively).

Table 1 shows two important developments of multinational companies. First, there has been a distinct increase in the foreign activity of manufacturing firms, in contrast to a more gradual increase in the activities of traditional multinational companies within the petroleum industry. Secondly, there has been a noticeable switch away from Latin America as a target for

[1] Servan-Schreiber, Jean-Jacques. *The American Challenge.* Hamish Hamilton, London, 1968, p. 17.

4

TABLE I

Total book value of U.S. foreign direct investment by area and industrial grouping ($ billions)

	1929	1946	1957	1967
Areas				
Canada	2·0	2·5	8·6	18·0
Latin America	3·5	3·1	8·1	10·2
Europe	1·4	1·0	4·1	17·9
Other	0·6	0·6	4·4	13·2
Industry				
Manufacturing	1·8	2·4	8·0	24·1
Petroleum	1·1	1·4	9·0	17·4
Mining and smelting	1·2	0·8	2·4	4·8
Other	3·4	2·6	5·8	13·0
Total	7·5	7·2	25·2	59·3

Source: U.S. Department of Commerce. *Survey of Current Business.*

investment, toward Canada and, notably, toward Europe. These movements have been particularly marked in the last ten years, when U.S. investment in Europe quadrupled, while not quite doubling in Canada, and scarcely growing at all in Latin America. Similarly, when looking at specific industries, the foreign investment in manufacturing industries has trebled during this time, while the petroleum industry did not quite double its foreign-controlled assets. Mining and smelting, despite doubling in size, remain relatively unimportant.

Above all, these figures show a very real change in the nature of multinational companies. The typical multinational company in the past was a primary producer (petroleum, bananas, coffee, meat, cocoa, etc.) which had to invest abroad because that was the source of its basic products. These were multi-national because their supplies and markets were in different nations; they were thus forced to coordinate production, markets and transport on an international basis. In contrast, the more recent multinationals are relatively 'foot-loose', that is, less tied to any particular location for investment. The upsurge of investment in Europe and, to a lesser extent, in Canada is a result of such companies' investing where they expect the biggest market growth. The upsurge into Europe in particular suggests that the larger multinational companies have over the last ten years felt considerable confidence in investing in manufacturing facilities which must be controlled across a 3,000-mile-wide ocean.

A number of technological advances have aided the development of organisations capable of such global coordination. The American tycoon who visited Europe in 1920 risked jeopardising his company or his position. His five or six day crossing by ship, followed by rail or road trips to towns whose postal, wireless or telephonic links with America were primitive, meant that for practical purposes he was out of communication with his firm. One early Hollywood immigrant tycoon, for instance, rashly made a sentimental trip back to his fatherland in Europe leaving behind an ambitious personal assistant. This assistant, realising he had two or three months during which the tycoon would be out of contact with the studio, took over total control and, since there were no written instructions to the contrary, instituted a complete revolution in company policy. Within the three months he had changed the organization so much that his returning boss had to retire to the sidelines since his 'assistant' was now the only person knowing what was going on.

Since then, personal communications have been revolutionised through improvements in the international telephone service, the institution of airmail and the growth of communications satellites allowing intercontinental television communication. Passenger aircraft help managers to move around the globe, so that trips that once took weeks can now often be made in a day. To show how important such improvements in communications technology are, Warren J. Keegan (1968) surveyed 13 multinationals and found that the average travel budget of their international executives (that is area directors, their deputies and key executives) came to $10,000 per annum; one middle manager had run up a travel bill of $25,000 in a year.[1]

[1] Keegan, Warren J. 'Acquisition of global business information.' *Columbia Journal of World Business*, Vol. 3, No. 2, Mar.-April 1968, pp. 35–41.

Moreover, the development of increasingly efficient freight services means that the flow of goods on a world-wide basis has become easier. For small, relatively valuable goods, the advent of air freight has allowed the integration of manufacturing plants which are often in different countries. In particular, air freight allows real savings by sometimes making it more economical to maintain one major centre for spare parts, flying those spares to other countries whenever they are required. On the ground, containerisation has revolutionised the economics of trains, ships and lorries by cutting down the handling costs involved when goods change from one mode of transport to another. Thus Ford in Europe sends a daily supply of components by containerised trains from Britain to their plant in Belgium for assembly.

The development of computers also aided the organisation of world-wide operations. The multinational oil companies like Shell or Standard Oil (New Jersey) have computerised models of their entire world operations allowing them not only to optimise the movements of their tanker fleets, but also to tackle more difficult tasks such as calculating the impact that a new source of crude oil will have on their operations, given its peculiar chemical properties. One important recent development is the practice of connecting computers directly, even across oceans. I.B.M., for instance, is slowly phasing out the chore of flying computer tapes from one location to another.

Which nations are most affected?

A glance at Table 2 shows that direct American investment is strongest in Canada, the United Kingdom, West Germany, Australia and France—in that order. Without doubt, the Canadian economy is most dominated by it; in 1960 the U.S. owned 43% of the capital of Canadian industry and in 1968, 60% of Canadian mining and manufacturing were in the hands of foreign-controlled companies. Australia is the next most dominated of the advanced economies, with somewhat over 25% of her company assets under foreign control. At the latest count, U.S. firms were supplying 10% of the output of British factories and 17·5% of Britain's visible exports. For Germany the 1966 equivalent figures are 4% and 5%.

7

TABLE 2

U.S. direct investment abroad, 1967. Selected nations.
Value of assets ($ millions)

European Economic Community		Other European Nations		Others	
Benelux	856	Denmark	273	Australia	2,354
France	1,904	Norway	183	Canada	18,069
W. Germany	3,487	Spain	480	Japan	868
Italy	1,242	Sweden	438	S. Africa	667
Netherlands	917	Switzerland	1,332		
		U.K.	6,101		
		Others	669		
Total	8,405	Total	9,477		

SOURCE: U.S. Department of Commerce. *Survey of Current Business*, October 1968.

TABLE 3

Proportion of foreign affiliates of U.S. firms which made no purchase of U.S. exports for further assembly in 1965
(Sample of 330 U.S. firms with foreign affiliates)

Country/Region	All Industries	Manufacturing Industries
Canada	51·9%	33·7%
United Kingdom	60·5%	43·8%
Japan/Australia/South Africa	61·9%	49·1%
European Economic Community	70·2%	59·3%
Less Developed Nations (outside Europe and Western Hemisphere)	83·5%	60·0%
Other Western Hemisphere	69·4%	65·4%
Other Europe	81·3%	70·9%

SOURCE: Marie Bradshaw. 'U.S. exports to foreign affiliates of U.S. firms.' *Survey of Current Business*, May 1969.

What is even more interesting is that the countries which have received most U.S. investment tend to attract U.S. subsidiaries which maintain particularly close links with the U.S. economy. Table 3 demonstrates the degree to which U.S. affiliates were independent of U.S. exports, and shows that such firms in Canada, the United Kingdom, Japan, Australia and South Africa are particularly dependent on such exports. This is an interesting fact: it suggests that the uneasiness about overdependence on U.S. firms which has recently gripped many of these nations may well be justified.

The technological gap

The unease felt by many in the countries receptive to American investment is increased because the American firms they must deal with are often those research-based, capital-intensive industries linked to defence interests. And it is precisely these industries which promise to be the growth area of the future. There is a feeling that American firms lead such industries because of the sheer size of the marketing and research effort they can sustain. The bulk of this investment has gone into industries producing cars, computers (overwhelmingly), pharmaceuticals, tractors, microelectronics, chemicals and petroleum. In 1968 General Motors, Ford and Chrysler controlled 30% of the European car market; similarly American firms control 25–30% of the petroleum market in the U.K. and the Common Market. With computers, the situation is particularly clear: one firm, I.B.M., manufactures around 65% of all the computers sold in the non-communist world; in only two non-communist countries, Britain and Japan, does I.B.M. have less than 50% of the market; the largest non-American computer firm, International Computers Ltd., has between 1 and 2% of the world market. The American lead is almost as serious in crucial fields such as microelectronics and scientific instruments. One writer, D. N. Chorafas in *The Knowledge Revolution*, estimates that 75% of Europe's science-based industries may be U.S. owned within 10 years.

It is tempting to blame the technological gap on the fact that European and Japanese firms are smaller than their U.S. competitors. In fact, the situation is considerably more complex. The Organisation for Economic Co-operation and Development

(O.E.C.D.) has sponsored a number of studies in depth of various industrial areas with such a gap, notably semi-conductors, electronic components, scientific instruments and computers.

Paradoxically they suggest that Europe's chief failing is its inability to stimulate the formation of small, highly techno-logical companies which 'spin-off' from existing academic or industrial laboratories. In semi-conductors, for instance, the present 'giants', Texas Instruments and Fairchild Semi-conductors, started as small companies formed by groups of scientists and engineers who pooled their expert knowledge of the relevant technologies. In scientific instruments, a field where commercial success may depend on having a range of products, not one of which is more than $2\frac{1}{2}$ years old, the U.S. boasts a number of very small firms. Thus only 13% of the 309 U.S. firms in this field employ over 100 people, while 62% of the U.K's 87 firms and 64% of Japan's 131 firms do so. This finding contradicts the conventional wisdom which insists that only large firms can survive in such research-based industries.

These studies suggest that the success of the U.S. in fostering these small, highly vigorous companies is due to several factors. First, the site of many of these Boston and San Francisco com-panies suggests that they locate near excellent university establishments. Boston, for instance, boasts of the famous Route 128 complex, a cluster of small firms set up on a Boston ring-road by entrepreneurs who have 'spun-off' from the Massa-chusetts Institute of Technology and the surrounding defence-oriented electronics firms. This process is helped by the fact that American universities do a relatively large amount of applied research for important government departments. Scientists working in such projects will have a very clear market orientation. Secondly, once established, they apparently find it much easier than their European equivalents to raise the risk finance for the initial investment and, just as important, for the rapid expansion of production facilities needed when their products are successful. Banks in Europe tend to be more cautious than their American counterparts; and only fairly recently have bodies been set up in Europe to back small science-based firms. Scientific Enterprises Associates, for example, was created for the purpose in 1969, with the backing of Fiat's Signor Agnelli, Bosch's Herr Merkle and French financier M. Paluel-Marmont.

Ultimately, however, much of the lead that American firms have in advanced technologies can be traced to the large and adventurous U.S. consumer market—(though others would put more emphasis on U.S. defence spending). In the field of electronics, the large colour television market has been an important stimulus while computer designs have benefited from the sophisticated services U.S. banks offer their clients. The important thing about this affluent consumer market is that any world-wide demand for a specific product will normally first appear in the U.S. Thus American firms can capitalise on their American experience when the market becomes international. Not surprisingly, when European competitors try to reinvent processes which the Americans have already mastered, they find themselves handicapped. This situation is particularly noticeable in fields like microelectronics. Here firms like Texas Instruments, Fairchild, or Motorola maintain their lead both through the economies of scale made possible by the size of the U.S. market and through their heavy expenditure in research.

Not all American world-beaters are like Texas Instruments. Many dominate strategic industries basically through their size, marketing prowess and managerial skill. I.B.M., for instance, furnishes a marketing success story, not one of technological leadership. Starting from a dominant position in the punched card market, the firm was reluctant to tackle the new computer technology which would render its existing products obsolete. Once having decided that computers were a logical addition to their product range, however, they went into the field with a vengeance, selling extremely hard to their existing business-equipment customers whose needs they have been extremely adept at satisfying. They achieved this while selling products not as technologically advanced as the models of several competitors. Thus their System/360 range of computers did not completely adopt the integrated circuits which were the most advanced form of electronics at the time the range was announced in 1964. Moreover, attempts to produce the largest capacity computers have been troubled with models being withdrawn, allowing Control Data Corporation to gain a useful foothold at this end of the market. Again, in developing

11

the 'software' for System/360 models, the firm got into difficulties and delayed deliveries. Despite this, I.B.M. has such a hold over its clients, and knows the market so well, that it is extremely difficult for competitors to make significant inroads, even with superior products.

Basically, the U.S. environment produces two types of firm: the small, fast-moving unit which produces the basic technological breakthroughs in the research-based industries; and the large, financially strong multinationals, whose resources enable them to exploit these developments on the world market. National-based competitors can do little but try and compete against a limited part of their range.

Nevertheless, much persuasive opinion holds that the 'gap' is finally a managerial one. After all, the American success in the European car market owes little to technological innovations. In fact, it is the Europeans who have experimented with front-wheel drive, unconventional suspension systems, radial tyres, etc. Yet, it is the American manufacturers who have seemed the most dynamic. Ford's successes, the Cortina and the Capri, have been conventionally engineered products made for a specific sector of the market which they have successfully filled. They have been more successful in identifying market opportunities and producing models to meet them which are convenient to manufacture and can sell at the desired price. In other words, the American firms have, in the past, been better managed, as one would expect of firms in a nation which has put so much emphasis on management education. The consultant, John Diebold, cites a similar case of British firms who are producing numerically-controlled machine tools which were capable of performing with extreme precision. Their American competitor observed that the market was perfectly happy accepting considerably larger tolerances. It therefore produced a simpler and considerably cheaper product which the customers actually bought. This suggests that good management does not necessarily produce technologically perfect products if the market does not want them.

In a later chapter, we will show first that not all U.S. firms are invincible, and second, that the gap between European and American management standards is closing. With one possible exception in Scotland, there is as yet no sign of a European

'Route 128' complex of small trail-blazing technologically oriented firms. Until one appears, there is good ground for assuming that the most important commercially viable technical breakthroughs will be made in the United States; but where U.S. power is based primarily on management which is considerably better than that of the non-American competition (cars, tractors, aerospace, computers even), then one would expect the gap to close.

CHAPTER II

Multinationals Illustrated

Most international institutions like the United Nations or the various common markets are still in their formative stages and are slow to react. The multinational company stands out as the one institution powerful enough to make speedy and effective, world-wide decisions. With increasing ease, company headquarters coordinate and control the decisions of subsidiaries all round the globe. But this has not always been the case.

In the early days, an ambitious firm might well set up subsidiaries abroad, but distances required each subordinate plant to operate more or less independently. Mars Inc., for example, was a successful American manufacturer of Milky Way candy bars until its founder declared to his Yale-educated son in 1932, "This company isn't big enough for both of us. Go to some other country and start your own business."[1] Frank Mars, the father, then sent his son Forrest abroad with $50,000 and the foreign rights to Milky Way and other Mars' bars. Settling in Britain, Forrest Mars created Mars Ltd., which soon became one of the foremost confectionery firms. Diversifying into petfoods with a firm, Petfoods Ltd., which now has 50% of the British market, Forrest was successful enough to succeed, in 1964, in taking over the American company after the death of his father. The story is similar in the case of Hoover. In Britain, the subsidiary made 'Hoover' synonymous with vacuum cleaners, while the American parent led a fairly undistinguished life in the States. The result was considerable tension when the parent company tried to reassert its authority in the 1950's.

Around this time the upsurge of American investment interest in Europe began. Partly U.S. firms were attracted by the booming European market and the chances offered by

[1] Quoted by *Fortune*: May 1967.

European economic integration; partly they were forced to expand abroad because tough U.S. anti-trust laws specifically forbade international cartels and market-sharing agreements. Thus safe links with European competitors were impossible. In the case of computers, I.B.M's hard-pressed competitors were forced into Europe in order to survive at all, since their chances of surviving on the 15–30% of the U.S. market not held by I.B.M. were considered slim. Finally, modern communications technology now made it possible for company headquarters to keep a meaningful degree of control over its overseas subsidiaries. It also became obvious, however, that for a number of industries, national markets were no longer large enough to provide the optimum economies of scale. But if a number of national markets were treated as one unit, then the firm's activities could be integrated into one profitable operation.

The integration of production

In its simplest form, product integration involves a policy of manufacturing particular units of a product range in different nations, while selling the complete range to a number of national markets. Thus, a company might make trucks in one nation, passenger cars in another. This is basically what General Motors has done in deciding that its British subsidiary, Vauxhall, should produce all General Motors' trucks outside America, while its German subsidiary, Opel, should export passenger cars. A similar strategy has been evolved by the U.S. automakers in the wake of the U.S.-Canadian automotive agreement which eliminated all tariffs on cars and parts shipped across their common border. Previously there had been a 17½% import duty levied on U.S. cars being shipped to Canada. Demand in Canada was enough to justify manufacturing a number of basic models in Canada but the market was not large enough to make it a particularly economic proposition. Since the pact, there has been an increasing amount of specialisation. Chrysler previously turned out relatively small numbers of 6 different models in its Ontario plant; now it uses the same plant to manufacture just two models, the Dodge Polara and the Plymouth Fury. By selling these two models both in Canada and the United States, they are able to achieve the economies of scale which come from extended production runs. Ford and General Motors have followed similar policies. The models they have stopped making in Canada they now supply from the U.S. Thus both the models manufactured in Canada and those made in the States are sold throughout the two nations.

Some industries have taken this principle of production specialisation even further, integrating components on an international basis. In 1966, the managing director of Massey-Ferguson Holdings Ltd. told a British audience how his firm, producing tractors and earthmoving equipment, integrated its production:

'By this we mean having interchangeability of product and common design everywhere as far as possible, so that components can be produced from a high volume centre to be exported to an overseas factory making the same finished machines. . . . We can now, for example, take a transmission and an engine from England, a rear axle from France, sheet metal parts and other components from Detroit, and assemble tractors for the domestic market. Or we can vary the sourcing of components as cost or currency dictate.'

He illustrated this last point with a case in which India was short of sterling, which made it difficult to export components from their British plant. They were still able to supply their Indian subsidiary by switching to a supply of the same components made by their licensees in Yugoslavia. Similarly, Ford has three main tractor plants, one in Britain, one in Belgium, one near Detroit. The Belgian plant makes all the transmissions for the three plants, Britain produces all the hydraulics and engines, while the Detroit plant makes their selecto-speed gear system.

When firms start coordinating their activities on this sort of scale, they are obviously becoming special institutions. The example of Ford (U.K.) shows how this happens. Up until the early 1960's, Ford owned 100% of a German subsidiary and 55% of a British one. Both companies acted independently, producing distinct ranges of trucks and cars for their respective home markets. But tensions arose in British Ford over matters like deciding which subsidiary was to service certain orders. Ford obviously got the biggest profit from the German operation, while the British shareholders wanted their share. As a result, Ford bought out the British share, taking 100% control. They have now taken this control a stage further by producing models which are designed to be standard for the whole of Europe. Ford's Transit range of vans and its European version of the Mustang, the Capri, have both been designed to be produced as identical models in both Britain and Germany. As long as tariff barriers exist between the two countries, this is as far as they can go. But should Britain enter the European Economic Community, then one would expect Ford to follow the policy they have followed in Canada: the British plant would produce certain models for the whole of Europe, while the German and Belgian plants would produce the rest.

It is important not to overestimate the extent of this integration. Mostly, it will be confined to industries in which the end product is standardised over a wide geographical area. The most quoted examples come from industries like office machinery, and agricultural or earthmoving equipment. The automobile market is less standardised, being closer to the consumer. For instance, whereas the European, Japanese or American farmers will be satisfied with tractors which are basically similar, there is much less scope for integrating the manufacture of passenger cars for the U.S. consumers and the rest of the world, since the type of car needed in the United States is basically unmarketable elsewhere because of its size. The major area for product integration lies in the major U.S. auto firms which supply some of the demand for small cars from their European subsidiaries. Thus General Motors through its Opel subsidiary in Germany is the third largest importer of cars into the U.S., coming behind Volkswagen and Toyota. Ford similarly imports cars from its British subsidiary into the States, being the ninth largest importer.

Such integration is, however, a relatively minor activity of the U.S. major auto manufacturers, simply because the markets across the world are far from identical. For the auto makers, their best chance of international integration of production comes from continents like Europe where the national markets for autos are reasonably similar. Even so, a car like Ford's Capri only uses around $35 worth of English components when assembled in Germany, despite the fact that Ford assembles the

17

car in both countries. Indicating the degree to which such integration has gone, the strike by British unions against Ford in the early part of 1969 led to 2,000 workers in Ford's Belgian plants being laid off after one week, when their plant ran short of components. It is not surprising that Ford's German subsidiary is now making itself independent of parts made by its British counterpart, thus negating the whole principle of component integration. In practice, therefore, Ford is if anything moving away from such integration, though it now uses common designs for its European subsidiaries. This means, of course, the future will eventually see some form of integration—either of components, or of the production in one country of models for the whole of Europe.

There is a tendency to see short-sightedly only car or tractor manufacturers who can switch components around the world if they so choose. This kind of operation is possible only where the final product is reasonably standardised. The closer one must deal with individual tastes, the more market variations have to be taken into account. But despite this fact, a firm supplying consumer goods to a wide number of different markets may think as much in global terms as any tractor firm. For instance, the Dutch firm, Philips n.v., makes transistor radios and simple television sets for underdeveloped nations. It therefore has to adjust its subsidiary factories to the economic scale, the supply ratio of labour to capital, and the skill level of each country. To help, it runs a pilot plant in Utrecht which trains both the Europeans and the developing countries' nationals who will be running any new factory. This plant is always experimenting with ways of adjusting industrial processes to people who may be industrially inexperienced. For instance, they have developed techniques for keeping paperwork and administration to a minimum; they have used pictorial means of instruction for countries where illiteracy is still a problem. To make the production process simpler, they use a domestic iron as a heater for coil and soldering processes; similarly, ordinary sewing machine motors provide the power for certain processes. Using the experience gained in this pilot plant, the managers of the new unit are able to go out to less-industrialised nations and start up factories from scratch. Thus, in 1964, a complete plant designed by the Utrecht section was installed in the Congo in a single week. Four days later, it was in production, and by the end of the month it had turned out 1,000 radios. In achieving this sort of flexibility, Philips' thinks as globally as any other multinational.

As an executive from International Harvester puts it, "When you have a joint venture in Turkey with engines from Germany, chassis from the U.S. together with local sources of components, you just have to be centralised." In this book, we will consider the implications this centralisation of decision-making has for the nation-state.

I.B.M.—A case study

A brief case study of I.B.M. will dramatise the issues. This company, the sixth largest in the world, is only one of a number of American-owned multinationals. Outside the United States it has 17 plants in 13 nations, which is not a particularly large number for companies in this league. The major multinational oil companies often have production facilities in at least forty countries, while Ford and General Motors each have manufacturing facilities in 20 nations. The integration that I.B.M. has achieved in its manufacturing and research facilities, however, is a model for other multinationals.

I.B.M.'s physical assets are worth around 7 billion dollars. At its peak, it has been valued by Wall Street at 40 billion dollars, roughly double the Gross National Product of nations like Sweden, the Netherlands, Belgium or Spain. It employs directly about 250,000 people round the globe, and controls roughly 65% of the computer market in the non-communist world. Moreover, this market is expanding in most parts of the world at a rate of at least 20% per annum, and there is no sign as yet of slowing. Rumour has it that light-hearted executive projections of I.B.M.'s likely growth by the year 2000 suggested that the company's turnover would equal that of all other industrial combines put together. This is not impossible, since the current largest firm in the world, General Motors, is in an industry which is virtually static; and petroleum has a fairly modest growth rate. I.B.M. is sixth largest in the world despite the fact that the computer market outside the U.S. is less than half the size of the American market. This fact, however, gives some idea of the size of the U.S. market for advanced industrial products, and also of how much potential market there will be when the rest of the world catches up with the States.

Interestingly, throughout the 1960's, I.B.M. became more centralised. Historically, the firm has had reasonably strong international involvement. Directly owned subsidiaries began manufacturing in Canada and Germany in 1924, France in 1925, Brazil in 1931, and in Italy in 1934. After 1945, the internationalist leanings of Thomas Watson Sr. ('World peace through world trade') led to renewed interest in the firm's direct manufacturing operations outside the Americas. In 1949, an international division, World Trade Corporation, was set up to supervise this expansion. They saw the potential world market ready for electric typewriters, which were then manufactured in Britain; but, amongst other things, they realised that supplying the world from one nation was dangerous, should national governments decide to protect themselves. They therefore developed the 'interchange' plan, whereby the manufacture was divided among nine nations, each one making certain parts. They thus reduced the risk of becoming too dependent on one country, and earned good will from nations in which they had manufacturing plants. This has basically remained their policy ever since, though they have added to it a fairly explicit policy of trying to balance their import-export transactions within each nation. Thus where a major market develops, they try to open a plant of some sort to compensate for this outflow of funds from that country.

Historically, the World Trade Corporation was given a lot of freedom. For a while in the late 1950's and early 1960's, it tried to develop computers independently. It did in fact produce some viable models. The British research laboratories developed a computer called SCAMP which performed well but was rejected because it was not compatible with the existing I.B.M. range. I.B.M. headquarters, always conscious of marketing realities, saw considerable market advantages to be gained from producing a compatible range of computers which would allow customers to move up from one model to another, or even to have a number of I.B.M. computers of different sizes. Therefore, in the mid-1960's they produced a complete new range of third generation computers, the System/360, which used a large proportion of microcircuits and made obsolete the former transistor-based models. What was new about this operation was the simultaneous production of a complete range of computers which would be standard for the whole world. The investment needed for this was vast, running to $4·5 billion dollars between April 1964 and April 1967—more than double what it cost the U.S. Government to develop the Atom Bomb before Hiroshima.

The System/360 marked the end of the era in which I.B.M.'s World Trade Corporation was free to try and produce models to suit different national markets. In practice the company had concluded that a good computer in one part of the world would sell equally well in any other part of the world. Although the design of most of the 6 models was done in America, one model, model 40, was designed at Hursley in the United Kingdom. To facilitate this work, special transatlantic lines were used to link company headquarters with the British and German laboratories. This was a trying time for some of the research laboratories which had grown used to a considerable amount of independence. There was, for instance, the San Jose laboratory which refused to stop working on one aspect of the System/360 range where it was in competition with the German laboratory. It had to be broken up to some extent. The company now gives each of its laboratories round the world the responsibility for some aspect of research or development. The System manager has a planning and coordinating role toward research activities taking place in three or four I.B.M. laboratories round the world. Once a project becomes marketable, then he is responsible for seeing the product into production normally in two locations, one in the U.S. and one outside. He is also responsible for keeping the product updated technologically while it is on the market. This may involve changing production techniques in the two factories.

An example of the process at work comes from the 360/40 model developed in the British laboratories. Although the computer was basically developed in Britain, it was to be manufactured in France and in Poughkeepsie, New York. This involved transferring a number of production engineers from France and the U.S. to the British laboratories for 12–18 months, so that development would take production needs into account.

21

To say that the final model was manufactured in France, however, is to be misleading: its memory was manufactured in Scotland; its solid logic components near Paris; and its boxes and peripheral equipment came from the Netherlands, Sweden and Italy.

A further example of the centralisation necessary to keep I.B.M. running is the fact that all orders emanating from outside the U.S. are given to one centre, again in Britain. In the past, the marketing centre, say in Japan, would pass on orders to the plant which had been given prime responsibility for a given computer. This plant would then break the order down into its elements such as central processors, memory, peripherals, etc. and would distribute these among the appropriate plants elsewhere. If a customer changed his order, the situation could get confused. Now all orders come to Havant in Britain. The European marketing centres send their orders overnight by private line, while Japan and Australia store theirs on computer tape and airfreight it to Britain. They are currently examining the economics of having a direct private line from Japan to Havant so that computer can talk to computer.

Obviously, such a system needs a supply of internationalised managers. The company realises that one of its biggest problems is maintaining informal links between managers in different locations round the world. They therefore encourage extensive travelling between people working on the same problem. The most effective way of encouraging world-wide cohesion is to post people to jobs in other countries for a couple of years. Obviously, problems arise when competent managers do not wish to be uprooted. I.B.M. is now developing an international career path for which selected managers can opt. If they do so, they can no longer expect to be posted back to their home countries every couple of years; but in return, they will obviously tend to become the élite from which top management will be drawn in the near future. At the moment, the company headquarters is still very much in the control of Americans. The highest non-American is a Frenchman, Jacques Maisonrouge, who has been steadily climbing the I.B.M. ladder, and was promoted in 1967 to President of the World Trade Corporation. He is the only non-American among I.B.M.'s top 38 personnel. This fact should, however, be put in perspective.

22

First, the top management of any firm generally reflects those recruited thirty years previously; in the 1930's and 40's I.B.M.'s international involvement was mostly a matter of marketing subsidiaries which were relatively unimportant when compared with U.S. activities. Second, there are very few firms of any size which do in fact have internationalised top management. Volkswagen, for instance, which owes much to the success of its American subsidiary, has no Americans on its board. A study reported by Rose (1968) of 150 U.S. Corporations revealed that only 1·6% of their executives were non-Americans. I.B.M. does claim that they are consciously developing non-American vice-presidents, but they do not expect to see the results before another four or five years.

I.B.M. parallels many other multinationals in the past decade in gradually tightening control over its international division. But the case of I.B.M. is particularly important for two major reasons. First, they have consciously tried to de-centralise and internationalise their research and development effort, a function normally kept close to company headquarters; and second, they have implemented policies of international integration which are among the most advanced in the world. These two achievements have one essential factor in common— the need for advanced techniques of communication. The scale of the exercise is readily apparent when one considers that in 1968 I.B.M. was employing some 24,000 R. & D. personnel in 26 completely separate laboratories; 19 in the U.S. and 7 in Europe. The World Trade division in the same year was operating in 104 countries through 331 sales offices with 228 service bureaux and data centres, apart from its manufacturing facilities. Coordination is achieved by maintaining a network of 307 communication centres throughout the world, linking the organisation by some 10,000 tele-typed messages per day— letters are virtually obsolete. Reinforcing this system at the executive level is a heavily used method of automatic informa-tion retrieval through desk-top microfilm readers. Immediate world-wide access is provided to I.B.M. reports, details of new developments, and a wide range of material including selections from 200 journals and 330,000 documents, plus a profile of the information needs of the 2,500 European and American executives equipped with the system to ensure that they receive everything of interest.[1]

Such clearly defined policy backed up by efficient direct-line communication makes national boundaries seem somewhat irrelevant. Surely many non-commercial organisations would do well to take a leaf out of I.B.M.'s computerised book.

[1] Heller, Robert. 'The march of the multinationals.' *Management Today*, April 1968, pp. 98–103.

CHAPTER III

The Fallible Multinationals?

In the recent rush of defensive mergers aimed at creating internationally competitive firms, many Europeans and Japanese seem to have assumed both that American firms are inherently invincible and that multinational companies are the logical corporate shape for the future. Both assumptions need stringent examination. It is easy to find large U.S.-owned firms which have made mistakes equivalent to those of European companies. And it is possible to show outstanding disadvantages to multinational operations in particular industries. We will argue that, once the rest of the world has taken management ideas and practices from some American multinationals, their futures are probably limited.

Before the 1960's, U.S. businesses experimented with investment activity round the world. Around the turn of the century, American life insurance companies frightened their European competitors by setting up branches in Europe; but once the latter had learned to use American marketing techniques, the invaders could no longer compete effectively. And in the world depression of the 1930's, a number of American firms sold off their European interests and withdrew to the U.S. market. One such firm, General Electric of America, is now having considerable difficulties in its European comeback.

U.S. firms trying to import cake mixes or bowling equipment into Europe have also retired defeated. And when one looks hard he finds many examples of muddled American management. Many middle-sized American firms (large by the standards of the rest of the world) which have faced competition only in a U.S. market boasting unified language and business practices founder when they attempt to cope with a range of languages, customs, mores, and habits of mind. Many of these firms went international because it was fashionable in the late

25

1950's and early 1960's. There was a general feeling, during the economically sluggish Eisenhower era, that future growth would come from outside the United States. Developments like the creation of the European Economic Community led to a surge of investment which was not always well conceived. In the spring of 1966, the U.S. Secretary of the Treasury warned the smaller American firms that the last ones into a market are the ones left holding the bag—a warning valid even for firms the size of Chrysler. Once they made their investments, some American firms found they had simply made commercial mistakes. Some have made these worse by completely misunderstanding the business cultures in which they are working.

The larger multinationals seem to have learned from some of their more glaring errors. In August 1962, the Frigidaire division of General Motors, having misjudged the willingness of French housewives to buy large American refrigerators, and finding themselves harassed by Italian imports, discharged 685 employees at their French plant. Ten days later Remington Rand headquarters in the U.S. ordered the dismissal of 1,000 workers in their French subsidiary. Despite the fact that the Frigidaire employees, at least, had no difficulty getting other jobs, the resulting storm of protests led, among other things, to President De Gaulle's limiting the freedom of incoming U.S. firms. Most major U.S. multinationals thus learned that they had far less freedom to lay off employees than their European competitors. France and Italy, in particular, retain cultures which believe that firms should support their employees even when near bankruptcy. Even so, some firms still have to learn.

Raytheon is a medium-to-large American electronics firm whose Sicilian subsidiary had a history of losses and labour unrest. Finally, with sublime timing, they announced the closing of the plant which employed 1,000 in the midst of an Italian election campaign. The mayor of Palermo promptly occupied the plant; so Raytheon declared its Italian subsidiary bankrupt, repudiating various unsecured obligations which Italian banks had granted assuming the U.S. parent company was ultimately responsible. Since then, Raytheon has been trying to auction the plant off in order to get some of its invest-

26

ment back. But the Italian government through the nationalised corporation, I.R.I., has scared off all buyers by announcing that I.R.I. will eventually take the plant over. At the time of writing, Raytheon has offered the plant for sale twice, lowering the asking price each time but getting absolutely no bids. Their $20 million investment is thus virtually worthless.

Italy, and particularly Sicily, seems to attract such comedies of errors. The European-owned oil multinational, Royal Dutch-Shell, made some abortive investments in the Italian chemical industry only to withdraw within a couple of years. Union Carbide and Rheem Manufacturing, both American, have similarly withdrawn from Italian ventures. Not all these fiascos can be explained through the leisurely business culture found in parts of Italy. Some of these withdrawals were the results of straight commercial mistakes. In 1968, for instance, the Celanese Corporation (the 75th largest firm in the U.S.) wrote off its Sicilian pulp and paperboard subsidiary losing at least $75 million. Amongst other disasters were a Eucalyptus plantation in Sicily which was too young to produce pulp, and further disadvantaged by unexpectedly higher transportation costs to north Italy and by competition from Scandinavia. Celanese also sold off plants in Canada and Britain and has retreated into the American market where it is making good, safe profits. Basically, however, the problems which drove these companies out of Sicily were forseeable ones which a true multinational should have assessed accurately.

In the rest of Europe, the mistakes may not be so glaring, though occasionally major U.S. firms obviously miscalculate the effort needed to pull round an ailing European firm. Two major examples are General Electric and Chrysler. General Electric spent two years trying to get permission to take over the hopelessly cash-starved French computer firm, Machines Bull, and finally succeeded in 1964. It promised President De Gaulle to continue research in France and to maintain Bull's level of employment, despite the fact that a French firm had calculated they would have to halve Bull's 10,000 employees. They have poured cash into the company ($69 million by 1966) and have had no worthwhile returns in exchange. G.E. made similar mistakes when purchasing Olivetti's computer interests. But Chrysler is in worse trouble, being late into the

European market where Ford and General Motors have been established since the 1920's. As a result, they have had to take over what firms they could find. In France they bought Simca, a successful investment outweighed by misfortunes in Britain and Spain. In Britain they bought into Rootes, a manufacturer which was losing hand over fist. They took over a firm which had about a tenth of the British market behind General Motors' Vauxhall subsidiary, Ford U.K. and British Leyland Motor Corporation; and their share of the British market has slightly declined to 8·5%. Meanwhile Spain's Barreiros Diesel S.A. has further drained the company. Spain was opened to foreign investment in 1960. In 1964 Chrysler signed a contract with the Barreiros firm to manufacture Simcas and Dodge Darts, an American model selling for more than double the price of the next most expensive car available in Spain. The appeal of the Dart was further diminished when the English slogan "Dart is power," translated into Spanish, hinted that the purchaser lacked masculinity. Their market share in this society which stresses 'machismo' fell from a peak of 20% to 10%, though Chrysler injected more capital at every stage. By 1968, the venture had lost $14 million, not including Chrysler's original investment and another capital injection in 1967. Finally, in 1969, this saga was capped when Don Eduardo Barreiros who founded the company 20 years previously resigned as president amid considerable recrimination. Simultaneously Chrysler's bid to get into the Japanese market ahead of its competitors via a minority holding in a joint venture with Mitsubishi has been falling into difficulties with the Japanese government. To cap it all, 1969 was also a year in which the firm saw its market share in the United States drop as well, forcing it to cut back on capital expenditure it had been planning. At the time of writing, there would seem to be clear indications that Chrysler will find it increasingly difficult to finance the capital investment needed if it is to raise significantly its world market shares. It would appear to be one multinational which may have to retrench.

Obviously, this list of firms which have had unhappy careers in Europe should be treated cautiously. The best American firms still remain superbly managed; though even Ford or General Motors have their weaknesses. For all their brilliance in producing good quality, popular passenger cars, their attempts to break into the really profitable 'prestige' car market against competitors like Mercedes-Benz, Rolls-Royce, B.M.W. or Rover have failed. Similarly, they have not succeeded in breaking significantly into the heavy truck field which is still dominated by European specialists like Mercedes, Leyland or Berliet. Currently, the Americans hold 30% of the European car market, but it is by no means certain that they will increase this lead against an aggressive Fiat, a revamped British Leyland Motor Corporation or Volkswagen. The European competition has stiffened considerably over the last five or six years, and the Japanese have still to tackle Europe in a major way.

A European fight-back?

What has been heartening to Europeans over the last five years is how the better managed European firms are holding their own and how the whole atmosphere has become more receptive to better management techniques. Later chapters will deal with certain approaches which Europe and Japan have been using to consolidate their firms; but at this point one can mention certain phenomena suggesting that the differences between European and American management are decreasing. First, management training is being introduced in Europe. This revolution has been led by Britain which *Business Week* suggests is five years ahead of continental Europe in this field. Two large business schools on the Harvard Business School lines have been set up in Manchester and London, supported by money from both the government and British industry. These are surrounded by rapidly expanding, graduate-level, management courses at practically all universities and technical colleges. On the Continent, the picture is not quite so encouraging, but there is now a nucleus of outstanding business schools gaining support from European firms: I.E.S.E. in Barcelona, I.S.I.D.A. at Palermo, I.N.S.E.A.D. near Paris, I.M.E.D.E. near Geneva. The Germans have set up four chairs of management studies in economics faculties. In France, the former N.A.T.O. headquarters has been converted into a business school handling 3,000 students, 600 of them doctoral candidates.

This movement is paralleled by the growth of journals aimed

at thinking managers. *Fortune*-inspired magazines are flourishing in Italy (*Successo*), France (*Expansion, Entreprise*), and Britain (*Management Today*). American managers sometimes express admiration for the financial and management writing in British newspapers; for all tend to follow *The Times*, which has had a daily business supplement analysing the business environment since 1964.

The management gap is thus probably closing, helped considerably by the substantial raids European firms make on the management of their American competitors. Thus British Leyland, Britain's standard bearer against the U.S. auto manufacturers has ex-Ford men as finance director, sales director, purchasing manager, production control manager and, for a time, styling manager. John Rhodes, a much travelled management consultant, argues in the September 1969 *Harvard Business Review* that when this management gap is narrowed, certain long-term factors will favour Europe. The U.S. has been trading in deficit with the European Economic Community since 1960. By 1968, it was buying $650 million more in machines, transport equipment and other manufactured goods than it was selling to the E.E.C. Moreover, the American self-sufficiency in iron ore is being eroded, and oil protection has reversed the pre-war situation in which U.S. oil was cheaper than other kinds. Once management skills become more equal, then the cheaper labour will also become a factor in Europe's favour. Rhodes therefore expects European industries to start catching up with the U.S., even if he does not expect them to overtake it.

This movement is dramatised by the fact that European firms are now investing in the U.S. In the 1970's, such investment may be flowing into the States at $1 billion a year. In 1969 British Petroleum, one of the world's 25 largest firms, tried to break into the American market via a complicated arrangement whereby oil produced on its land in Alaska would gradually give it control of the U.S. oil distribution company, Sohio. Similarly, Britain's Imperial Chemical Industries and Germany's Badische Anilin und Soda Fabrik announced major plans to build new plants in America. B.A.S.F. put in a bid for one of the U.S. chemical manufacturers, while the Dutch chemical firm Koninklijke-Zout-

Organon (K.Z.O.) has bid for America's International Salt. Such moves, which challenge the supremacy of the American multinationals in their home market, have much to commend them. A reasonably secure foothold in the U.S. market can serve as an invaluable source of experience for a multinational's activities in the rest of the world. This seems to be particularly noticeable in the marketing field. Beechams, the U.K. pharmaceutical firm, will regularly send its marketing men for extended tours of duty with their U.S. subsidiary. Unilever has been able to benefit from the experience of its U.S. subsidiary, Lever Inc., by transferring striped toothpaste from the U.S. to Europe. Likewise, with the coming of colour television to Europe, the parent company can now draw on the advertising experience it has gained through long acquaintance with the medium in the States. Pirelli keeps a general representative's office open in New York, totally independent of the sales office they also have, in order to keep in touch with all the latest scientific, technological and managerial developments. The information gleaned is then fed back into Pirelli's activities in the rest of the world.

What competitive advantages does the multinational gain?

For obvious reasons, multinational companies will survive only if they gain real competitive advantages. The disadvantages of being multinational tend to be ignored. It is therefore worth examining those industries in which one would expect multinationals to have an advantage over purely national based firms, and those industries in which one would expect to find no such advantages.

Having a number of plants which each produce one thing allows firms to supply a large market with a range of products, each produced in long enough runs to be profitable. By adding new national markets, multinationals can generate demand for products which are best produced in runs no single national markets could support. To some extent, this is what the U.S. car manufacturers have been doing in the Canadian and U.S. markets. Again, I.B.M.'s policy of manufacturing components for the whole of Europe in specialised plants within 7 or 8 different countries is influenced by the economies of scale they can thus achieve.

31

One has reason to be sceptical, however, about the degree to which such manufacturing economies contribute significantly to the success of most multinational companies. Obviously oil and mining firms need to be multinational in order to reach the requisite markets: they are tied to fixed supplies of raw materials which must be extracted, processed and transported at an economic value. What is less clear is why many national markets cannot support manufacturing operations which achieve the maximum economies of scale. The classic study in this field, by J. S. Bain (1959),[1] examined 20 U.S. industries and concluded that at least half had leading firms which were beyond the optimum size for 'static' efficiency—that is, efficiency in production and distribution. Bain's earlier study in 1956 suggested that the optimal car plant had an output equivalent to 10% of the U.S. national market. The plants of other industries like rayon, soap, cigarettes, tyres and tubes, and liquor needed an output of less than 5% of the national market. (In the case of cement and petroleum, optimal plant level was less than 5% of the largest recognised sub-market.) These figures suggest that a 30–40% penetration of one of the larger European national markets would give just as great an economy of scale as a 5–10% share of the whole European market. Therefore, an adequate strategy by a national firm might be to attempt gaining the maximum share of the home market, thus reducing unit costs as far as they can go. The multinationality of the competition would seem to carry relatively unimportant advantages as far as the size of plants is concerned. This is particularly true of industries in which transportation costs are relatively high—for example, coal, steel or drinks. Coca-Cola, the archetypal multinational, has expanded despite having to have the drink produced in numerous, relatively small plants all round the world. The advantages of the multinationals are much clearer in research. Industries like chemicals, aircraft and computers are based very heavily on expensive technical research and development. Increasingly the policy of survival in such industries is for the leading companies to plough back as much as they can into further research in order to maintain their market position. Increased turnover and profits, gained through multinational organisation contribute vitally

[1] Bain, J. S. *Industrial Organisation.* Wiley, New York, 1959.

to the spiralling costs of keeping up in the more capital-intensive industries. If one ignores the very special case of the $4 billion which I.B.M. spent on the System/360 range of computers, one still finds that even the firms fighting for the remaining share of the world market have to spend $150 million to develop a computer range. Just to remain competitive, such firms have to spend $25–50 million a year on research budgets which, if one assumes they are spending a rather high 5% of their turnover on this, implies an annual turnover of $500-1,000 million per annum—something which only the U.S. market is likely to be able to support. This is basically why I.B.M.'s competitors had to launch out into Europe in order to get back at least some of the development costs they were incurring. Similarly, these figures lie behind the official encouragement given outside the U.S. to mergers which create larger units in such fields. However, in aircraft, and increasingly in computers and nuclear power, it has become obvious that the research costs are so enormous that national markets are not enough. Great European interest has therefore been aroused in joint purchasing agreements by governments and consortia agreements by manufacturing firms in different countries.

Rather more problematical is the advantage gained by multinationals in marketing. For here, a number of separate factors are working, sometimes in different directions. First, world markets are not uniform. There are very few products with the global appeal of uniform tins of sardines. With the majority of products reaching the consumer market directly, uniformity is impossible. An off-beat example of the difficulties faced by the multinational is what happened to the soap-manufacturers, Lifebuoy. They tried unsuccessfully to sell soap with a carbolic scent in France: the French associate the smell with brothels. Other enterprises have fared as badly. French housewives prefer dark coloured clothes while American ones prefer light colours; the British and Far-Easterners drink tea, which elsewhere is associated only with snobbish dowagers; whole continents have different tastes in fish, which affects efforts to market palatable versions of high-protein fish-meal concentrates in underdeveloped countries. Campbell Soups, apotheosised by Andy Warhol, controls 90% of the U.S. canned soup market, but has had an uphill struggle elsewhere. It tried to break into the U.K. soup field dominated by Heinz, which in the U.S. controls a mere 5% of the market. Between 1959 and 1962, Campbell lost $6·1 million in finding that the British taste in canned soup was different from the American (for one thing, the British prefer a sweeter version of tomato soup). In a more advanced industry, the U.S. car firms have had difficulty breaking into the executive car market because the Detroit headquarters have tried to lay down styling policies which do not appeal to Europeans.

As further complication, different countries are at different levels of economic development, so that the standard of luxury required may be different. There are now even a few European firms catering in what is known as 'intermediate technology'— that is, machines and processes which are obsolete in the developed nations, but which still make economic sense in economies where, for instance, unskilled labour is in big demand.

However, the fact that markets are at different stages of development does give the multinational one advantage. We showed how Unilever was able to transfer marketing break-throughs like striped toothpaste to Europe from the U.S. In fact, the U.S. consumer, affluent, innovative, and willing to accept mass-produced products may well be one of the key competitive advantages available to U.S. firms. Similarly, Unilever, which has extensive interests in the underdeveloped world, uses what it calls the 'executive' countries in Europe (that is, Germany, France, Belgium, Holland and the U.K.) to test and develop products which, once proved in these markets, will then be released to remoter parts of its commercial empire. Such a multinational spread of interests can even pay off in less obvious ways. For instance, a number of countries which still have non-decimal currencies, have recently been bringing themselves into line with the rest of the world. These switches to decimal currencies carry a lot of business for the business machine firms which have to convert cash registers, calculating machines, etc. A firm like National Cash Register which has an Australian branch has been able to feed the information gained from the Australian conversion to the subsidiary in Britain which is converting at the time of writing. In many ways, therefore, the multinational can be seen as an organisation capable of learning from its experience in one part of the world and applying this knowledge to other parts. But does this process really need the existence of multinational companies? Could not well-managed national firms learn from the experience of other countries just as well?

The case of the Ford Mustang car model is interesting in this context. The Mustang, aimed at the young, sports-minded customer who wanted a car with a genuine whiff of the racetrack about it, illustrates beautifully how marketing experts found a niche in the market and exploited it ruthlessly. With the Capri, Ford has apparently succeeded in identifying a similar market in Europe, which they have filled with a car which has in common with the U.S. Mustang only the type of buyer it is designed for and the general styling. Now the Capri's success owes nothing at all to concrete links with the U.S. It is the extension of an idea which any European manufacturer could have considered when the Mustang was successful in the U.S. The Capri does not have parts in common with the Mustang. Its European advertising does not even mention the Mustang, which is unknown in Europe except to the motoring cognoscenti. Therefore, it is getting none of the conventional production or marketing synergies (management jargon for the act of combining different activities and getting results which are proportionately greater than the mere act of addition should apparently provide) from the Mustang's American success. What would appear to have happened is that Ford, emboldened by success, decided to test a good idea elsewhere. Ford's multinationality was not, in fact, a crucial element in this case. Any firm watching the American market closely could have done the same thing.

Marketing is becoming an increasingly expensive business and some would claim that it is often easier to get better economies of scale from research in consumer rather than producer goods industries. For instance, washing powders have become a field in which market breakthroughs will only be made by research which produces something on the scale of the new 'enzyme' powders currently sweeping the world. The food industry has become a field in which the company researchers look for new ways of drying, freezing, packaging

35

products. A firm like Campbell's must keep its market lead in the States by carrying out extensive agricultural research to develop tomato strains which mature early, give high yields and resist diseases, or corn with conveniently shaped kernels. Obviously production costs can be lowered not just by producing tins and packages to suit the animal or vegetable, but, perhaps more economically, by adapting the product to the packaging. The search for square apples which don't roll about may not be just a myth.

This sort of research is really akin to the car manufacturers' investigation into various sources of propulsion. But it is not the only type of research cost faced by consumer-oriented industries. Launching costs are a very heavy drain on company resources. For instance, test marketing often gives equivocal results and forces firms to launch products nationally; in an economy the size of the United States, this can run into millions of dollars. But when a multinational can spread launching costs over a number of national markets, it has a considerable advantage over its competitors based on a single market. Thus multinationals can take more marketing risks because they are able to exploit market breakthroughs on a larger scale. In fields like washing powders, where competition is increasing from 'store brands' sold by retailers who cash in on the marketing successes of Procter & Gamble or Unilever, this multinational spread is a useful way of getting the maximum return from any one breakthrough. Not many consumer goods are as expensive to develop as the small car planned by General Motors for the North American market in 1970. The plant to manufacture this model set the firm back at least $100 million, costs high enough to make entries into new national markets a useful strategic step.

Access to international sources of finance

A major advantage open to multinationals is easy access to the growing pool of Eurodollars and to the cheapest of the wide range of national capital markets. A purely national competitor may well be unable to expand because of, say, high interest rates in its home market. The firm may find that currency regulations make borrowing from foreign sources impossible, and will certainly find it difficult to compete for loans with the multinationals. The size and recognised names of most multinationals give them relatively good credit ratings wherever they go for money. In any case, having subsidiaries in a number of countries makes it relatively easy to borrow from low interest markets and often to transfer these funds to high interest ones.

Such advantages have increased since the advent of the Eurodollar market—a supply of 'internationalised' dollars, Deutschemarks, Swiss francs, etc., which are not returned to their home countries but are deposited with banks elsewhere and then loaned to other borrowers. This market was created by the 1963 Interest Equalisation Tax. Through this tax the U.S. government made it unprofitable for firms to finance foreign activities by borrowing U.S. dollars, up to that time, the prime source of finance for multinationals. Relatively high interest rates in Europe have meant that firms or individuals with idle dollars have had no incentive to ship them back to America. Thus a growing pool of finance, free from national restrictions, has been growing. From around $2·5 billion in 1965, the pool grew to around $25 billion by the end of 1968. Originally the bulk of financing from this source was short-term, but more recently the importance of long-term borrowing has increased. Straight loans are being edged out by convertible issues as the prime way of raising long-term finance from this market.

Originally the American multinationals were the chief borrowers, but their European competitors are now in the field as well. Despite the fact that interest rates in 1969 reached 12%, it is still a popular source of finance for multinationals because it is outside purely national currency restrictions. A firm borrowing, say, sterling in Britain would find itself unable to transfer the money abroad except under the most stringent conditions. A firm which raised the same sum by borrowing sterling legitimately earned outside Britain is very much more free to use it.

Scepticism about the inevitablity of multinationals

When one looks at the logic behind multinationals, one becomes a bit wary. Certainly no strong case can be made for production economies, except in a few cases. The marketing advantages are problematical, but more convincing all the

37

same; one has to balance the differences in markets against the advantages of spreading launching costs widely and of being involved in markets which give the firm valuable experience; however, well-managed national competitors could do as well by using very good market intelligence. The advantages seem greater when one considers the need to spread research costs, but this is only a major factor in certain science-based industries. Access to the world finance markets is more a question of the firms' size and credit rating; as the sophistication of the international financial community grows, then a well-managed, profitable, non-multinational company will probably have no serious difficulty raising money either. If these 'advantages' seem less than major, the long-term future of the multinational looks even less rosy in terms of organisational complications.

The major European firms have tended to be more genuinely multinational than their American counterparts since European markets have been smaller than the U.S. ones. Thus Du Pont only has 11% of its sales abroad, General Electric only 18%, General Motors only 14%; and even in 1967–8 when U.S. Ford was hit badly by strikes, foreign markets still provided only 36% of world sales for the Ford empire. In comparison, Volkswagen sells 67% outside Germany; Imperial Chemical Industries 50% outside the U.K.; German chemical producer Hoechst, 46% outside Germany; British Leyland, 42% outside the U.K. To compensate for their lack of expertise, American firms take great care with the organisation of their international operations.

This anxiety has led American companies to set up international divisions, a device rare among European firms. Managements with relatively slender experience of foreign markets decided that their best strategy was to create a division concentrating on the world market. However, the more complicated the range of products on sale, the more transient has been the international division. Since 1963, a steady stream of firms has abandoned this relatively simple organisational framework. In its place, they adopt structures which eliminate the domestic-international dichotomy and instead group the firm's activities by product or market or both. There is some evidence that the more advanced firms are moving toward what one can call a grid strategy in which product and area divisions are jointly responsible for sales abroad. This is the thinking behind Caterpillar's 'double boss' policy.

The president of Caterpillar Tractor is in charge of two sets of vice-presidents; one lot are normal line managers with responsibility for production and sales within specific world regions; the second set are functional officers (financial operations, marketing, personnel, etc.) who control such functions throughout the world. As a result, many managers have two bosses. If something goes wrong with a specific function in a given area (say, sales in Europe), then both the overall marketing officer and the European line manager must initiate steps to put things right. Likewise with I.B.M., production difficulties of a computer model affect both the I.B.M. management of the specific country involved and also the I.B.M. team which has world responsibility for that specific model.

Once firms start playing about with organisational structures this complicated then a number of problems arise. It becomes much more difficult to assign direct responsibility, and conventional ideas about the unity of command, profit centres, etc., totter. Moreover, organisations as complex as these start destroying the informal networks which often allow firms to avoid ghastly mistakes. Formal organisation can only set down minimum routines to avoid such glaring blunders as, say, people in different parts of an organisation working against each other. However, to be really vital and fast-moving, a firm often has to rely on informal communication between its members; if something goes wrong, then it helps to have friends one can phone for advice, knowing that they will not use one's troubles as evidence against one at some future date. In a multinational, the people who can help each other are often in different nations, perhaps speaking different languages, and probably only casual acquaintances. Since one is likely to be more hesitant in chatting over problems with semi-strangers than with friends, the multinational is likely to be slow in reacting to certain kinds of trouble. Such lack of intimacy may be significant when a new product is transferred into actual production, if oceans separate the people who have developed the product from the production engineers. Even if the relevant personnel are flown to each other, differing languages and cultures may cause communication breakdowns and simple errors. A purely national competitor might well gain an advantage in the possible speed of reaction, since the relevant decision-makers are more likely to know each other on an informal basis as well as a formal one. In particular, a purely national firm should also gain advantages from not having to reconcile the interests of one nation with those of another. For instance, a multinational deciding where to locate a new investment will have to decide between the claims of a number of subsidiaries; similarly, decisions about which subsidiary may export to which market may also lead to conflict; a subsidiary may be unable to act until the parent has ruled on potential conflicts—and this all takes time.

This chapter should end with a note of caution. Few writers are seriously examining the limitations of multinational companies. This is probably because we are still at the stage in which the multinationals are far better managed than their national rivals. Some delay is inevitable before the managerial gap is significantly closed. As it closes, however, it should become obvious that the advantages of certain manufacturing multinationals have lain in their management skills, not necessarily in their multinational spread.

CHAPTER IV

What do Governments stand to Gain—and Lose?

A strong case can be made for welcoming foreign investment into the national economy: it creates new jobs; it trains personnel in modern management techniques which are in turn diffused into the rest of the economy; it increases local technological expertise by the use of sub-contracting; it mobilises capital and technology from outside the country faster than purely national firms can; it offers access to export markets which would not otherwise be available. Alexander Hamilton summed things up when discussing European investment within the American economy in 1791:

> Rather than be judged a rival, it ought to be considered an auxiliary all the more precious because it alone permits an increased amount of productive labour and useful enterprise to be set to work.[1]

The most obvious area in which foreign countries benefit from multinational investment is in regional development. Countries which have particularly vigorous policies to divert firms to depressed regions benefit most. Thus Italy encouraged a number of American firms like Standard Oil (New Jersey) and American Cyanamid to invest in the depressed, agricultural South of Italy, the Mezzogiorno. Since Italian private industry had strongly resisted suggestions that it invest in the South, the Italian government has obvious cause for satisfaction that foreign firms have been willing to gamble there, even if some of the ventures (Raytheon, Celanese, Rheem Manufacturing, Union Carbide) have been unsuccessful.

Britain has enjoyed unusual success in luring foreign firms into development areas. A government survey shows that 30% of the foreign-owned firms (mostly American) setting up in

[1] Layton, Christopher. *Transatlantic Investment*. Atlantic Institute Press.

Britain between 1945–65 have gone into Scotland, an area of the United Kingdom troubled since the decline of its traditional industries, coal and shipbuilding. In particular, the electronics industry has settled strongly, attracted by good universities, large quantities of cash (in 1969–70, the U.K. is offering £350 million as incentives for firms locating in such areas), new towns, clean air, golf courses (definitely an attraction to foreign managers) and whisky. Since 1945, so many firms like National Cash Register, Remington Rand, Honeywell, Olivetti, Burroughs Machines, I.B.M. have established plants there that Scotland now claims to be the second largest computer complex outside California. There are now plans afoot to develop a 'Science park' on the lines of the Route 128 complex round the Massachusetts Institute of Technology, an ex-professor from which is running the technical university, Heriot-Watt in Edinburgh. Whether such a scheme succeeds or not, it remains true that an industrial structure which was doomed to decline has been revolutionised by the careful cultivation of subsidiaries from the multinationals. Similarly, in Germany it is possible to point to Bochum in the declining Ruhr-Rhine region: in 1952 half its employed population worked the coal mines and another quarter worked in iron and steel mills which were becoming progressively more uneconomic. On land made available from the closing of the mines, General Motors constructed two large factories for Adam Opel A.G. which in June 1969 were churning out 1,500 Opel Kadett cars a day, and employing 17,500 people. Firestone has done a similar job in Belgium's Béthune, as had Kodak at Châlon-sur-Saône.

A logical conclusion of this argument is that a successful regional development policy depends on attracting investment from multinational companies. Existing national companies are informally 'locked' into prosperous areas by their past investments. An Italian firm in Milan may be put at a disadvantage if forced to locate new investments in Sicily because it would end with a number of geographically scattered plants which would be hard to coordinate. But multinationals establishing plants in a country for the first time are in no way prisoners of their past. They are able to respond to the incentives that are available, provided these compensate them for investing in areas which may well be less than ideal. A complication can result for national governments protecting national industries from foreign competitors while heavily subsidising the same competitors through regional investment incentives. However, any country which tries to keep regional imbalances in check will find itself paying foreign companies a lot of cash. This is the price of a successful regional policy.

As well as reinvigorating declining regions, the multinational can stimulate specifically inefficient, or maybe infant, industries. French planners in the early 1960's actively encouraged Libby's $10 million investment in the Rhône basin, hoping that those operations would revolutionise the marketing and distribution methods of French agriculture. The British government body, the Industrial Reorganisation Corporation, is, at the time of writing, toying with a similar strategy. In this case, certain sectors of the British mechanical engineering industry are considered technologically backward. Since larger firms would not guarantee the use of progressive technology, they are being urged to form links with German or American firms which may be world leaders. Similarly, West Germany has used agreements with the leading U.S. constructors of nuclear power plants to build up German firms which are internationally competitive. Also Siemens, the West German electronics firm, has built up its computer capability through licensing agreements with America.

Moreover, a country which is receiving investment from multinationals is dealing with firms which are likely to be far more efficient than their national competitors. Professor Dunning (1969)[1] demonstrates that American subsidiaries are likely to be more efficient than their British competitors in any regard. Such subsidiaries in Britain make more profits, export more, invest more into new manufacturing facilities, and produce more with a given share of the labour force, than their British competitors. The only explanation that satisfies him is that the U.S. firms are simply more efficient. Alternative explanations (accounting conventions, concealed subsidies from the U.S. parent, location in the very profitable industries) do not fully explain his findings.

Obviously the multinationals also transfer the latest techno-

[1] Dunning, John H. 'The role of American investment in the British economy.' P.E.P. Broadsheet 507. London.

43

logies to the host country. Examples range from breakfast cereals to automatic car transmissions to pneumatic road-drills. In Britain, Woolworth's pioneered high-turnover, low-margin retailing, while Sears Roebuck did the same for other parts of the world like Latin America. Similarly in a field like tractor manufacturing, North American production processes forced the European industry to revolutionise its own methods. And the transfer can work the other way. Currently the U.S. tyre firms are fighting against the introduction of radial car tyres produced in Europe by Michelin, Pirelli and Dunlop. Gillette was forced to introduce costly improved razor blades round the world because its British competitor, Wilkinson Sword, marketed a revolutionary blade in Britain (based on Gillette patents).

The multinational also is sometimes able to take risks which national investors cannot do. When the West Australian prospectors, Hancock and Wright, found the Hamersley Iron deposits, they could not find a single Australian capital source willing to back further prospecting, let alone investment. It was the multinational mining operations like Rio-Tinto-Zinc, Consolidated Gold Fields, Kaiser Steel, UTAH Construction and Mining who were able to locate the Japanese markets, arrange for the building of bulk ore carriers, find the finance on the world markets. The Hamersley Iron operation was financed by North American bank loans of $120 million for the initial financing alone. Gambles of this size in which $50 million may have to be spent before any metal is actually mined could not be taken by purely national firms. Only a real multinational can put together the necessary packages of finance and customers which can get a mining operation quickly under way.

Finally, the host nation can gain much from the spin-off in general management efficiency which the subsidiaries of multinationals provide. Earlier, we mentioned how Ford (U.K.) has produced a cadre of finance and purchasing officers, lured away for their management expertise, who have fanned their way through British industry. Even in the notorious area of U.S. labour relations, one finds convincing examples of trail-blazing agreements which are well in advance of anything tried by the national competitors. For instance, Esso (the subsidiary of

Standard Oil (New Jersey)) pioneered in Europe the large-scale productivity bargain in which management and union leaders trade restrictive practices and promises of higher productivity for the cash of higher wages. I.B.M. throughout Europe has pioneered 'staff' schemes and fringe benefits for all its employees. Similarly, in the British car industry the traditional piece-rate payment schemes have tended to contribute heavily to the anarchic industrial relations environment. It has been the U.S. subsidiaries which have been moving away from such pay schemes, while the one British firm, British Leyland, is unwilling to take the initiative.

The political problems

For obvious reasons, politicians of host countries often view multinational companies with highly-charged emotion. Gaston Defferre, one-time challenger to De Gaulle for the French presidency, exclaimed in 1966, "The economic invasion by the United States is a clear and present danger . . . the beginning of the colonisation of our economy." (*Quoted by Oglesby, 1968.*)[1] Others talk of 'neo-colonialism' or 'industrial helotry', or use other terms which express the concern of politically sensitive individuals from both ends of the political spectrum. How justified are their fears?

Both the left and the right have cause to be frightened. The right-wing nationalist is concerned about foreigners usurping control of his fatherland, while the left-wing nationalist is concerned about the political complexion of those running the multinational and the government in whose country the multinational's headquarters are based. Both believe that accepting subsidiaries of multinationals lays the host country open to pressure of a political nature. While such problems exist, at least some of the danger comes from engagement in international trade of any sort. Multinational companies are not the only instruments for applying political pressure across national boundaries.

President De Gaulle was a leader who faced a great deal of political pressure through industrial channels, though Sweden, among the developed nations, now seems to have superseded

[1] Oglesby, Carl. 'The new Roman wolf.' *Interplay*, November 1968, pp. 30–8.

him as the prime target of industrial pressure for political ends. De Gaulle's independent foreign policy toward the communist world more than once clashed with the U.S. Trading with the Enemy Act which lists strategic goods which cannot be sold to communist countries by N.A.T.O. countries. There was one occasion when he wished to show his appreciation to Chairman Mao by sending Red China three or four Caravelle jet airliners. The U.S. State Department blocked this gesture since the plane contained a significant amount of American 'strategic' electronic equipment. More recently there were rumoured difficulties in getting a French colour television factory set up in Russia. Although France had deliberately decided to use a French-invented system named SECAM, the components still contained enough American electronics to run into trouble.

The most interesting case in which a multinational fell afoul of the Trading with the Enemy provisions was that of Fruehauf-France S.A., the French subsidiary of the American trailer manufacturer. The French managing director was approached by the truck manufacturer, Berliet, which had won a contract to provide tractors and trailers to Communist China. Would Fruehauf provide the trailers to go with Berliet tractors? Fruehauf's man in France agreed and was promptly sacked when the American parent learned of what had happened. The situation worsened when Berliet prepared to sue for damages should the contract be scrapped. Worse still, the French government has legal powers to forcibly run companies which are in legal convolutions like this. Finally, the U.S. State Department let the U.S. parent company off the hook by agreeing that this particular incident was out of the parent's control. The contract was honoured and the French management was restored; but it was agreed that the subsidiary would not deal with Red China in the future. Some governments, in particular the American government, claim the right to control the policies of the subsidiaries of multinationals owned by their nationals. Such manipulation can interfere with the interests of the countries in which the subsidiaries are located.

De Gaulle was not only harried for his friendliness to the communist world. His attempt to build the 'force de frappe', his independent nuclear deterrent, was not appreciated by the

46

U.S. State Department. In 1964, this agency prevented Control Data Corporation from sending De Gaulle one of their latest 'number-crunching' computers capable of dealing with the complex calculations needed to develop nuclear weapons. This form of embargo can even be used to stop wars. In 1967 the war between India and Pakistan rapidly came to a halt because the nations supplying them with their weapons deliberately kept them short of spare parts; when a tank or a plane was immobilised because of a defunct part, neither side could repair the equipment.

Not all pressure on a government need be so politically inspired. For instance, from 1964–7, France under De Gaulle adopted an extremely hostile attitude toward foreign investment, particularly from the U.S.A. General Motors was originally planning a $100 million investment in a plant for making automatic transmissions in Strasbourg. It became obvious that unless the investment climate became more relaxed, this plant would, instead, be located in Belgium. However much the French Government was afraid of the American investment, it could not let such an investment go, so French policy toward foreign investors has been gradually modified. The lesson from De Gaulle is obvious. It is possible to maintain an independent foreign policy if one so wishes, but it will be difficult to make such gestures as giving communist countries gifts which are partly dependent on work done in militant non-communist nations. There is also a danger that some multinational investment may be located into nations whose politics are more acceptable to the directors. There is thus an economic cost in the form of potential investors who are lost, though this is not normally on a scale which forces a nation to follow a given political line. For instance, Rhodesia has been under what is supposed to be a blockade by the manufacturing nations of the world, who aim to force her government to make concessions to the African majority. Though the economy has suffered, the political results have been nil. If a government is following a policy which is popular with its people, then economic pressure through the subsidiaries of multinational companies is not to be feared. In the last resort the militant local politician can always nationalise such subsidiaries.

In practice, this pressure can work both ways. American

47

multinationals find themselves hindered because they must work under tighter interpretations of 'strategic' goods than their world-wide competitors. Their non-American competitors happily sell buses, cars, computers, etc., to Cuba, Russia, Red China or Eastern Europe. In Vienna, a number of American firms keep what they call 'listening posts' (i.e. offices to keep them in touch with developments in East Europe). The list includes I.B.M., Dow Chemical, General Motors, Honeywell, Remington Rand, Union Carbide, U.S.M., National Cash Register, Ingersoll Rand and Westinghouse Airbrake. Such companies, finding that their European competitors are making heavy inroads into the East European markets, are potential lobbyists for a relaxation of the U.S. State Department trade regulations.

Currently, Sweden is coping with some of the pressures De Gaulle once faced. Swedish-American relations have deteriorated during the late 1960's to the point that there is no U.S. ambassador appointed to Stockholm. The basic disputes revolve round the Vietnam war with anti-American feeling running high and Swedish protection for deserters from the U.S. forces. The Swedish foreign minister even announced in October 1969, that the country might aid North Vietnam ($38 million was mentioned) beginning in July 1970. This policy has caused increasing uneasiness amongst the Swedish business community since they face the brunt of American retaliation. Firms such as ASEA with contracts with the Tennessee Valley Authority feel vulnerable. Other firms have had U.S. customers refuse to sign contracts being discussed. A genuine Scandinavian multinational, the airline S.A.S., finds itself heavily dependent on finance from the U.S. Export-Import bank and is thus vulnerable to counter-pressure in retaliation to the Swedish governmental policies.

There is therefore a need for governments to try to keep significant parts of their most crucial industries free from multinational control. Partly this concern is a commercial matter: American owners would doubtlessly have prevented firms like British Leyland or Fiat from significant involvement with markets like Cuba or Russia. Partly it is political: one obviously has greater freedom if not entirely at the mercy of foreign decision-makers in key industries. However, a strong-minded

48

government need not be influenced by such pressures, providing it is aware of the economic costs of its actions. Finally, political pressure is also exerted through the subsidiaries of the nation which gets out of line.

Anti-trust and extraterritoriality

Like a number of Europeans, I feel somewhat ambivalent on the issue of the American anti-trust authorities. On the one hand I admire the single-mindedness with which they have pursued their expressed purpose of encouraging competition and discouraging price-fixing, carving up markets or the other hobbies of businessmen who would prefer an easy life at the expense of the consumer. When one considers that anti-trust activities have actually imprisoned businessmen (some unfortunate General Electric employees) for price-rigging activities which in most other nations would have received an apologetic reprimand or a trifling fine, one can only marvel that such a body has sprung up in the nation which is the capital of business. At the same time, it is possible to see that the decisions of U.S. anti-trust authorities affect nations which may not agree with their policies.

The U.S. authorities invoke the 'effects' principle whereby any events which have actual or potential implications for the U.S. come under the jurisdiction of U.S. authorities and courts. The strongest example of this claim was the notorious Swiss Watch case in the early 1960's: a U.S. court, understandably concerned about the rather cosy non-competitive practices of Swiss watchmakers, decided that their restrictions amounted to a conspiracy to unlawfully restrain the domestic and foreign commerce of the United States—i.e., that they were carving up the American market for their mutual benefit. The indignant court delivered an all-embracing decree which insisted that the Swiss manufacturers should not only scrap all restrictive agreements between themselves, but also should scrap similar agreements with the British, French, and German industries. The court thus decided to impose American competitive concepts on a Swiss industry, much to the disgust of the Swiss Government which appeared in an American court to argue that its sovereign rights should be accepted. Whatever one's feelings about Swiss trading practices, it is generally conceded that the

49

Americans went too far in this case; they were virtually trying to dictate an anti-trust policy to a national government.

The U.S. anti-trust authorities still claim the right to control the foreign activities of U.S.-owned firms. They also believe that it is their duty to block mergers which may lead to a lessening of competition in America at some unspecified date in the future. This has resulted in American courts preventing mergers which European shareholders are perfectly happy to accept. Thus Gillette bought a German appliance manufacturer, Braun A.G., a family firm with a successful electric shaver, but no cash to expand. The U.S. Justice Department sued Gillette, ordering them to divest themselves of Braun since the latter company might conceivably have entered the U.S. market itself at some future stage.

Similarly, Litton Industries has run into anti-trust trouble over its plans to take over Triumph-Adler, a West German typewriter manufacturer. This is because Litton owns Royal McBee, the second largest U.S. typewriter manufacturer. Another instance relates to the Monsanto-Bayer joint venture in the U.S., Mobay. To the companies this agreement made sense since Bayer was ahead in developing flexible polyurethane but lacked a U.S. base. Monsanto got access to the German technology and provided the U.S. marketing knowhow. The Justice Department argued that Monsanto would stop researching in this field and that Bayer would have no incentive to move into the U.S. market independently. In an out-of-court settlement Monsanto sold its half share to Bayer.

What should one make of such cases? If one believes that the competitive principle is worth fighting for, then the U.S. Justice Department cannot really be faulted. Takeovers are a very easy way of buying up competitors. And in the present stage of U.S. and European development, the larger American firms are usually those buying up the smaller European firms which might develop into effective competitors. Obviously one sympathises with the shareholders in Braun, but then there is no reason to suppose that Braun might not have been able to develop into a competitor of Gillette's as Wilkinson in Britain did. Similarly, it is difficult to fault the thinking in the Monsanto, Bayer case. Both firms were taking the easy way out and might be tempted not to compete in other fields.

In fact, when one looks at European industry one sees the need for continuing watchfulness on the part of U.S. authorities as well as European ones. The Common Market's anti-trust authority has only gathered momentum in 1969, when it felt powerful enough to fine most of the major European chemical firms for fixing the prices of dyes. Similarly, the six leading quinine producers in the European Economic Community who control at least 50% of the world market have also been fined in 1969 for price-fixing offences. These first stirrings of a tough European anti-trust policy are to be welcomed; but it will be some time before European firms fully outgrow the 'gentlemen's agreements' existing all over Europe. For instance, many European firms still have 'no poaching' agreements whereby they refuse to hire personnel who have been employed for their competitors. Again, European industry seems very attracted to the idea of joint ventures with alleged competitors, which indicates a certain unwillingness to compete openly with them. But as they gain self-confidence they can be expected to provide that extra source of competition which the U.S. anti-trust authorities see as being 'potential'.

In the meantime, non-American governments sometimes see fit to follow policies countering principles which the U.S. anti-trust authorities support. For instance, Europe and Japan are currently going through a wave of mergers which are officially supported to provide internationally competitive industrial units. Since these often involve firms which have previously been in competition there are several long-term implications. It may be that European firms with significant American interests may find themselves at a handicap. Thus the merger of the Swiss chemical firms CIBA and Geigy is complicated because they have American interests which will concern the U.S. Justice Department. The Combines Investigation Branch of the Canadian Government has also expressed worry that Canadian measures to stimulate industrial action may not operate effectively because of the fears of U.S. subsidiaries about the legal situation. In particular, they cite the formation of export consortia specifically permitted under Canadian law, presumably considered suspiciously by the U.S. authorities. Another case illustrating the issues comes from Europe where Russian aluminium flooded in. The European producers decided to buy the Russian output providing it was kept to a limited amount. European companies were allocated purchases *pro rata* and European governments agreed to the deal. The European companies obviously wanted to bring in the American-owned subsidiaries who were benefiting from the stabilisation of the market. They were unable even to discuss the deal because of the U.S. anti-trust provisions.

Obviously, when governments are supporting policies which are sometimes seriously in conflict, there is need for considerable consultation. Members of the Organisation for Economic Co-operation and Development (O.E.C.D.) have agreed to consult each other wherever national trust laws may involve the important interests of another country. Similarly, there is definite need for arbitration courts to protect the rights of those firms and nations which are caught in the middle of disputes about the scope of various anti-trust agreements. A number of nations have protected their interests by passing legislation obliging subsidiaries to owe first allegiance to the laws of the nation in which they are located. Denmark, Finland, India, Holland, Norway, Panama, Sweden, Switzerland, the United Kingdom and the provinces of Ontario and Quebec have now all got some legislation prohibiting the compliance with foreign anti-trust measures (Rolfe, 1969[1]).

The remaining difficulty in the anti-trust field arises when European firms finally try to compete in the United States, for they suspect that the anti-trust laws may be used against them. In fact, the situation has been further complicated by a new toughness in anti-trust policy apparent under the Nixon administration. Although some firms like Unilever and Beechams have long had subsidiaries in America, it has only been since the mid-1960's that a significant number of European firms have become interested in entering the market by direct manufacturing. Britain's Imperial Chemical Industries and British Petroleum, Germany's Badische Anilin (B.A.S.F.) and the Dutch chemical firm Koninklijke Zout-Organon (K.Z.O.) all announced major plans for the U.S. market in 1969. It was at this point the U.S. authorities stepped in, using British Petroleum (B.P.) as their main target. Forty-nine per cent owned by

[1] Rolfe, Sidney. *The International Corporation.* International Chamber of Commerce, Paris, 1969.

52

the British Government (Winston Churchill was once worried about ensuring the supply of oil needed by the British fleet), B.P. was the third largest firm in the world outside the U.S. in 1968. Unlike all its major competitors, it has had no supplies of crude oil in the United States. Thus it had been losing the advantages of the very generous tax provisions made for the benefit of the U.S. oil producers. Earlier attempts to get into the American market by supplying Middle East crude oil to Sinclair came to naught when the U.S. Government introduced quotas on imported oil. In 1968, B.P. acquired 10,000 service stations from Atlantic Richfield (Arco) and Sinclair Oil. These companies were merging and needed to sell the stations to a potential competitor in some areas where the merger would noticeably decrease competition and thus arouse the U.S. Department of Justice. This acquisition was to cost B.P. some $400 million, or more than the total book value of all German investment in the United States. This deal made sense only if B.P. managed to find significant amounts of American oil. It found them in Alaska. By September 1969, it became clear that B.P.'s share of the Prudhoe Bay oilfield on the North Slope contained reserves which should exceed the total of the East Texas field, heretofore the largest oilfield in America. B.P. now owned a series of rundown service stations on the East Coast and an excess of Alaskan oil. A merger was therefore arranged with Standard Oil of Ohio (Sohio), which had always been short of crude and which was well-respected for the quality of its management. At that point, the U.S. anti-trust authorities stepped in.

The Justice Department claimed that it was merely following rules applying to companies of any nationality. Early in 1969, Attorney General John Mitchell announced that the U.S. authorities would probably oppose mergers between any of the top 200 manufacturing companies, or between any such company and the leader in a concentrated industry. Sohio, the 18th largest U.S. oil company, is well within these limits. And the properties B.P. took over from Sinclair would put its American interests alone into the top 200 U.S. companies in terms of both sales and assets. If one considers B.P.'s worldwide activities, then the company was roughly equal in sales to Boeing, the 18th largest American firm. Given the standards that Mitchell had set then the B.P.-Sohio merger obviously deserved to be blocked. After all, B.P. had the resources eventually to become an effective competitive force in the U.S., even without the help of mergers. On the other hand, the U.S. oil industry is notoriously feather-bedded; so arguing that it needed protecting from unfair competition was absurd. Through allowances firms get as they deplete their oil reserves and through their ability to set exploration costs against tax, American-based oil companies are heavily subsidised at the cost of the American consumer: an American company like Texaco may pay roughly 32% of its income in taxes while British Petroleum pays around 60%. Protecting a truly competitive industry is one thing, but protecting the highly-padded profits of the U.S. oil firms is another. However sympathetic one was with the U.S. anti-trust guidelines, this particular case was somewhat disturbing.

The British were particularly sceptical about U.S. attitudes toward foreign investment since Courtauld's subsidiary in the U.S. before World War II, American Viscose, met an extremely hostile reception and was almost forcibly sold to U.S. interests at a basement price as part of the Lend-Lease deals. In the meantime, the Dutch firm K.Z.O. was testing the attitude of the Justice Department to the idea of 'foothold acquisitions' by bidding for International Salt, with which it did not compete.

The basic paradox is that U.S. companies in Europe have found themselves virtually free of significant anti-trust restrictions. Traditionally, countries like the U.K., West Germany, Belgium, the Netherlands and Italy have freely allowed U.S. firms to open up subsidiaries even when the management gap meant that for any given market share, the American subsidiaries would compete more effectively than European firms with similar shares of a market could do in America. Yet, it is the latter who were more likely to meet resistance from anti-trust pressure. On balance, the long-term losers could have been these American subsidiaries who were more likely to face increased pressures from Europeans learning what a rigorous anti-trust policy really was.

As it happens, the U.S. anti-trust authorities relented and permitted all three of these arrangements. B.P. was allowed to proceed with its Sohio scheme, providing it got rid of enough service stations in Ohio to reduce its monopoly there. Similarly, B.A.S.F. and K.Z.O. were allowed to go ahead with their acquisitions. But the basic fact remains. The U.S. has the most effective anti-trust record in the world. A similarly militant body would benefit many countries. But for firms actually entering the U.S. market, what matters is how liberally the U.S. authorities interpret the doctrine of 'potential competition' and how generously they allow such firms to get a foothold in a market before applying the full weight of the anti-trust provisions. Otherwise, the main problem is still going to revolve round 'extra-territoriality'. Increasingly, governments will not accept the right of another nation's anti-trust authorities to decide what goes on in their economies. In theory, this is fair, but in practice it really only works against the U.S. authorities who, in this case, are the only people likely to make the sort of tough decisions that matter. All one can hope is that any move toward an international anti-trust authority will be heavily influenced by the U.S. ethos.

Decisions taken elsewhere

Ultimately, the worry of most nationalists is that crucial decisions affecting their interests are taken outside the country. Fred Catherwood, the director-general of the National Economic Development Organisation in Britain discusses the need for maintaining portions of key industries in national hands:

> This is not an emotional condition although it could of course become one. It is simply that the British citizen does not have votes in the U.S. congress and does not like decisions which affect his destiny to be completely removed from his control. No U.S. senator represents Dagenham (Ford's main U.K. plant) and no British member of parliament can hope to have the same influence on Detroit as the U.S. senator and congressmen representing Michigan or the administration of the United States.

Such worries become obvious when the time for rationalisations and sackings come round. Part of the French concern about the Remington Rand sackings in 1962 was due to the fact that the final orders very obviously came from the U.S. headquarters. Similarly in Britain, a firm called Roberts-

55

Arundel was taken over by a U.S. company which tried to get rid of certain union personnel by replacing them with women workers during a vacation period. The resultant labour strife led to intervention by the British Government which called a conciliation meeting between the U.K. head of this firm and the relevant union leaders. On the day of the meeting, the U.K. managing director had to admit to the government representatives that the night before he had received a cable from the U.S. headquarters telling him not to negotiate. This sort of 'management by telex' is like a red rag to union leaders and all others suspicious of foreign motives.

Obviously multinational headquarters have become increasingly sensitive about such events. It is now rare for such headquarters to draw significant attention to their subsidiaries' dependence on their instructions. However, there is plenty of scope for further trouble. One of the more worrying problems will arise when the first major manufacturing multinational finds itself bankrupt, or more likely, finds itself significantly overextended. At the moment catastrophes of this nature take place entirely within individual nations. Thus the British firm, General Electric (no connection with the American firm of the same name), after taking over the struggling Associated Electrical Industries (A.E.I.) and merging with the other major British electrical engineering firm, English Electric, found itself overmanned in a number of divisions. Over 1968-9 they totally closed down one plant employing 5,500 and, toward the end of 1969, announced the end of another 4,300 jobs. When one considers that General Motors and Remington Rand aroused France by sacking around 1,000 workers each, it becomes obvious that the multinationals have to work within much more sensitive guidelines. Certainly, it is very difficult to think of a foreign-owned firm's sacking around 10,000 people, even in Britain, without running into very heavy political trouble.

At some stage, major multinationals will have to close down operations across national boundaries, which will basically mean picking between different nations, all of whom will want to preserve the subsidiaries in their own nation. So far we have merely seen firms like International Harvester pulling out of their Swedish operations, or Celanese and Raytheon pulling out of Sicily. What Europe has not yet faced is a multinational with really significant interests in Europe deciding to get out. The automobile industry might see this happen, since Chrysler's battle to establish itself as a viable force on the European scene is increasingly desperate. With serious troubles in its British and Spanish operations and with growing competition from European manufacturers like Fiat, British Leyland and Volkswagen, Chrysler may be unable to become one of the top three car makers in Europe. It may well decide at some stage to cut its losses and withdraw, leaving behind considerable problems, since its competitors would only be interested in buying a certain amount of plant and equipment. Obviously one cannot write off Chrysler like this. But some such major withdrawal by a multinational is more likely in the relatively slow-growing auto industry than in the faster developing chemical, petroleum or computer industries.

Other tensions arise when the country of a parent company runs into balance of payments difficulties. At that point, they may well pressure their foreign subsidiaries to remit greater shares of their profits than is otherwise normal. This is what happened with the U.S. Mandatory Controls on Capital Outflows of 1968: the U.S. Government intended to cut back capital outflows and the reinvested earnings of American subsidiaries by at least 1 billion dollars below the 1967 level. The world was divided into three sectors. Subsidiaries in the most advanced countries were limited to reinvested earnings which in total might not exceed 35% of the annual average investments financed by capital outflow and retained earnings in 1965 and 1966. In practice, the U.S. Government was telling these corporations how to behave. Since those orders normally meant that U.S. subsidiaries had to remit rather greater profits back to the U.S. than they normally would, the move obviously had its impact on the economies of the host nations. The impact on Canada, however, was likely to be so severe that she was exempted from the programme. In return, the Canadian authorities had to guarantee that Canadian banks, etc., would not help U.S. corporations evade their responsibilities through their Canadian subsidiaries. In the words of Polk (1968):[1]

[1] Polk, Judd. 'The new world economy.' *Columbia Journal of World Business*, Vol. 3, No. 1, Jan.-Feb. 1968, pp. 7–15.

The guidelines are simple enough, but the result is almost startlingly clear; the price of access to U.S. capital is 100% alignment of Canadian financial policy with U.S. capital controls!

So far no significant resistance has developed to such moves. But as a nation like the U.S. takes a greater share of the economies of other nations, it cannot responsibly solve its financial problems by demanding satisfactory behaviour from its 'own' subsidiaries in other nations, without considering the economic problems of the host nations. As the drive for greater freedom in capital movements grows, such arbitrary moves naturally meet with more disapproval. The recognition will grow that subsidiaries owe allegiance to two masters, the nation of the parent company and that of the subsidiary. Unilateral manipulation of world-wide industry for the interests of one nation is not likely to be encouraged.

Research and development

The research strategy followed by multinational companies has serious implications for national governments concerned in raising the general technological level of their own national industry. As we saw earlier, there is a danger that U.S. multinationals involved in research-intensive industries may be able to maintain a semi-permanent research lead over their European counterparts, partly because they can afford larger research budgets and partly because they are involved with the American market which will buy most technological developments first. A national strategy should aim at ensuring that U.S. multinationals in the rest of the world will be unable to stifle the research efforts of other nations.

Basically, most multinationals will tend to keep the bulk of their research activity in their home country. Thus they may be able to delay the spread of research results to their subsidiaries in other nations; they may be tempted to remove the research activities to the parent company when they take over potential competitors in foreign countries. As a result, lesser countries are left with second-best research efforts and lag behind the real pioneering research increasingly creating the breakthroughs which provide the basis of long-term market success; as long as the research effort in the countries relying heavily on multinational subsidiaries remains second-rate, there is little chance of spinning off the stream of small, technology-based companies which seem to be the source of so many creative ideas in the U.S.; therefore one may validly argue that over-reliance on multinationals leads to a permanently secondary world role.

The first concern of any government should be the location and quality of a multinational's research effort. Obviously, in any situation in which a multinational is trying to take over a national firm, conditions should be laid down to prevent transferring the national firm's research effort to company headquarters. For instance, when Raytheon took over the British electronics firm A. C. Cossor, in 1962, rumours spread that they removed most of the advanced research to their U.S. laboratories. The managing director of the subsidiary disputes this, claiming that there was no important research going on. Certainly in the computer field, however, one hears similar stories of U.S. firms buying up European ones and then removing their research activities to the States.

Even if the multinational does leave a research effort with a given subsidiary, the work may entail little more than developing products for the national market. The Stanford Research Institute did a survey of 200 U.S. firms, half of whom did research in Europe. Most of these spent 4% or less of their total R. & D. budget there, and many viewed such efforts as means of monitoring European R. & D. activities and of gaining access to the European scientific community. In other words, their purpose was not significant research.

This argument should not be overstated. Even without its own research, a subsidiary will have access to world-wide research which may well be far ahead of anything it could have launched. W. G. Jensen (1969),[1] in studies on the U.S.-owned subsidiaries in the British pharmaceutical and electronics industries, found one electronics subsidiary with access to company research costing over $280 million per annum. In pharmaceuticals he cited a subsidiary which could call on company research equal in expenditure to the total United

[1] Jensen, W. G. 'Two case studies of the role of American investment in the British economy: pharmaceuticals and electronics.' Appendix to Dunning, *op. cit.*

Kingdom spending on pharmaceutical research ($32·5 million in 1965).

The interesting question, then, is whether subsidiaries have free access to the research carried out in the parent company. Fred Catherwood (1968)[1] suggests that the largest customers of a multinational may demand commercial benefits greater than those given their foreign competitors. Since multinationals find most of their important customers in the United States, there is a danger that the American multinationals may phase access to research so that the U.S. market has several months' advantage before new technology is passed on to subsidiaries elsewhere. This situation might well arise where component suppliers are multinational themselves as is the case in microelectronics (Texas Instruments, Motorola, Fairchild) and car components (Borg-Warner, Timken, tyre firms like Goodyear and Firestone). Any delays in transferring their most advanced technology from the U.S. to their foreign subsidiaries can only put non-U.S. competitors of the U.S.-based multinationals at a disadvantage. One condition potentially forestalling this unfairness could be that new subsidiaries should have immediate access to any knowledge available to their foreign parents. Delaying the transfer of such technological developments to give specific commercial advantage to another party of the multinational should be considered an unfriendly act toward the host nation.

In the long run, however, multinationals must locate a significant proportion of their basic research in the countries of their subsidiaries. The technological gap can be closed only if the quality of research done outside the United States is improved. A quick way to do this is to transfer some of the pioneering research to other countries. This move is important because research workers who are a couple of years behind the best work going on in the world will remain there unless they get the chance to work in the forefront. It is the pioneering research organisations which are most likely to spot the commercial applications of any technological advance; individuals doing secondary research can only pick up opportunities which have been unintentionally overlooked. Thus governments have

1 Catherwood, H. F. R. 'United States investment in Britain.' 1968. Conference Paper. National Economic Development Organisation, London.

every reason to try and persuade multinationals to spread their research activities round the world.

Obviously, multinationals will protest that diffusing research will be inefficient. To some extent they are right. Commercial success in the long run depends on fitting market opportunities to technological possibilities. It therefore makes sense to have the research effort near the company headquarters. This is not, however, absolutely necessary. I.B.M. has shown how to coordinate research on a global basis. Though they must take very firm steps to coordinate this research, the system obviously works. Other firms, too, are using their subsidiaries for research. Thus its British subsidiary performs most of Ronson's research on cigarette lighters and allied products, leaving the investigation of electrical products to the American parent. Ford's British research establishment looks into machining, that is the suitability of laser beams, electrochemicals and ultrasonic techniques for metal cutting, while the U.S. parent company does the more basic research on the 'wedding' properties of materials (i.e., how they can be combined). Standard Oil of New Jersey has located in Britain its largest internal combustion engine testing facility, which has special responsibility for work on fuel oil, natural gas and potentially pollution-free liquid petroleum gas.

These examples show that multinationals can spread their research effort around. In fact, the head of Standard Oil's Esso Research Centre in Britain points out that a development project in America costs three or four times what it costs in Britain. The cost of a project in continental Europe is likely to be 30–50% higher than in Britain; but such projects are still very much cheaper than the same research would be in the U.S. Lockheed Aircraft, with strong ties to the U.S. defence agencies, finds it profitable to maintain a development unit in Britain, and to fly results and communication across the Atlantic each day. After all, given the high wage costs of research workers in the U.S., and given the difficulties of persuading European scientists to settle for good in the U.S., it makes sense to hire European brains in Europe where they can be bought considerably cheaper. As it becomes easier for computers to talk to each other across oceans (flying the tapes from one site to another is a reasonable alternative for the moment), the difficulties of coordinating world-wide research activities should disappear, allowing cost advantages (backed up by some political pressure, perhaps) to swing the location of research activities toward the subsidiaries of multinationals. Certainly, any government worried (as they should be) about the location of research, would do well to follow a two-point strategy. First, governments should persuade the multinationals to allocate their research effort in proportion to their involvement in the nation. Second, having got their 'fair share' of the multinational research effort, they should make sure that they are not being left with simple development activities which will be of little use.

Neo-colonialism?

Many on the political left see multinationals as agents of the old imperialist powers who are now conquering national cultures with a new, subtle form of imperialism. Carl Oglesby, the 1965 national president of Students for a Democratic Society (S.D.S.), put it this way in an article in 1968:[1]

> Multinational companies for progress around the world? This only means that (the) . . . U.S.-European ruling elite wants now, as usual, to expand and rationalise the world political space in which it is free to pursue its profit making, and that it has prepared itself today for an order of global integration which was heretofore impracticable.

Probably no major multinational can afford to take a visibly active stance. In the advanced countries, governments can normally resist the political pressures of multinational subsidiaries. That they normally follow lines similar to American policy is more a matter of inertia than subservience to multinationals. After all, De Gaulle and Sweden have followed noticeably independent foreign policy lines from the U.S. without being forced to make significant concessions. Similarly, Trudeau's maverick N.A.T.O. policy has not been curtailed, despite Canada's economic dependence on the U.S.

For the less-developed nations, the situation is obviously less happy, if only because it is still possible for single firms to dominate their national economy. However, the growth of

---

[1] Carl Oglesby, *op. cit.*

economic nationalism in the petroleum and copper mining industries and the increasing freedom of nations to play off multinationals against each other (this will be discussed fully in a later section) suggest that power is slowly moving from the multinational companies to national governments of independent inclinations. These questions will be discussed at length later, but for the moment let us consider the simple question: if a nation has a reasonably stable government, does it really make any difference who actually owns the firms making the country's baby-foods, cars, computers, newspapers, razor blades, margarines, etc.? Discounting national pride and the strategic issues, and assuming that research policies and financial strategies do not harm the nation, would it matter if the Americans, or the British, or the Japanese totally owned another country's economy through multinationals? In practice, it would not, just as it does not really matter that a Californian's cars are made in Detroit. In the words of Servan-Schreiber,[1] "The economic satellisation of Europe would not prevent the French from discussing politics or the Germans from going to concerts." Culturally, it does not matter who owns the firms that run one's economy since there is less and less room for companies which give customers what the company thinks they ought to get. The vast marketing expenditures of the multinationals are not there to force totally unwanted goods down the throats of captive customers. These expenditures ensure, instead, that they produce products close enough to consumer demand in world markets so that national competitors cannot exploit any significant untapped market.

Foreign domination matters most in the field of the mass media, and several countries have legislation to protect certain media from foreign control. Thus New Zealand passed the News Media Ownership Act in 1965 to block Canada's Lord Thomson from acquiring a major newspaper. Again, Canadian advertisers have not been able since 1965 to claim as business expenses their advertising in non-Canadian owned publications with the exception of Canadian editions of *Time* and *Reader's Digest*. Generally, the takeover of newspapers by foreigners is one of the supremely emotional occasions in national politics;

[1] Servan-Schreiber, Jean-Jacques. *The American Challenge.* Hamish Hamilton, London, 1968; Atheneum Publishers, New York.

such occurrences are normally discouraged everywhere. One wonders, however, if this practice really matters to such an advanced, capitalist nation as Canada. Newspapers are slowly dying. The average person takes more of his views and information from television, which tends to set or reflect the general standards upon which the national culture is based. But the daily newspaper, which to survive must assume its readers have homogeneous interests, must also compete with rapidly expanding numbers of specialised magazines which cater to minority tastes.

Governments recognise the importance of television by exercising fairly tight control over the number of programme hours which must be produced in the home country. Otherwise economics would dictate the exclusive use of American programmes which can be sold cheaply to foreign stations because they normally recoup their cost in the lucrative home market. Of course, one nation, South Africa bans the whole medium, on the grounds that television would have to rely at least in part on the programmes of other nations which are tainted by undesirable views. While this case is extreme, various other nations have become concerned with the impact that 'westernised' culture is making through television; what often follows such anxiety, of course, is attacks on western popular music, mini-skirts, long hair, or whatever other manifestation of decadent westernised culture is currently gaining acceptance.

And yet, it may well be that the battle against the 'decadent' west has already been lost; that future action can only minimise some of the worst cultural damage. The concept of a mass culture controlled by a few centralised institutions is gradually changing as minority tastes are recognised and catered to. But one tends to forget that in the 1920's and 1930's the cinema became a popular, mass cultural medium which was virtually synonymous with Hollywood. During this era, Hollywood studios turned out between 70–80% of the world's films, and their impact was probably even more completely universal. Competing film makers in Europe often had to disguise their films as American, because the public wanted nothing but Hollywood. In practice, Hollywood probbably made the greatest world-wide cultural impact in the shortest time of any institution in history.

The important thing about Hollywood film-making was that the industry was run by people with popular tastes. The film makers were often immigrants or small entrepreneurs who accidentally hit a gold mine. They found themselves free to film subjects which interested them in the way which appealed to them. It was not until the late 1920's that the wrath of conventional America caught up with them and censorship forbade the treatment of subjects like abortion, adultery, or other controversial issues. This censorship, however, did not stifle the élan with which Hollywood trumpeted the glories of the American way-of-life—a life style which included a very basic interest in material goods or money.

In America itself, Hollywood's films are given major credit for introducing waves of immigrants to the culture and language of their newly adopted home, the United States. Secondly, Hollywood's independence in the 1920's was probably a major force in defeating Prohibition and in launching the 'Jazz age', a phenomenon which had its impact outside the States as well. More subtly, it revolutionised the female role, fashion and, even, courtship patterns (if only to provide models for kisses). Outside America, it is obviously more difficult to chart such an impact. International distribution of silent films was easy (only new titles in the relevant language were required) and many non-American directors longed to travel to California as did the great Russian director, Sergei Eisenstein, around 1930. The prestigious swarmed to the place: at the age of 7, Shirley Temple received visits from H. G. Wells, Noel Coward, Eleanor Roosevelt, J. Edgar Hoover and Thomas Mann. Another child star, Jackie Coogan, was received in private audience by the Pope.

For twenty years, then, until the advent of television, the popular culture of much of the Westernised World was produced in one American city. The output from this centre was heavily affected by the materialistic goals of much of American society at that time. The rest of the world's fascination with the place must have been paralleled in a revolution in their expectations of the new way of life, so alien to their traditional cultures but so much more attractive. Hollywood's power has been broken, but its message continues to spread. New film makers from Britain, France and Italy make films to the old

65

'escapist' formulae, while the international world of pop music spreads a message of youthful abandon. Governments wanting to fight these values have probably already lost. The masses will demand such films and records if they are banned. All that many governments can do is to try and keep up the quality of the imports they receive. What they cannot do is to keep out the basically materialistic or secular values. Such values become a neo-colonial force. In comparison, the nationality of a breakfast cereal or computer manufacturer is trivial. Their activities may be economically objectionable; but culturally, they are unimportant.

CHAPTER V

The Financial Implications

Balance of payments implications

It would be convenient if simple calculations existed which showed exactly how much multinationals contributed to or took away from a given country's balance of payments. Most of the world's economic managers give highest priority to balance of payments problems. But unfortunately there are complications. First, one must consider such advantages as the 'spin off' effect on the efficiency of national competitors, or such disadvantages as political pressures. However, there is a second, more fundamental difficulty. Kindleberger (1969):[1] "There is no way of judging the balance of payments effect of a single transaction without knowing what would happen if it did not occur and the complete chain of consequences if it does occur." For instance, when balancing the remission of profits back to the headquarters of an American car firm, one would have to calculate what would have happened had the firm not invested in the given country. Would the national car firms have taken over completely the space that the U.S. firm has filled? . . . Or would their partial success in producing the type of cars sold by the American firm have resulted in a higher level of imports? The exact assumption made can completely alter such calculations.

Two studies based on similar assumptions attempt to evaluate the effects on Britain and the United States of their traditional capital-exporting roles, to determine whether the nation benefits from a manufacturing subsidiary abroad. Britain's Reddaway report (W. B. Reddaway. 1968)[2] concludes that

[1] Kindleberger, Charles P. *American business abroad: six lectures on direct investment.* Yale University Press, 1969.
[2] Reddaway, W. B. *Effects of U.K. direct investment overseas: final report.* Cambridge University Press, 1968.

such direct investment does lead to a long-term net gain to the British balance of payments on current account. This conclusion rests, however, on the assumption that the competition would take over 100% of the market in the absence of British investments. If one assumes that they would only capture 90%, leaving room for British exports, then direct investment is not necessarily advantageous to Britain. Second, the initial outflow of capital may well be heavy, creating a large, short-term problem. The size of the difference between these short-term and long-term effects depends on the extent to which the initial investment is financed by overseas funds such as Eurodollars. A similar study sponsored by the U.S. Treasury (Hufbauer, G. C. and Adler, F. M., 1968)[1] largely agreed with Reddaway, though it suggested that direct U.S. investment was more profitable than Britain's.

From the viewpoint of a host nation, Dunning (1969)[2] concludes that Britain actually benefits from receiving American investment. He compares the extra exports generated by U.S. subsidiaries in Britain, and the imports which have been saved, with the earnings and royalties sent back to the U.S. headquarters, the licence fees necessary to pay if the Americans had not invested in Britain, the components such subsidiaries import into Britain, and concludes:

> . . . this gives a small positive contribution of U.S. firms to the balance of payments of £12 million. To this figure must be added an inflow of (net) new investment in manufacturing industry which in 1965 was £73 million.

We thus end with a somewhat paradoxical situation. Both Reddaway and Hufbauer/Adler suggest that direct foreign investment benefits the donor nation. Dunning suggests it benefits the recipient nation. None of the studies is entirely convincing in its assumptions (Dunning lacks up-to-date figures on the imports generated from countries outside the U.S. by American subsidiaries in Britain. His final calculation may be too optimistic as a result). But these findings do not necessarily conflict: American investment in Britain could

[1] Hufbauer, G. C. and Adler, F. M. *Overseas manufacturing investment and the balance of payments.* U.S. Treasury Department, 1968.
[2] Dunning, John H., *op. cit.*, 1969.

benefit the U.S. through higher American exports and royalties; at the same time, the British economy could benefit from the same investment since the U.S. subsidiaries usually have significantly higher export ratios than their British competitors.

Whatever the truth, it would seem to be too early to make any serious policy decisions. What one can do is show the type of impact multinational companies are having in given financial areas. From this, it is possible to see the need for caution when examining certain activities of the multinationals.

Multinationals and exports

We noted at the beginning of this book that the multinationals were downgrading the importance of direct exporting. Thus at a conservative estimate in 1967, the value of output resulting from direct foreign investment by the 10 leading capital exporting nations came to $240 billion; their combined exports totalled $130 billion. As Rolfe put it[1], the major economic channel between the U.S. and the rest of the world is international investment and production, not exports: in 1966, the U.S. exported $24 billion while U.S. companies produced at least $110 billion directly abroad. The drive for free trade may now be less important than a drive for the free flow of capital between nations.

However, even within the export field, we find the multinationals play an important role. Marie Bradshaw[2] surveyed 330 U.S. Corporations with 3,579 foreign affiliates which had total 1967 exports from the U.S. of $8·5 billion (total U.S. exports from all sources that year were $24 billion). She showed that $4·4 billion (52%) of this sum was channelled through the foreign affiliates of U.S. firms. Out of the total $8·5 billion, 48% went directly to unaffiliated foreign purchasers, 29% went to affiliates for direct resale; 18% went to affiliates for further processing; 3% was made up of capital equipment purchases of affiliates from the U.S., and the remaining 2% went to affiliates but was unallocated. If one adds in the exports from other sources in America which the U.S.-owned affiliates

[1] Rolfe, Sidney. 'Updating Adam Smith.' *Interplay*, November 1968, pp. 15–19.
[2] Bradshaw, Marie T. 'U.S. exports to foreign affiliates of U.S. firms.' *Survey of Current Business*, May 1969, pp. 34–51.

generated, then the total figure of U.S. exports passing through these affiliates comes to $5·1 billion. Assuming that this was a survey covering only a third of U.S. exports, one can state that 'within the family' trading (i.e., from one part of a multinational firm to another part of the same firm) across the U.S. frontier accounted for at least 18% of the United States exports in 1967. Likewise, the overseas affiliates of U.S. firms handled at least 21% of U.S. exports. Since this was only a partial survey of U.S. firms, there are grounds for claiming that 'within the family' trading may well have accounted for around 25–30% of total U.S. exports that year.

Similar figures have been produced for Britain, the second largest home of multinational companies. A Board of Trade survey in 1968 showed that in 1966:

> . . . exports to related concerns in overseas countries represented about 22% of total exports [the U.S. experience noted above would suggest that another 3–4% of U.K. exports would be created by purchases of such affiliates from British companies, other than their owners].
> . . . among the branches and subsidiaries of U.S. companies based in Britain, 56% of their exports went to affiliates outside Britain.
> . . . subsidiaries and branches of U.S. auto companies in Britain sent 80% of their exports to overseas affiliates.
> . . . other industries with particularly high ratios of exports being channelled to foreign-based affiliates were chemicals, electrical engineering and rubber.

Obviously, much of this exporting activity reflects firms exporting to sales subsidiaries which they own abroad. Particularly interesting, however, were the American figures produced by Bradshaw[1] showing that $1·5 billion (at least 6% of the total U.S. exports in 1965) went to foreign affiliates 'for further processing'. This figure is a direct reflection of the degree to which U.S. firms are organised with global logistical flows. What the figures do not show is the degree to which subsidiaries of U.S. firms trade amongst themselves, without either importing or exporting across the U.S. frontier. For instance, the American car and computer firms in Europe are now manipulating the flow of components and products round the continent on a scale which should begin to be economically important.

[1] *Op. cit.*

Unfortunately, statistics on this movement are non-existent, and our picture of American multinational firms is therefore incomplete. Needless to say, no statistics exist to throw light on the activities of multinationals owned by other nations. We shall see later in this chapter that this statistical information is particularly scanty about multinationals' import strategies—a gap which must be filled in the interests of sound economic management. Perhaps some body like the O.E.C.D. should call a conference of statisticians for the major trading nations to see whether the standards of statistical information in this field could be raised. What evidence there is suggests that multinationals are now playing a vital role in the trading activities of the major nations. But national policy makers should not have to rely on such "guesstimates".

Integration with the American economy

The figures on the pattern of U.S. exports show that American investment integrates certain countries with the U.S. economy more than others.

TABLE 4[1]

The proportion of foreign affiliates of U.S. parents making no purchases of U.S. exports in 1965

Location of the Affiliate	All Industries	Manufacturing Industries
Canada	32·2%	19·1%
United Kingdom	39·8%	29·3%
Japan/Australia/South Africa	40·8%	34·8%
European Economic Community	47·2%	44·6%
Other Europe	52·1%	54·3%

[1] The figures are abstracted from tables presented in Marie Bradshaw's 'U.S. exports to foreign affiliates of U.S. firms.' *Survey of Current Business*, May 1969.

These figures suggest not only that countries like Canada, Australia, and the United Kingdom receive a relatively high proportion of American investment, but also that their

American subsidiaries look toward the U.S. for supplies. There is clear evidence that Canada is significantly more integrated with the U.S. economy than any other nation. But more interestingly, clear evidence also points to the importance of language as a factor in deciding the degree to which a company is centrally organised. Particularly for manufacturing industries, U.S. subsidiaries in continental Europe are noticeably less integrated with the American economy than their English-speaking compatriots in the United Kingdom, Canada, Australia and South Africa. Of course, historically the early U.S. subsidiaries were easiest to establish in English-language countries. By 1965, however, the major swing of U.S. investment toward non-English-speaking Europe had begun. One can expect a surge of integration in the future, as U.S. parents begin to rationalise their investments.

Export allocation

Multinationals' power in the export field has serious implications for national governments. In the past, one could assume that imports and exports were controlled by a number of reasonably small concerns which responded to economic fluctuations in the classical way: if the prices of one nation's goods went up, cheaper goods from other countries were purchased; goods for sale were marketed in the most economic foreign market. The coming of the multinationals has meant that the relatively undistorted flow of goods can now be heavily influenced by decisions taken in the multinational head-quarters. Such headquarters may find themselves influenced in turn by past investment decisions, or by long-term company strategies which do not include short-term manoeuvres taking advantage of temporary fluctuations in different markets.

Increasingly, multinationals are able to supply markets from two or three sources. They therefore must choose between subsidiaries. Most multinationals consider wasteful leaving their subsidiaries free to compete for export markets. They can allow markets to be decided by strictly economic factors, ruling that orders should be given to the manufacturing subsidiary which can land the produce at the cheapest over-all cost, taking transportation into account. But this rule, though simple, has its disadvantages. It may well pay the over-all firm to channel orders through subsidiaries located in low-tax countries, even if their manufacturing costs are relatively high. Again other subsidiaries may have tax-losses to utilise.

When the central headquarters rules that one nation shall be preferred over another, national suspicions often rise. For example, General Motors could have supplied the Japanese markets from either California or Australia, but chose California. But recently, Australia has been worried about the quantity of her Japanese imports, an anxiety fed by the General Motors decision. General Motors has also been forced to choose between using autos from its German (Opel) or British (Vauxhall) subsidiaries as additions to its range sold in the United States. Chrysler, faced with a similar problem, chose to distribute in America cars from both its Simca and Rootes subsidiaries, thus ducking the problem. Finally, the decision of all three major American auto-manufacturers to produce a U.S. manufactured small car to fight the growing tide of imports hits not only Volkswagen but also their own European subsidiaries' exports.

Anti-trust authorities do not approve of formal schemes for carving up world-wide markets. It is therefore unlikely that multinationals will agree formally that one subsidiary will not export to a given market, though obviously what was permitted would be clearly understood by the relevant managers. However, as Catherwood[1] points out, the central headquarters of such companies are not likely to approve investments leading to vast excesses of capacity which operate at the expense of other subsidiaries. He points out that it is unlikely the manager of a German subsidiary will suggest setting up American agents in competition with the multinational parent.

'Runaway industries'

Equally important is the growing tendency of multinationals to move their manufacturing activities away from high-wage nations, and thus incidentally become net importers into their parent nation. U.S. watchmakers have constructed plants in Switzerland and Japan; Singer now sells its U.S. customers two

[1] Catherwood, H. F. R. 'United States investment in Britain.' 1968. Paper available from the National Economic Development Organisation, London.

73

machines produced in its overseas plants for every one made in the U.S. Its Elizabethport, New Jersey, plant once employed 10,000 but has now shrunk to 2,000. Electronic firms find the cheap labour of Hong Kong and other parts of South East Asia a reason for manufacturing there and then exporting the products to the United States. One can hear the grumbles of patriotic American electronic firms who find themselves being undercut by their less homebound competitors. Finally, the U.S. auto manufacturers, who have so far only toyed with importing cars made by their European subsidiaries, may find that the drop in transatlantic freight costs resulting from the commercial introduction of the massive Lockheed Galaxie air freighter justifies building their smaller cars in Europe. It might even become economical at long last to design a car which would serve simultaneously both Europe (as a medium-sized, high-powered car) and America (as a small, economy car).

This trend will grow, even though resistance to it will increase. There will obviously be heavy nationalistic pressures put on these multinationals. They may well feel forced to produce in their home nation, even if it is increasingly uneconomical. However, there are disguised ways of becoming a 'marketing shell' (a company which once manufactured in a nation but which now supplies its market with products from lower cost nations). One can, for instance, gradually build a larger and larger number of components abroad.

In many ways, the development of 'runaway industries' is a logical result of companies going multinational. In the past, one of the chief obstacles to firms taking full advantage of world-wide production cost differences has been sheer ignorance of the high cost markets. Transportation developments have lessened this ignorance, but the genuine multinational which is well established in a number of different nations is the competitor best able to take advantage of such opportunities. The United States will be hit first, since it is the country with the most expensive labour. And as the European multinationals start fighting back, American mutlinationals will find that long-term survival depends on their manufacturing outside the United States. However, as the lesser-developed nations grow in economic stability, Europe will face similar problems.

The implications of this pattern are extensive. Unions must face the danger that jobs will slip away from their members. Developing nations will gain a good chance to capitalise on their one common marketable commodity, cheap labour. But the faster that transportation costs fall (and containerisation, bulk carriers and air freight are lowering them the whole time), the more inevitable this process becomes.

Financial speculation

The positive side to the financial power of the multinational is that it is able to take full advantage of various bases by borrowing in low interest areas and transferring the money to operations in high interest ones. Such money movements are relatively simple but also quite hard to detect, even if governments are trying to scrutinise the process. A subsidiary in one country might be told to stop borrowing while a subsidiary in a low interest area might be told to borrow for both of them. The latter can transfer the money by such devices as speeding up payments for internal transactions with the first subsidiary, in effect giving it a loan. A vice-president of U.S.M. Corporation (formerly United Shoe Machinery Corporation) explained this feat:

> One of our Danish subsidiaries had excess cash which it lent to another Danish subsidiary which was receiving goods from the Swedish subsidiary. The Danish company pre-paid its account with the Swedish subsidiary and this money financed the movement of Swedish product into the Finnish subsidiary. What did this manoeuvre accomplish? If Finland had been required to have paid for the goods, it would have had to have borrowed at 15%, the going Finnish rate. If the Swedish subsidiary had financed the sale, it would have had to borrow at 9%. But cash in Denmark was worth only 5–6%. Moreover Danish currency was weak in relation to the Swedish. By speeding up payments to Sweden, we not only obtained cheap credit, we hedged our position in Danish kroner as well. (*Fortune*, 15th September 1968.)

This financial freedom can be used, however, for chicanery such as tax evasion. A multinational benefits by making as much of its profit as possible in low-tax areas, or in areas in which the tax authorities are notoriously incompetent and/or corrupt. Transfer pricing makes this possible.

A well-integrated multinational can manipulate the transfer prices of transactions between one nation and another. To maximise its financial return, the multinational may instruct its subsidiaries in a high tax area to fix prices so that they buy expensively and sell cheaply to subsidiaries in low tax areas. This means that the paper profits will fall in the latter area. minimising the company's immediate tax obligations. A good example of this is given by George Thayer (1969)[1] in his account of the activities of International Armament Corporation, a U.S. company which is the world's largest private dealer in weapons: he describes how between 1958 and 1963 the company's owner was able—quite legally—to channel substantial sums of virtually untaxed money from his American operations into a purchasing fund in Geneva:

> Interarms (U.K.) might buy a large quantity of surplus Lee-Enfield No. 4 Mark 1 rifles from the British government for, say $1.50 apiece. It would then resell them to Interarms (Canada), a company domiciled in Monaco (to take advantage of the low corporation tax), for $1.65, a 10% profit added. To take advantage of a low rate of import duty, the rifles had to be invoiced into the U.S. at a value below $5, so Interarms (Canada) would resell them to the parent company for $4.95. The Monaco-based company would thus make a profit of $3.30 on each weapon ($4.95 less $1.65) purely by a paper transaction. The money was paid into a purchasing fund in Geneva. No American taxes would be paid on the outgoing $4.95 because it was picked up by a foreign company as gross income which was not taxed.

None of these transactions was illegal, though Monaco's tax rates have since been raised under pressure from France; and the U.S. has become stricter about the conditions under which American firms can do this sort of thing. Governments have retaliated by coming to double taxation agreements, whereby a company's activities will be taxed first in the country in which the activity takes place (a U.S.-owned subsidiary in Britain will first pay taxes in Britain); but if these initial taxes are lower than the parent country's rates, then the company will have to pay a second set of taxes to make up the balance. If the taxes in the first country are higher than those in the parent country, then the multinational headquarters will pay nothing

[1] Thayer, George. *The War Business.* Weidenfeld & Nicolson, London, 1969.

extra on those particular profits. Furthermore, taxation author-ities work as closely as they can with the customs services; they will increasingly demand that multinationals do their transfer pricing as though these were 'arms-length transactions', i.e. as though they were selling to an independent purchaser. If a company sets prices unaccountably higher than those of similar firms, then they may face a supplemental tax which assumes they are arbitrarily hiking their prices.

Although tax authorities in the most advanced nations have been increasing their surveillance, multinationals still boast a great deal of freedom. Even if they eventually have to pay a second lot of taxes in their home country, making their profits initially in a low-tax area means that they can use the untaxed money during the inevitable time-lags before their own tax authorities make their balancing assessment. Second, profits are easier to make in countries where the taxation authorities are inefficient. Italian company accounts are notorious for their very tenuous connections with actual events. Selling an Italian firm poses problems, since it may well be worth far more than accounts actually show. A U.S. firm might agree to buy an Italian firm for $20 million, when the company has been declaring profits only of $200,000 and a book value of $2 million. The taxable gain left is $18 million. The Italian firm might then sell patents to the Italian firm's subsidiary incorpor-ated in a Swiss canton without paying any capital gains tax. The Italian firm would then be purchased at, say, $4 million, giving the Italian tax authorities a $2 million capital gain to tax. The Italian subsidiary in Switzerland could then be sold for $16 million, tax free, making everybody happy. Similarly, the Vatican banks in Italy will often help companies in this predicament by buying a firm at one price, selling it at another, and transferring the extra cash to the seller.

So long as tax authorities exert differing degrees of pressure, the ruthless multinational will find it pays to manipulate prices, even if few firms go so far as to have all their transfer prices set by tax lawyers and international accountants—a known practice. In the meantime, a number of smallish nations have set themselves up as tax havens. Traditionally attractive nations like Switzerland (which has over 4,000 holding companies based there), have been joined by Luxembourg, the Bahamas,

Panama, Curaçao (the Netherlands' Antilles), and Liechtenstein. Many other small countries have ambitions; as soon as the Greek military junta took power it announced a number of tax incentives for foreign business.

These nations can play a valuable role in international finance. By offering a base for financial transactions with no accompanying restrictions on currency movements, they allow companies to manipulate funds without having to tie down a lot of capital in one place or without having to check constantly with government officials who are concerned about their national balance of payments. Channelling major financial movements away from the great trading nations does not affect the major economies as much as continuous massive flows of funds across their borders might. However, there are also disadvantages.

Every so often, companies find themselves disputing with regulatory authorities in certain nations, at which point it may become desirable to base the company in a tax haven offering a fair amount of secrecy. The individual who smuggles money into an anonymous Swiss bank account is not too different from the company which chooses to operate in a country where the shareholders' identities are never disclosed. *Fortune* (March 1968) discussed the career of Bernard Cornfeld's Investors Overseas Services (I.O.S.), a company with 14,000 employees and at least $1 billion in its investment funds. Basically, I.O.S. is a world-wide organisation, taking investment from anywhere and placing it in whatever market it chooses (most often, Wall Street, where on some days I.O.S. has accounted for 4% of the dealings). The company has been brilliantly run, taking advantage of all possible international tax and legal concessions. It paid a 1966 tax bill of $375,000 on $6 million profits.

I.O.S. is scrutinised carefully by national authorities since it can furnish the rich a convenient way of shipping capital out of a country; and I.O.S.'s career has been marked by such ingenious manipulation of the world currency regulations that it remains attractive as a suitable investment vehicle. In 1965, U.S. Securities and Exchange Commission, concerned about a number of the company's activities outside the U.S., demanded I.O.S. customer lists and operating information. I.O.S. argued that compliance would be a breach of faith with customers

78

who included 6 heads of state and many nationals from the Iron Curtain countries. The case dragged into court and I.O.S. lost. Finally, I.O.S. agreed to sell its U.S. subsidiary and promised not to deal with U.S. citizens or in the U.S. securities market. In return, I.O.S. no longer comes under U.S. jurisdiction and can thus preserve the confidence of its clients.

In fact, this case only highlights a probable source of future concern: the way money of dubious origins is obtained through bank accounts and firms based in nations lax about such matters. The U.S. authorities are increasingly concerned about government officials who 'cream off' a large proportion of the international aid going to certain nations; businessmen dealing with some developing nations find that they are asked to make large payments to numbered Swiss bank accounts in order to get key contracts; the Cosa Nostra (the Mafia), with a turnover estimated by U.S. Government officials at $30 billion or one-third more than General Motors, the world's largest private company, is alleged to smuggle money out of the U.S. into anonymous accounts in places like Switzerland and the Bahamas, and thence back into legitimate businesses serving as covers for large quantities of 'hot' money. Increasingly, this is a problem which the U.S. authorities cannot solve by themselves. Anonymous bank accounts which are justified in some circumstances (the genuine political refugee), become less desirable when they cloak world-wide corruption. The military government in Brazil has tried to break this anonymity by opening mail and searching homes. In the U.S., the chairman of the House Banking and Currency Committee has called for legislation against banks which refuse to open their records to U.S. regulatory agencies.

This kind of problem reappears in a slightly different guise in the Caribbean. Outside direct U.S. control, many small nations find that the best solution to their economic problems is to encourage tourism by lures, such as gambling, which are strictly controlled in the U.S. A typical development is the gambling centre of Freeport in the Bahamas, 100 miles from Miami and an easy flight for the more determined gambler. While Freeport's rivals in Nassau, Haiti and Puerto Rico are further away from Miami, all cash in on the gambling boom. However, evidence suggests that U.S. gambling interests,

79

increasingly controlled in cities like Las Vegas, are turning their attention to such sources of new income. During 1969, the U.S. Department of Justice intercepted sophisticated electronic cheating equipment—remote-controlled roulette wheels, radio transmitters and assorted magnetic devices—en route from Las Vegas to Haiti. *The Economist* quoted an F.B.I. agent as saying:

> With its remote radio controls, this table will do everything but reach into a player's pocket and remove his money. With a little practice the magnets can be tuned by the remote radio transmitter so that objects will dance on top of the table or stand upright with no visible means of control.[1]

In one of these interceptions, agents seized a man they claimed was a Mafia associate, whose papers showed he was in touch with men working for casinos in London, Madeira, St Maarten, Bonaire and Haiti (the last three places being in the Caribbean). In the Bahamas, the gambling is probably straight; but in setting up casinos, Freeport sought advice from Myer Lansky, supposedly the head of Florida's illegal gambling. To set up a casino one must know the credit rating of all major gamblers, and the relative honesty of all key staff. Only the Mafia has this sort of knowledge.

One of the growing problems in this area is the mini-state which may become easy prey for big-money interests whose motives do not bear close scrutiny. Britain actually sent troops into the small island of Anguilla partly to stop such a takeover. Tourism, the industry such islands attract best, also depends on operations attracting some unscrupulous businessmen. Property developers, hoteliers. casino-operators are all flooding into this area marked by the vital absence of company legislation. Local officials are under incredible temptation. Bahamian politicians raise political funds in Miami, where co-operative business interests expect preferential treatment when their candidates are re-elected.

The U.S. Securities and Exchange Commission (S.E.C.) is increasingly worried about the status of large businesses based in this area. The American Department of Justice has named individuals who they claim are helping the Mafia move the

[1] *The Economist*, June 28, 1969, p. 68.

profits from its American rackets into Swiss accounts and from there into the Caribbean. Some of these companies are now starting to buy their way into the U.S. market. In a recent case, the Justice Department limited the stake of one Bahamas-based company in Pan American Airways.

This discussion may seem a bit removed from tax havens, *per se*. However, many tax havens are small nations who attract money because they do not enquire too closely into its source. After all, if Switzerland, an eminently respectable nation, can so doggedly protect its numbered accounts from outside investigation, despite the overwhelming evidence that some are being used by criminal interests, it is unlikely that newer competitors will look any more closely at the funds they attract.

In any case, large-scale crime increasingly is internationally organised. One can even argue that the Mafia was one of the earliest U.S. multinationals: it started with the procurement of native Italian prostitutes, progressed to the importation of alcohol during prohibition, then diversified into drugs, setting up supply lines from the Middle East through France to the United States. More recently the growth of tourism has added further opportunities. In the immediate future, the development of these tourist spots will provide the Mafia with a chance to pull away from the U.S. market, which becomes more dangerous as law enforcement agencies slowly uncover the extent of Mafia infiltration throughout the U.S. economy. In so doing, they move into politically weak nations where their form of corruption should guarantee them the freedom from surveillance unavailable elsewhere. The opportunities for less scrupulous multinational companies, too, will increase. Basing operations in one of these less reputable areas may allow them to 'lose' profits which might be taxed elsewhere. The task of the U.S. tax authorities will get considerably harder, and the advantages for the less scrupulous of going multinational should increase.

Financial speculation

One area in which the rise of the multinationals has been particularly important is international parities. A company with a global spread of interests finds itself increasingly vulnerable to unforeseen devaluations of national currencies. Such events can lead either to a company's assets or to its profits suddenly declining in value. Major companies now have economists, one of whose jobs is to predict such events. Ford's devaluation experts, supported by a library on leading national decision-makers, claim to have been usefully correct in 69 out of 75 crisis situations up to 1968.

A company which is convinced that a devaluation is imminent can take evasive action. It can manipulate transfer prices and vary the speed with which one subsidiary pays another. Thus it makes sure that the bulk of its money is on the right side of the national border when devaluation takes place, as U.S.M. did in operations quoted earlier. *Fortune*[1] claimed that most firms asked their European subsidiaries to defer payments for goods from the United Kingdom for 6–7 months to insure that considerably more money than usual was outside the country when devaluation finally occurred in November 1967.

A second manoeuvre is also possible. Companies with assets to be affected by devaluations can actively speculate in the forward market so that they cover the loss in asset value by the profits made in forward speculation. One study showed that in the 1967 devaluation, 19 of 22 firms had fully hedged their U.K. investment. According to Brooks,[2] I.T. & T. (International Telephone & Telegraph) announced the day afterwards that their management had anticipated the event and that their yearly earnings would not be affected. International Harvester and Texas Instruments protected themselves by selling short on sterling. Singer even made an accidental profit, probably because some countries which might have devalued in Britain's wake did not do so.

The trouble with such activities is that they actually make the suspected devaluation (or revaluation) more certain. In fact, since the multinational can now actually influence the balance between exports and imports, they increasingly determine such currency activities. In practice, such a company may first hasten or delay the flow of exports and imports in order to hedge its bets; then it may do the same with its payments between subsidiaries; next it will hedge in order to cover assets which may be affected; finally, it may go further and

[1] September 15, 1969.
[2] Brooks, John. *Business Adventures*. Victor Gollancz, London, 1969.

actively speculate in order to make profits totally unrelated to any other considerations. Business ethics would generally frown on the latter behaviour, but in the absence of any real evidence, one cannot say with any confidence that some firms do not speculate openly in a situation which is profitable for one who guesses right.

The end of fixed parities?

With rare exceptions, the international financial system is built round fixed parities, which are protected desperately by governments who feel that devaluations somehow signal defeat. In fact, they may sometimes reflect unavoidable misfortunes such as the loss of traditional markets or the growth in competition from other nations. The 1960's, however, have been so marked by increasingly severe financial crises that respectable financial commentators openly admit the flow of speculative money has grown so large, the international banking community cannot contain it.

Between 1967 and 1969, four of the world's most important parities were toppled by sheer speculative pressure. In November 1967, the pound was devaluated. On one day alone, the Bank of England lost $1 billion, a loss which meant that the maximum sums provided by the international banking community to an ailing currency like the pound could vanish in three days under speculative pressure. Four months later the dollar was forced into a partial devaluation of its currency in relation to gold, when there was a similar massive flight out of the dollar into gold. It then took the speculators a mere fifteen months to bring down the franc. This was no mean achievement since De Gaulle had, up to May 1968, gradually built up the French reserves to around $7 billion. By insisting that a large proportion of the dollars in this total should be converted into gold, he played a major part in forcing the U.S. authorities into accepting a two-tier price system for gold, an acceptance which was tantamount to admitting that U.S. reserves behind the dollar were not enough to maintain the pledge made by the U.S. authorities in 1934 to exchange gold in any quantity for dollars at the fixed price of $35 an ounce. Then came the events of May 1968, when rioting students and industrial workers brought about wildly inflationary wage increases and finally De Gaulle's resignation. At this point, the international financial and business communities realised that the franc rested on an economy which was not particularly strong in the first place and which now looked decidedly vulnerable. In the ensuing months, speculation against the franc so increased that not even one of the strongest reserves could save it from the inevitable devaluation which took place in August 1969.

In October 1969, the Deutschemark in turn bowed to speculative pressure, this time being forced into revaluation. This was a slightly more complex affair, with West Germany's consistent balance of payments surpluses leading to demands from other nations for a revaluation to restore the competitive positions. There was some demand from within Germany for such a revaluation, since the cost of such international commercial success was a growth rate in Germany which meant higher inflation than the Germans (many of them mindful of the 1920's when one needed handcarts to carry his valueless paper money) were willing to tolerate. The main objections came from the industrialists who did not relish a move aimed to make them less competitive in the international arena, and from local politicians who saw any change in the parity as an admission of national weakness. The General Election in September 1969 added to the uncertainty. The steady flow of funds into Frankfurt became a torrent, leading to the enforced closure of the foreign exchanges in the last days of the election. This was followed by three weeks in which the mark was allowed to 'float' (i.e. find its own level without official backing), finally culminating in an official revaluation at 3·66 D.Marks per U.S. dollar.

These successful attacks on four out of the five or six most important international currencies would suggest that there is no reason whatever for expecting the new pattern of currency parities to last. Each devaluation or revaluation merely means that another currency is put under pressure. It is now thoroughly clear that the best defences of the international financial community are no longer strong enough to maintain any currency which is under attack. There is no evidence that the introduction of devices like the 'paper gold', Special Drawing Rights (S.D.R.'s), which are designed to expand the reserves of the major nations, is going to change the balance of power in the immediate future. If anything, the rapid growth of floating sources of international finance like the Eurodollar pool suggest that the situation facing vulnerable fixed parities will get worse.

The full implications of this situation are complicated. It would seem to make sense for nations to adopt some form of adjustable exchange rates. International monetary circles buzz regularly over new proposals with bizarre names like 'crawling pegs', which are designed to give the international financial scene this greater flexibility. The merits and demerits of such schemes do not matter too much in this context since they are all designed to mitigate the growing influence of massive international currency speculation. What is important to emphasise is that the activities of multinational companies are a significant part of this speculation and that to some extent such companies can make predictions self-fulfilling since they control a significant proportion of the trade between the largest nations. When their decisions are made on purely economic grounds, there can be no real complaint. However, it is possible that they might over-react in certain situations because they are affected by subjective reasons as well. For instance, deservedly or not, left-wing governments are felt to be less trustworthy as economic managers than right-wing ones. Thus, the final run on the Deutschemark began when it became clear that the left-wing Social Democrats might win the 1969 general election, just as the election of the British Labour Party in 1964 was followed almost immediately by massive speculative raids. In the less-developed countries, the international business community obviously feels safer under right-wing governments. Such subjectively based decisions do not usually matter, but when such decisions can effectively help or hinder national progress and thereby affect the fortunes of political parties, one can only become uneasy. In particular, the power of the multi-nationals both to hedge on the financial front and to affect a nation's balance of trade is new, and needs careful watching.

Implications for economic policy makers

This chapter has argued that the basic international commercial transaction has changed from a small importer's or exporter's unimportant decision to the giant multinational's manoeuvre, which may affect a nation for years. In this situation, the conventional means of regulating an economy by changing interest rates or tariff barriers may be irrelevant in the future, since the largest multinationals will command international flows of components and products which can only be altered slowly, having been planned as an integrated system. Such conventional economic manipulation may have only long-run effects on the largest companies and even then may be ignored; such companies will be looking ten years or so ahead, assuming that a country can only be out of step with its neighbours for a limited period of time; thus they undertake investment decisions that apparently make poor economic sense at the time they are made.

In this kind of situation, direct pressure on firms may be as effective as conventional fiscal policies. Thus, Ford needs a third major plant in Europe for the early 1970's. This will probably go to France, since placing a second major plant in Britain or Germany would risk considerable French resentment. The French Government's view will be that the impact of such an investment is so important, no risks should be taken to lose it. Thus, we find Mr and Mrs Henry Ford II wining and dining in the French presidential palace while the decision-making process was proceeding. After all, Henry Ford is running an organisation equivalent in size to a small nation and his firm can have a large impact on France. Leading multinationals are right when they claim that they no longer make entirely economic decisions. Like it or not, they are caught up in the political process.

National leaders, however, make decisions without adequate information. We have seen that most nation's statistics fail to analyse the impact of multinational companies on their economies. This could be rectified by breaking up the export and import figures so that the transactions of foreign-owned firms and foreign-based subsidiaries are clearly identified. In fact, perhaps multinational companies should break down their activities on a country-by-country basis, showing their monetary flows across national boundaries.

Though multinational companies would obviously object, such reports would be desirable since informed public debate should be possible over decisions which can alter a country's balance of payments by £10 million a year. This is becoming more important as multinationals create more products and become more footloose. Thus the Dutch multinational, Philips Lamps, the largest non-American electrical and electronic manufacturer, makes everything from small computers to colour television, washing machines and refrigerators. During the 1960's it depended increasingly on Italian refrigerators, which for various reasons, are excellent value. During 1969, Philips and Ignis, the largest Italian refrigerator manufacturer, announced that they had agreed on formal links, thus joining Philips' financial strength and marketing expertise to Ignis' volume. The logic of this move is that Philips will be marketing more Italian-manufactured domestic appliances in the rest of Europe, where the competition is relatively inefficient and fragmented. Countries other than Italy will therefore be relatively worse off since they will be taking more *imported* machines under the Philips label. By itself, this may not matter, but suppose a similar decision was taken about the manufacturing location of computers and colour televisions; this might, taken cumulatively, lead to a serious relative deterioration in Philips' balance of trade with one or two nations. In the case of this firm, a union delegation from the International Metalworkers Federation visited the Philips' headquarters in 1967 to enquire after company strategy regarding rationalisations which were taking place in the company. It came away reassured that the company was not giving undue favour to any one nation.

Without adequate company statistics one cannot make such judgements on a really informed basis. The impact of investment decisions and the resulting 'within the family' trading flows of European multinationals like Philips, Unilever, and Imperial Chemical Industries, or of American multinationals like I.B.M., Ford, General Motors, etc., cannot be accurately assessed because companies are not forced to give any significant information about their activities in different countries or trading blocs. Knowing, for instance, the company sales or number of employees in a given nation is not particularly important. Given the central role played by balance of payments considerations in national politics, it becomes important that multinationals should be required to give information about their international financial transactions. In a later section, we will discuss the move to set up a 'European' company with freedom from purely national control within Europe. If such a scheme does get approved, then it should be linked with requirements for fairly detailed information about the company's activities in each nation. Lacking such information, we will continue to see important decisions taken without informed comment or criticism. This is thoroughly undesirable.

After analysing the relationship between governments and multinationals, one feels that governments must increasingly attract major investments within their borders. This means that they must become more sensitive to issues which seem important in such investment decisions, especially when other nations nearby are following different lines. Thus British Governments, long worried by the contrast between Britain's lively strike record and the docility of the West German labour force, have attempted to tighten up British legislation governing industrial relations. More important is the competition between governments in investment incentives. In Europe, nations keenest to attract such investment will offer incentives reducing a company's capital commitment in a new plant between 30–40%. If anything, the competition is increasing, with the Dutch and the Belgians vying in their generosity to foreign investors; in 1966, the Belgians were offering capital grants of 30%, only to be topped by the Dutch who offered 40%. Moreover, as governments realise the importance of new investment in stimulating the growth of backward regions, this competition with subsidies will increase.

Some nations, in their enthusiasm, might go too far with these incentives. Kindleberger[1] cites the case of Puerto Rico, which offers U.S. companies a ten-year freedom from corporate tax. The policy undoubtedly works (101 of *Fortune*'s top 500 companies had manufacturing facilities in Puerto Rico in 1969) but raises a serious question about the economy's actual gains. What happens after the 10 years if other investment sites in the region will give similar tax exemption?

[1] Kindleberger, Charles P. *American business abroad: six lectures on direct investment.* Yale University Press, 1969.

Such competition must increase. When a single investment decision can be so important governments have strong incentive to swallow their pride and bargain hard for the investment. But one unanswered question is left: just how much of investment grants and foregone tax revenues should each new job be worth? At what point does this competition become ruinous?

CHAPTER VI

The Union Response

So far we have seen how the changing nature of large multi-nationals is destroying the balance of power between government and industry. If it is true that certain decisions are moving out of reach of governments, how much further must they be moving from trade unions, whose traditional weapon—withholding labour—is becoming obsolete. In the past a 'national' union would strike a company in the last resort; the balance of power, although normally in the company's hands, was not lopsidedly so. Today, however, if a company has only 30% of its production in any one country, a national union cannot affect more than that 30% of the firm; the remaining 70% in other nations can go on producing, even supplying the normal markets of the branch being struck. Belatedly unions have discovered that they must organise on an international basis themselves.

For a number of reasons, unions have found this difficult. The international union movement has always split along religious and political lines. Collective bargaining practices also vary from region to region (some unions are used to plant bargaining, others to area or industry bargaining, while others are used to getting their conditions of work improved through parliamentary means). While one of the more effective international groupings, the International Metalworkers Federation (I.M.F.), started considering the creation of a union structure parallel to multinationals in 1956, nothing much happened until they called a world-wide conference of auto workers in Frankfurt-am-Main in 1964. During the 1960's, however, there has been evidence of a significant growth in international union cooperation which has already won a few isolated, but potentially significant victories against the multinationals. The credit for this in the first place seems to belong to the United Auto

Workers (U.A.W.) under the leadership of Walter Reuther. Reuther gave the initial support and stimulation to a movement which by the end of the 1960's was showing signs of becoming self-sustaining.

By and large, it is the size and spread of the multinationals rather than their ultimate ownership which matters to union leaders. Ownership can be significant when the headquarters are militantly anti-union, and there are a number of American-owned firms which unionists particularly suspect on these grounds—for example, the 'yellow' union policies of Du Pont de Nemours and Union Carbide are often mentioned. On the other hand, in developing nations little difference may be evident between the local subsidiaries of Ford or British Leyland; the local managements may be equally keen to rid their plants of union organisers.

The multinationals' threats are relatively new to union strategists. It is now quite common for multinational managements to stress to uncooperative union leaders that continuing troubles will mean locating further investment in another country where a more docile labour force will welcome the extra work. The Canadian-owned multinational Massey-Ferguson was hit in 1968 by a 10-week strike aimed at getting equal pay for Canadian and U.S. employees. The management bluntly told the strikers that if they were forced to concede equal pay, then all expansion would be made in the U.S., where labour productivity is good, while the Canadian activities would be allowed to run down. Similarly, Ford in the U.K. threatened not to invest further in the British plant at Dagenham which struck in early 1969, a threat that carried some conviction because Ford has plants in Germany and Belgium.

It is difficult for a union to know how seriously to take such threats. No firm is going to close down a plant in which it may well have invested hundreds of millions of dollars, just because the work force is particularly unruly. Once a firm has made an initial investment, it is to some extent trapped by the size of its past involvement. Significantly, despite the considerable ill-will stirred up by the Ford strike mentioned above, the company still went ahead five months later with an £18 million expansion of an engine plant there. If one assumes that the Ford management was genuinely furious about the disruption this particular strike caused its European activities, he can still point out that they had no option in this case: £18 million spent on a totally new engine plant in another country would not have provided as many engines as the £18 million extension to the existing engine plant.

If there is discrimination, it is likely to take place considerably later when the multinational plans a totally new operation involving new plants. With a 'green field' project the location could be in a number of countries; in this decision, the union situation could be the determining factor. Without any really convincing analyses of the factors which determine multinational sites, one cannot state confidently that threats against unions in collective bargaining situations are totally unfounded. In the short run they almost certainly are, but in the long run, there is really no evidence one way or the other.

A further problem faced by unions in conflict with a multinational's subsidiary is that the firm can break strikes with output from other countries. Charles Levinson of the International Chemical Workers tells of Goodyear, which has plants in the U.S., Sweden and West Germany. Around 1966, the Swedish subsidiary stockpiled in anticipation of a strike in the U.S., but was persuaded that the strikebreaking attempt was not worth the company's trouble. A year later, the same stockpile was a threat to union strategy in Germany. Michelin was reported to be influencing a strike in its Spanish subsidiary by supplies of tyres from other plants. This problem can only grow with time and the answer can only come through collaboration between unionists in different countries. This involves a considerable amount of advance planning; management can normally tell when a major conflict is likely to arise, and can take the necessary steps well in advance. Moreover, the union strategy in this situation may be eroded by developments in transport technology. In the old days when most international commerce went by road or rail to the docks where it was unloaded, the dockers might help. Today, a firm may send 'blacked' goods by air freight. Alternatively, it could use a roll-on, roll-off ferry where the lorry can be driven straight on to the ship without help from dockers. Finally, the spread of containerisation, the practice of putting goods into standardised, anonymous boxes, has meant that dockers have a much harder time identifying the 'blacked' goods.

Finally, there is the highly debatable problem of the 'runaway' industry which sets up production facilities abroad, phasing out production at home. Many American unionists are beginning to feel that this development is more important than the traditional bogey of technological unemployment. They point out that between 1961 and 1968 there were only 3·5 million jobs created in the U.S. economy, despite the Vietnam war and widespread prosperity. They begin to suspect that non-defence industries have actually lost employment as a result of growing imports. They feel that the U.S. is facing economic disaster by encouraging firms to invest abroad, while neglecting to develop domestic manufacturing facilities that will absorb a growing American work force.

In a previous chapter we mentioned companies like Singer who faced Japanese imports by filling out its product line in the U.S. with low-cost models made in Scotland. Other firms in the electronics, garment, and watch-making industries are under suspicion. Few, however, run away with the panache of that labour-intensive industry, the cinema. In the early 1960's Hollywood discovered Spain as a cheap, sunny location. As a result, Lawrence of Arabia rode his camel on a Spanish beach; *The Fall of the Roman Empire* took place ten miles from Madrid; Spanish villagers played Chinese revolutionaries in *Fifty-Five Days at Peking*; artificial snow fell while the *Battle of the Bulge* and the Russian revolution (*Dr Zhivago*) were filmed there. Even greater anachronisms occurred when 'westerns' were shot in South Italy or Yugoslavia. Even more studio-based films are being shot outside Hollywood, where union pressure has pushed salaries so high that films are cheaper to make abroad, even though the American reservoir of technical expertise is universally renowned. The producers of Stanley Kubrick's brilliant space epic *2001: A Space Odyssey*, admit that it probably could not have been made in the United States because it would have cost too much.

Runaway industry is not just an American problem. The Scandinavians are uneasy about the paper industry. Billerud has opened a mill in Portugal producing viscosa pulp for the Swedish parent company; the Norwegian Borregaard has constructed a similar mill in Brazil. These plants use eucalyptus wood which is the best raw material for viscosa pulp and is much cheaper than the resinous wood of Scandinavia. Although the latter is being used for other operations, there has been a clear production transfer. Similarly, the Norwegian shipping fleet (the fourth largest in the world) has discovered the disadvantages of paying Scandinavia's relatively high wages when competitors hire crews at half their rates. So they have been chartering foreign ships which sail under foreign flags, with 'foreign' operating costs. Some 100 foreign ships are believed in Norwegian service at the moment. This strategy is also used by U.S. shipping firms who cannot stay competitive while paying U.S. level wages.

Trade unions are understandably worried about such trends. Unless protective action is taken, they mean the end for certain labour-intensive industries in high-wage economies. The International Union of Electrical Workers in the U.S. has sponsored a bill to enforce explicit labelling on products which are manufactured, produced or assembled outside the U.S. One cynically wonders about the efficiency of such a measure, since the consumer is not usually so consciously patriotic in making expensive purchases. Under further union pressure, President Nixon established a commission to investigate the whole problem of goods which are assembled in cheap-labour nations from parts originally manufactured in the U.S.A.

One's emotions are divided in such cases. One must obviously sympathise with employees in industries rendered unviable by the growth of competition from low-wage economies (such as textiles), by the growth of competitive technologies (coal) or by changes in transportation economics (inland steel industries). On the other hand, all intellectual trends urge accepting the decline of such industries. Reports on the Third World all stress the need to reduce protective tariffs in industries where developing nations have a competitive advantage. Unionists representing these industries in the developed nations are obviously justified in fighting to protect their members during the enforced run-downs, perhaps even insisting that these should be carried out at a slower rate than the developing countries demand. However, no strong moral case can be made for protecting such uncompetitive industries in the long run.

The United States is an interesting case study because the problem of 'runaway' industries is probably about to pelt her. The U.S. is a notably high-wage economy which has been protected both by its relative isolation from potential competitors in Europe and Japan, and by the productivity of its labour force which has been high enough to offset high wages. This protection is disappearing fast. Relative productivity levels are to some extent a function of efficient management; and we have seen elsewhere that the gap between American managers and others is narrowing. Above all, however, developments in transportation technology now render the U.S. market vulnerable to competition from other continents. Certainly, wage differentials between Central American nations like Mexico and the United States will be fully exploited by non-American multinational firms eager to attack the most lucrative market in the world. In the short run, therefore, the strategy of American unionists may be to seek protective measures; but over the long term international political realities will make such protection impossible. Their optimal strategy would therefore seem to be raising wages and working conditions toward the U.S. levels in the nations receiving their runaway industries. To achieve this, they have every incentive to strengthen international ties with other unions.

Reuther's United Auto Workers (U.A.W.) have been most active in this field. By 1962 they were talking of international information pools, cooperation with international agencies, and carefully selected American pressure on U.S. corporations in behalf of foreign workers. These plans made little headway until 1966, when four automotive councils were created under the auspices of the International Metalworkers Federation (I.M.F.). This Geneva-based federation of world unions involved in trades like the auto industry appears to be heavily influenced by the U.A.W., with Walter Reuther, the U.A.W.'s president, acting as president of the I.M.F.'s automotive department. Each of these four councils (one each for Ford and General Motors; another for Chrysler, Fiat, Simca and Rootes; and the fourth for Volkswagen and Mercedes-Benz) was designed to bring together the unionists concerned with their companies' global activities.

So far, these councils do not seem to have advanced far

beyond 'talking shops', where information is collected. Their most radical steps have been to arrange informal discussion meetings between international delegations of unionists and the top labour relations personnel of firms like Ford and General Motors. These meetings are not collective bargaining sessions in which either side puts down demands. They consist of statements of positions. The most interesting result so far has been a discrepancy between descriptions of company labour policy: multinational subsidiaries normally maintain that their local labour relations policies are dictated from headquarters, while the company headquarters assert that in this field they leave their subsidiaries a great deal of autonomy. The I.M.F. also arranged meetings with the Dutch headquarters of Philips n.v. in 1967, in order to learn how the company operated within the European Economic Community, in which Philips has a number of large plants. The I.M.F. delegation seemed reasonably satisfied that Philips considered the employment situation in other E.E.C. countries no less than it did in the Netherlands.

All this is the initial sparring before really determined efforts get underway to establish equally good working conditions in all a multinational's subsidiaries. So far, there has been only one really successful attempt to achieve parity of wages between two nations; and this is, once again, the work of the U.A.W. One result of the U.S.-Canadian automotive agreement providing for free trade in cars and parts between the two nations was considerable unionist concern that American jobs might be undermined by low Canadian wages. The 1967 bargaining round therefore involved wage parity between the two nations. Ford, which suffered the major strike that year, managed to avoid any commitment to equal wages on either side of the border. However, the weaker Chrysler capitulated and guaranteed that the 40 cent per hour wage differential suffered by its 13,000 Canadian employees would be wiped out within $2\frac{1}{2}$ years. In some industries, Canadian employees actually earn more than their U.S. counterparts, but the Chrysler-U.A.W. agreement remains the first notable example of 'international bargaining'.

This attempt to get equal working conditions between nations—not just within nations—will grow, though it will be delayed for some time by the fact that most national unions are still fighting for parity within their own national borders. Multinationals have stimulated the awareness of these differentials, since they often force smaller 'national' competitors to merge, thus producing a few nation-wide companies for the first time. When a 'national' combine is formed, workers suddenly see that other workers within the same firm—doing much the same jobs in other parts of the nation—earn different salaries. This problem, faced also by the conglomerates who find that their subsidiaries accept incompatible labour relations agreements, has resulted in the low-wage parts of the British Leyland company's striking for parity with plants in traditionally high-wage parts of Britain. No significant drive for international parity within multinationals has yet been launched, although early in 1969, the Belgian subsidiary of Ford did strike giving as one of its reasons the fact that it wanted to close the differentials between it and the Ford plants just across the border in West Germany. However, as multinationals become better organised, employees will be increasingly aware of other employees' salaries in different subsidiaries. The growth of truly nation-wide firms in the U.S. had the greatest effect in reducing regional disparities in wage and interest rates. One can now expect the multinational to play a similar role across national boundaries.

Europe will be affected quickest. Here multinationals are superimposed on a jumble of nation-states which are only just beginning to coordinate their activities. Major differences exist in labour payment systems. For instance, different policies regarding management's contributions to social security benefits lead to the Italian Fiat's having overall man-hour costs equivalent to those in West Germany ($2 an hour), while costs in France are $1.90, and in Britain only $1.70. However, since social security and other fringe benefits cost Italian Fiat workers $0.70 per man-hour, compared with rates as low as $0.25 for the British, their actual take-home pay is lower than the rest of Europe—$1.15 against $1.30 in Britain and $1.66 in Western Germany. Italian industrialists therefore will find themselves under considerable union pressure to bring Italian take-home pay up to that in the rest of Europe. But this will be economically feasible for Italian management only if they can make considerably smaller social security payments.

How are union leaders likely to bring about significant improvements for workers? The U.A.W.-Chrysler salary breakthrough was unusual since the U.A.W. is one of the few unions to represent workers on both sides of a border. In more typical situations, the unions of different countries have to come together before any cooperative action can be contemplated. The major case in which this has happened involved the French glass firm, St Gobain, which found itself in 1969 facing concerted action by unions in eleven different nations.

St Gobain is a somewhat diversified multinational—the largest glass manufacturer in Europe, but also a manufacturer of chemicals, oil and paper. It has 143 plants scattered over 12 countries (including the U.S.) with a holding company, St Gobain Internationale, based in Fribourg, Switzerland. Toward the beginning of 1969, the contracts of its four subsidiaries in France, West Germany, Italy and the United States came up for negotiations, which went normally to begin with. In particular, the U.S. management argued against U.S. union demands, because the subsidiary had incurred losses in both 1967 and 1968.

Unfortunately for the St Gobain management, a smaller, aggressively-run French company, Boussois-Souchon-Neuvessel (B.S.N.), offered a bid to take them over, which aroused considerable antagonism. The French financial establishment rallied round St Gobain. In the course of a counter-attack eventually repulsing the B.S.N. bid, the St Gobain management suddenly announced that consolidated profits had risen 35% in 1968, that profits and cash earnings would double by 1971, and that dividends would increase 22% with a one-to-four stock bonus into the bargain. Naturally union negotiators reckoned that the work-force deserved some of the bounty themselves.

At this point, the International Chemical Workers (I.C.F.) came into the picture. I.C.F., another Geneva-based federation of trade unions, had been looking for suitable multinational firms to tackle. St Gobain's sudden announcement of added profits in the middle of a number of contract negotiations provided a perfect target. I.C.F.'s secretary-general, the Canadian Charles Levinson, called a world meeting in Geneva of union delegates representing workers dealing with St Gobain and its subsidiaries. Delegates attended from the U.S., Italy, West Germany, Norway, Belgium, Switzerland and France, while agreements to abide by any decisions taken came from the Netherlands, Argentina and Brazil. That the French delegation represented only part of the French labour force suggests the difficulties of getting international union co-operation. The communist union, C.G.T., and a couple of smaller ones representing over 70% of the French labour force, had already signed an agreement, while the I.C.F.-affiliated Confédération Française Démocratique du Travail representing 20% of the French workers, refused the offers of the management.

The conference decided to coordinate support for the negotiations taking place in the U.S., West Germany, France and Italy. Each was to continue with its purely national demands (i.e., they were not seeking parity of wages), but none was to sign an agreement with the relevant management until the other three unions concerned gave permission. The representatives from the other countries agreed to ban all overtime working if so asked. They also carried out a certain amount of contingency planning to prevent management's switching products from unaffected sources. Public announcements of support were made from shipping and transport unions.

Ralph Reiser, the U.S. union leader representing 24,000 workers, allowed his men to work three weeks after their contract expired to coordinate their action with the Italian demands. As a result of the Geneva discussions, Reiser also added a new demand for severance pay to protect U.S. workers from plant shutdowns. The West German affiliate granted its work force their demands, but union leaders delayed signing the agreement until the action had been played out in the other nations. On 2nd May 1969, the Italians asked the U.S. workers to strike, and followed with a strike of their own on 8th May. A day later the Italian management conceded, while the U.S. strike dragged on for 16 days with the management finally conceding defeat and granting a package of 9% per annum for three years, despite losses in the U.S. for the previous couple of years. The unions therefore feel that arguing their case with reference to the world-wide profit figures of the parent company rather than just those of the local subsidiaries was fully justified.

99

The I.C.F. which had coordinated the whole affair was left with a bill for 700 Swiss francs ($130 roughly), half of which was spent on alcohol for journalists. All the other expenses had been paid by the national unions concerned.

The I.C.F. was able in this instance to take advantage of some of those factors which have created viable multinational companies. Improved travel facilities made the Geneva meeting possible, while telephone calls adequately kept the participants in touch with each other. In fact, union activity on an international scale need not be expensive. Bodies like the I.C.F., the I.M.F., or the U.A.W. are often well placed to pressure company headquarters on behalf of union members elsewhere in the world. Thus I.C.F.'s Levinson has exerted pressure on Swiss-based multinationals in behalf of unionists in Japan; British union leaders have contacted the headquarters of British Leyland about the victimisation of union activists in Chile by a British Leyland subsidiary; similarly the U.A.W. has pressured Chrysler headquarters about anti-union activities in its Spanish subsidiary.

The power of unions in the long run is rather more problematical. In some ways, their power should increase, provided they can cooperate internationally. The policy of component interchange whereby a single plant may manufacture key parts for a product marketed on a world-wide basis means that pressure put on that plant will have repercussions throughout the rest of the company. If this occurred often, then the multinationals would presumably take the precaution of having at least two sources of supply; but even this need not trouble a really determined union. Again, it is increasingly difficult for companies based in developed nations to deny information about callous behaviour in parts of the world once well-hidden from publicity. Thus unions can exert pressure by threatening to run public relations campaigns should malpractices in other nations continue. The threat of international publicity was used in the mid-1960's when the U.S. ballpoint pen manufacturer, Scripto, ran its Georgia headquarters on a non-union basis, employing Negro women to handle highly automated machinery. Their plant was in Martin Luther King Senior's parish so the picket lines were soon studded with notables such as King, himself, and the Rev. Ralph Abernathy. After a couple of days, the company countered by flying down one of their directors, Douglas Fairbanks, Jr. I.C.F.'s Levinson then threatened to use national advertising and full coverage in all union media if the issue was not settled. The result was large wage hikes and almost 100% unionisation. A further cheap form of international union pressure is to brief popular representatives, Congressmen and Members of Parliament, on pressuring government purchasing officers to restrict purchases from multinationals with obstreperous subsidiary managements. Finally, supporting financially the strikes in developing nations is relatively cheap for American and European unions, since cheap wages mean cheap strike pay. Thus the international union bodies can back lengthy strikes in developing economies which would be burdensome if carried out elsewhere.

On the other hand, it is by no means clear in exactly what circumstances the workers of one nation would be willing to lay down tools on behalf of those in another. Thus the St Gobain case was to some extent unusual since the richest unions members, in America, happened to have the biggest incentive for supporting international action: they could hope for success only if they argued from the company's global profit-and-loss statements. It is less clear whether workers in the U.S. would strike in aid of workers elsewhere who might be trying to reduce the international differentials within the company. Although it could be in their interest to help their poorer paid competitors in increasing their relative wages, asking U.S. workers, for instance, to strike in aid of their Italian or Japanese colleagues might prove unenforceable. What is likely more workable is the coordination of bargaining so that contracts are negotiated at the same time in different nations. Naturally, financial help, backed with information and expertise, will also prove useful.

An interesting parallel exists between the transfer of technology resulting from the spread of multinational companies, and the transfer of important information and ideas accompanying international cooperation between unions. In the St Gobain case, the U.S. union leaders came away from the Geneva meeting with extra demands for severance pay. Describing the Metalworkers' activities, Victor Reuther (Walter's brother), in a speech to the I.C.F. in 1967, said the I.M.F. had

... set in motion a programme of technical assistance extended by confident, well trained and experienced members of affiliated unions of the I.M.F. We don't need a big bureaucracy continually on the payroll, but if we get an emergency call from a group of workers in Chile or steelworkers in Japan and they need an expert in job evaluation or they need some guidance in developing a pension plan, we would turn to that affiliate in the I.M.F. which has the most experienced persons in that domain and despatch them to the place where they are needed to complete that short mission and assignment.

Most important is the internationalisation of union demands, since unions in different nations have had different priorities. The growing internationalisation of union activities now means that the best aspects of union demands in one part of the world will increasingly be taken up elsewhere. Thus the International Chemical Workers are trying to introduce to the U.S. the job security won by German unions: workers over 50 years old cannot be fired; workers with 15–20 years seniority must be given 12 months notice, plus 12 months severance pay. In the reverse direction, U.S. unions' achievements in winning guaranteed incomes (United Rubber Workers have now won 80% of the gross wage of workers who are laid off through economic fluctuations, etc.: the U.A.W. have raised this guaranteed income to 95% in some cases) will be brought over to Europe as a demand. Similarly, the I.C.F. is interested in trying to 'internationalise' demands for continuous training, industrial democracy, and integration of manual and non-manual workers.

However, since the possibility of real direct international union action is likely to be restricted for the moment to isolated cases and individual firms, the main emphasis of union leaders must be to improve the quality of their information services. Thus the U.A.W. has struck a bargain with its counterparts in Britain, the Transport and General Workers Union (T. & G.W.U.) and the Amalgamated Engineering Federation (A.E.F.), whereby they will coordinate their bargaining against the major auto manufacturers and will swap information about agreements struck in all the plants of these firms. On a more ambitious scale, the I.C.F. is in the process of setting up a computerised data-bank on the collective bargains struck world-wide by the 30 major chemical multinationals. Levinson hopes to have this fully operative by 1972, based on computers owned by German and U.S. affiliated unions. Obviously, there are some difficulties in comparing different agreements, since earnings can be calculated a number of different ways (piece-work, salaries, overtime, etc.), but the idea is that any affiliated union will be able to arrange a printout of all relevant information about a firm's concessions round the world, other bargains in the same country, etc. There is no reason to think this data-bank should not become operational since the technology is exactly that used by the multinational companies.

Just exactly how successful unions will be in acting internationally still remains to be seen. For the moment they remain a potential counter-balance to the multinational firms which are able to make relatively quick decisions, without the delays inherent in the democratic process. The multinationals need some forms of check to their activities. The growth of international unionism could provide one effective check. Whether it will ever be strong enough remains an open question.

CHAPTER VII

The Less-Developed World

The relationship between multinational companies and the Less-Developed Countries (L.D.C.'s) is particularly controversial. On one side left-wingers recall past depredations carried out by multinationals. They refer to oil companies which once bought presidents or, failing that, engineered coups against the presidents owned by other oil companies. They remind one also of the atrocities committed by some of the world's mining, rubber and food companies in their exploitation of local labour. On the other hand, visionary businessmen argue that these days are long past and spin visions in which the developing world and the benevolent multinationals march together toward a utopia of full bellies, affluence, and ease. As usual, the truth lies somewhere in between.

Like most prosperous nations, the multinationals are not particularly interested in the L.D.C.'s, preferring to make their profits in safer markets. A 1969 *Fortune* survey of 300 top executives from the 500 largest U.S. industrial companies showed an overwhelming preference for foreign expansion in developed nations: 69% stated they would rather expand in developed nations, 9% preferred underdeveloped nations, and 12% were interested in both. Even more depressing, the larger the firm, the less interested it was in the underdeveloped nations; only 4% of firms with sales of $1 billion plus expressed interest, against 11% of the group with sales below $1 billion. This lack of interest shows in the fact that between 75-80% of international private capital flows between the rich nations. Within the total stream from the rich to poor nations, private investment contributes about 40% of the total, a proportion which has not changed much during the 1960's.

As we noted earlier, the trend in multinational investment has been in manufacturing ventures in advanced nations, meaning the U.S., Canada and Europe. In 1946, the book value of U.S. direct investment in Latin America was three times as great as that of its European investments; by 1967, the Latin American total was little more than half that of Europe. The traditional interest in mining and petroleum has not changed much as far as the developing nations are concerned. O.E.C.D. estimates that of the $30 billion book value of direct investment owned by O.E.C.D. countries in the L.D.C.'s in 1966, about 40% was in oil, 9% in mining and smelting and about 27% in manufacturing. If one assumes that manufacturing activities would provide the multinationals' greatest potential aid to the L.D.C.'s, then he notes sadly that only 22% of the rich countries' overseas investment in manufacturing activities is located in developing nations—against 46% for the petroleum industry and 47% for mining.

The trends of such investment patterns are not clear. In the late 1960's there was a burst of investment activity in L.D.C.'s connected with new petroleum and mineral discoveries. At the same time, manufacturing firms showed distinct disillusionment with the political temper of a traditionally 'safe' continent, Latin America; as a result, firms seem willing in some cases to pull out. Further, the Pearson report for Robert McNamara's World Bank (1969) stresses the need to start the flow of funds from the rich to the poor nations moving again after a decade of relative stagnation.

Technological transfer

To many policy-makers, the primary need in L.D.C.'s is reduction of the dependence on imported technology. To meet this goal, the help of multinational companies often seems necessary.

In the past it has appeared that using licensing agreements got technology into a country fastest. Japan's intelligent use of licensing agreements with foreign competitors is often cited as a successful example. However, as we saw when discussing the technological gap between Europe and the United States, relying on licenses is useless if the nation's management or basic technology is not developed enough to fully utilise the relevant machinery. A high-production, but expensive machine is no use if, say, the company's distribution network is so inefficient that it cannot handle the output, or if the workers are so inexperienced that they damage the machine. A license only gives the basic technological or scientific information; it does not include the managerial know-how necessary if the manufacturing process is to be successful.

On a simple level, a multinational will have this managerial expertise and will be able to implement a process quickly by anticipating the major danger points. On a broader level, this management may well have wide enough experience to see exactly what new improvements to the industrial infrastructures will make the venture a success. Therefore when one argues that direct investment is often the most efficient way of ensuring the transfer of technology to a developing nation, one assumes that such investment also gives the country management skills without which the technology is irrelevant. Certainly there is no virtue in spending money on research and development which has already been done elsewhere. The largest private firm in India, Tata, which accounts for something like 10% of the total Indian investment in organised industry, spends only £500,000 a year on research, mostly on work adopting ideas developed abroad. This compares with £20 million per annum spent by one of its partners in India, the medium-sized European firm Mercedes-Benz.

It is unrealistic to expect countries with little industrial background to be able to create a computer, car, aircraft or chemical industry from scratch without help from foreign companies which do have experience. After all, if the U.S.S.R., one of the world's great industrial nations, has to turn to the Italian car manufacturer, Fiat, for its first major car plant, there is no reason to think that less-experienced nations can succeed alone. What the question reduces itself to is not whether L.D.C.'s can do without help from multinational companies, but on what terms they should try to get this help so that they get the technology without the more obvious disadvantages.

Joint ventures

Many nations believe that their best strategy is to encourage foreign investment but to ensure that most of it comes in the form of joint ventures with local businessmen who get technical and marketing experience from working with foreign firms. The major country following this policy, Japan, has put an almost total ban on investment which requires more than 50% foreign control. Thus foreign firms wishing to invest there have to search for a Japanese partner. However, this strategy may suit developing countries less well.

Many firms will go out of their way to avoid such ventures. Firms like General Motors, I.B.M. and Dow Chemical will normally do all they can to avoid partners. I.B.M. even convinced the Japanese Government to accept their 100% ownership policy since they would not invest without full control. India has also bowed to the I.B.M. policy. However, the I.B.M. case is rare. A country does not often need one particular firm so desperately that it must accept company terms. For instance, Japan can play the world's auto manufacturers off against each other; if General Motors will not take Japanese partners, plenty of willing competitors will. Similarly, International Harvester's policy was once to invest only where it had 100% control over the venture; but it found the pressure of Japanese and Indian Governments too strong, since it did not have I.B.M.'s crucial market dominance. It has therefore accepted partnerships with local companies in both countries.

Multinational complaints against partnerships are not ungrounded, since the interests of multinational and partner need not always be identical. Heinz wanted to expand faster in Japan than its partner, and bought a larger share in the venture to increase its control. Coca-Cola found it difficult to persuade its partners, who bottle the drink round the world, to switch from 6-ounce to 10- and 12-ounce bottles, thus hindering the development of their global strategy.

The major objection to such partnerships comes when a company is globally integrated. If a given venture provides only components for a global range of products, then the multinational decisions about transfer pricing may conflict with the interests of the local partner. Similarly, deciding how to supply various export markets round the world will be hindered as long as a partner makes its profits on a single country's activities. This is why Ford bought out the minority shareholders in its British subsidiary in 1961. As long as its nearby German subsidiary was 100% owned, the parent company kept on having to look over its shoulders at the interests of the 45% of British equity holders, possibly leading it to decisions which were not in the long-term interests of Ford as a whole. The thought that I.B.M. might be forced to take local partners in various countries shows one how difficult this issue is. When a company is planned so globally, it would probably make sense to allow local interests to participate in the global company in proportion to the company's involvement with the local's country. Other ways may be found to guarantee that I.B.M.'s expertise gets transferred to the country in question.

In fact considerable evidence suggests that a country may be acting against its own best interests in insisting that incoming investors take local partners. A multinational will take a more relaxed attitude toward wholly-owned subsidiaries when fixing royalty, pricing and dividend policies. In any case, it pays such firms to make their profits in those nations where they control 100% of the local subsidiary and therefore receive 100% of the profits. As one executive expressed it, "we have 45,000 shareholders in company X, ranging from ministers to taxi-drivers. We transfer profits to them but not one bit of technology."[1] In Britain, admittedly not a developing nation, the export records of joint ventures were significantly less impressive than those of 100% foreign-controlled firms, as were their profitability, their labour productivity, and the proportion they spent on research.

Despite this, some firms do not object to local participation in their foreign investment. The more crafty firms realise that a number of partners in such schemes means they can dominate by playing the partners against each other so that any major disadvantages can be ruled out. But most firms who accept such schemes realise that they are buying themselves local experience which can be useful when knowing whom to approach is highly important. This arrangement can, of course, be disastrous if multinationals cooperate with individuals too closely linked to a fallen regime. But firms like Rio-Tinto-Zinc, or Kaiser Aluminum seem consciously to welcome local partners. And in 1969 a director of Unilever explained,

[1] Rolfe, Sidney. *The International Corporation.* International Chamber of Commerce, Paris, 1969.

Our policy is to be as flexible as possible. In India there was pressure on us to make our shares available locally when we expanded our business there a few years ago. We did not need the money but we sold the shares. Things are not always done for purely economic reasons.

The days when companies could insist on 100% ownership of ventures in developing nations seem to be passing. However, the policy-makers need to be aware that local participation is no industrial panacea. Quite possibly the tide of economic nationalism which seems to be swirling round the developing world may make joint-venture arrangements increasingly popular. A nation must simply be sure that it is not actually losing because of over-reliance on such a policy.

Assembly policies

One major advantage of multinational help is that they can transfer existing production to a developing nation. I.B.M. has transferred some of its lines from its Scottish plant to Argentina. Similarly, Olivetti has moved its portable typewriters from Italy to Spain, and has transferred the production of another line from Scotland to its Mexican plant. Above all, multinationals can choose to manufacture directly in markets which they have previously supplied from elsewhere. Hopefully, such transfers reduce imports and build up the capacities of local suppliers.

Manufacturing firms reluctant to open production in developing nations feel that such operations will be uneconomic. They therefore must be enticed. The simplest way is to put a tariff on imports of finished products, but leave unfettered the parts which can then be assembled by local labour. The end product may be identical to the import, but the plant will create jobs and train a wage-labour force vital to the nation's growth. Mere assembly, however, is not enough. Increasingly, nations require a growing proportion of local manufacture.

The auto industry in Australia illustrates this process and its accompanying difficulties. A fairly small market, Australia supports two to three models which sell over 30,000 cars per annum. The highly protected component industry pressured the government into pushing for more Australian content in the final cars. Therefore, in July 1966, high tariffs were raised against totally imported cars. Those models selling up to 7,500 a year were required to have 45–60% locally manufactured components; those selling over 7,500 had to have 95% Australian components. Unfortunately, the government had done its sums wrong. Using local components, a model would have to sell 30,000 cars a year to be profitable, a number that only three models approached. This left a large number of models selling around 10,000 to 15,000 each and losing money. Volkswagen consequently decided to cease production and to rely on importing vehicles into Australia under the less demanding conditions. As a result, the government has since modified its proposals to allow vehicles selling less than 25,000 units per annum to settle on 85% local content. But this adjustment still leaves Australian-produced cars expensive, particularly in comparison with highly profitable Japanese models. Importers merely bring in a wider range of models than they might otherwise.

In other words, steps taken to guarantee a certain degree of local manufacture often add to the high cost of the final product. On the other hand, it does give the local component industry a chance to expand. These two factors have to be balanced, especially since developing one's own auto industry this way can be costly. Baranson[1] has graphically shown the danger of ending with uneconomic runs: Chile's 7,800 vehicles produced in 1964 were manufactured by 22 companies at four times the cost of a car directly imported from abroad. Similarly, Argentina's 16 producers made 195,000 vehicles in 1965 (compared with 32,000 in 1959). The car which could have been imported for $2,000 in 1959 was being made in Argentina at a cost of $5,000. Moreover, imports had not been reduced, but had risen from $26 million in 1959 to $250 million in 1965, despite the goal to keep imports at 10% of the total output cost, which would have entailed only a $45 million import bill in auto parts in 1965.

How do you judge such cases? Obviously allowing so many

[1] Baranson, Jack. 'Will there be an auto industry in the L.D.C.'s (Less Developed Countries) future?' *Columbia Journal of World Business*, Vol. III, No. 3, May-June 1968, pp. 48–54.

firms in a market that none can produce models in economic numbers is self-defeating. The luxury of multiple models can probably wait, if restriction of choice leads to a considerable lowering in the costs of a few standardised models. On the other hand, the quickest way to get a proportion of the industrial structure used to working in relatively high standards is to insist on gradually raising the degree of local components in the product being assembled.

More recently, developing nations have gone further in their demands on multinationals and have started asking for guaranteed amounts of exports from their subsidiaries. Countries which have started requiring exports are Mexico, Brazil, Argentina, India, Spain and Yugoslavia. For instance, Fiat is helping set up an auto plant in Turkey with some participation by the Turkish Government. One of the conditions is that the venture will export to certain Middle East nations. Similarly, Fiat, one of the auto manufacturers which has come to terms with the demands of developing countries, now fully realises that it must not only help such nations establish car industries, but must also plan ways in which Fiat can help them export when they are set up. This may entail arrangements whereby the new industry supplies certain components for Fiat activities elsewhere, or it may mean Fiat will make its international marketing efforts available for the products of the new industry. Either way, the multinationals will one day have to put together deals in which they find export markets for the manufacturing ventures they set up. In fact, multinationals in the petroleum and mining industries have long done this. The oil majors are old masters at juggling the mix of oil production and world-wide markets they control. Australian mineral deposits were developed so fast partly because the mining consortia have been able to assemble not only the initial finance but also the necessary long-term contracts with nations like Japan which make the whole venture profitable.

The multinational is a world-wide package of management talent, market knowledge, financial acumen and sources, and production expertise. Countries benefit when such companies draw on experience which is not available to the country by itself. The only caution must be that the country should learn from the process, and that the cost should not be too high.

Regional groupings

At first sight, there is a simple answer to the small national markets which make mass production uneconomic: join three or four individual nations into a common market organisation. The larger market makes the area more attractive to foreign investors and, just as important, makes it easier for the combined national governments to bargain from strength. Thus we now find the Latin American Free Trade Association (L.A.F.T.A.), Central American Common Market (C.A.C.M.), a Caribbean free trade area (C.A.R.I.F.T.A.), the East African Community, the Central African Economic and Customs Union (U.D.E.A.C.) and a splitaway Union of Central African States (U.E.A.C.). Even within Europe where the two major trading groups, the European Economic Community (E.E.C.) and the European Free Trade Area (E.F.T.A.) still compete, the Scandinavians are talking about forming a further grouping called N.O.R.D.E.K., which would bind them even tighter as an economic unit.

The thinking behind such grouping is logical. One of the reasons why the United States and Japan in their respective eras have been so dynamic has been that industrialists have been able to plan from the start for a market of over 100 million people, instead of facing numerous tariff barriers, quotas, language barriers and downright prejudice. Significantly, India, despite her problems, can be tough with incoming investors because of her vast home market. The patient industrialist finds it worth accepting Indian partners, etc., in order to have freedom within India's protective barriers.

Unfortunately, most trading areas run into severe teething problems. National interests seldom disappear suddenly in deference to the overall good of the wider group. When Nicaragua and El Salvador can go to war over a soccer match between their national teams, it is clear that economic co-operation between highly suspicious nations will not come easily.

The second major problem faces all such economic groupings. Some nations are bound to dominate because of their size or their favourable location. Thus L.A.F.T.A. has been relatively disappointing because the larger nations like Argentina and

Brazil clearly had little interest in it. The government in Buenos Aires has made it clear that developing such lagging areas within Argentina as Patagonia must come first. As a result, some of the smaller nations in L.A.F.T.A.—Colombia, Ecuador, Peru, Bolivia and Chile—need a bloc within a bloc, and are actively investigating the creation of an Andean economic integration association. On another continent, Africa, similar problems have arisen with U.D.E.A.C. This customs union originally consisted of Gabon, Congo (Brazzaville), Chad, the Central African Republic and the Cameroon. However, land-locked Chad and the Central African Republic felt they were doing worse than their partners, so they broke away to form U.E.A.C. which also included the Congo (Kinshasa). Even this group encountered some murky political instability. Basically conflicting French and American interests in this area make any economic integration difficult.

It is naïve to expect immediate results from such regional confederations. In theory they effectively add to the bargaining power of nations with little individual investment appeal. Certainly, multinational interest in such schemes can be quite significant. In the early 1960's for example, I.B.M. calculated that Argentina, Brazil, Chile and Uruguay as a group could support a major manufacturing operation. They suggested that if these nations eliminated duties on I.B.M. components and ancillary items, I.B.M. would build plants in Brazil and Argentina, and would arrange for another American firm to license a Chilean paper producer to manufacture the business forms needed for the machines. The governments agreed, while maintaining a common tariff against imports of these goods from third countries.

Multinationals have a vested interest in encouraging the spread and success of such groupings. Without them, the multinational often operates at considerably less than full efficiency. However, it is also clear that the stability of such groups depends at least in part on the multinationals themselves. Companies have to realise that these groupings are often little more than loose confederations of suspicious nations. The multinational must therefore avoid the temptation to lump all its investment where economics alone dictates. If everyone does that then the less attractive nations will one day back out, thus destroying much of the investment's rationale. Rather the multinationals should investigate product or component interchange which will allow them to build some plants in the less attractive nations, thus buying some political stability at the expense of some economic efficiency. On a different plane, such firms might actually approach the political bodies running the groupings with a view to drawing up a series of incentives favouring the less attractive nations. Until such free trade areas realise their obligation to distribute the investment they attract reasonably among their constituent nations, they will never really be stable. The role of the multinational here is to look a little past the end of its nose.

Buffer institutions

The first major drawback to multinational investment in the Third World is their extreme 'visibility' in an environment often highly suspicious that such an organisation can be a tool of the 'neo-imperialists'. In such a context, however worthy the multinational's motives, their presence can be inflammatory. Second, in order to avoid spreading their management talent too thin, the multinationals will tend to invest in a few big projects rather than a number of smaller ones. But, the bigger the project the more small local entrepreneurs will be scared of being dominated by the multinational giant.

A need has therefore developed for joint multilateral ventures in which banks and corporations from the developed world can invest without actively dominating the activities being backed. Since 1964, such investment companies have been established for Latin America and Asia, with a further one planned for Africa. The most advanced company is the Adela Investment Company, S.A. which by early 1969 had 140 shareholders in 16 developed countries from Europe, Japan, Canada, the U.S. and Latin America. At that time, its biggest project was a $77 million forestry project in Honduras. Its Asian counterpart, P.I.C.A. (Private Investment Company of Asia) is backed by a consortium including First National City Bank, Alcan Aluminium and the Bank of Tokyo.

Such institutions promise a flexibility in private investment which may make them politically more acceptable to the developing nations. At the same time they may help reduce the vulnerability of foreign investments to the periodic waves of xenophobia which strike even the most 'stable' nations. Furthermore, they should prove useful in attracting private investment from sources which would not have had the expertise to initiate such projects themselves.

Do the L.D.C.'s need advanced technology?

Governments of the developing nations obviously face the temptation to press ahead with projects aimed at proving they can be as advanced as any other nation. Thus expensive steelmills are built; universities are established (at a cost per student sometimes higher than that of developed nations); a national airline and, sometimes, a national shipping fleet serve national prestige; and demands grow for auto construction. This is a doubtful strategy. Certainly the multinationals could help such projects, but they could also help with projects better suited to the medium-term needs of the L.D.C.'s.

The basic problem facing the L.D.C.'s is hunger. The U.N.'s Food and Agricultural Organisation released a major report in 1969 called the *Indicative World Plan for Agricultural Development* which predicts the bleakest future unless the whole scale and form of international aid can be revolutionised. Food production has been left largely to intergovernmental efforts since few multinational food-producing companies exist. The task of developing new, high-yielding strains of wheat and rice has been mainly carried out in government laboratories. One reason multinationals are ineffective here is that products will still be grown by the millions on millions of the world's small, conservative farmers. Persuading these to accept change is difficult enough, but persuading them to work in large amalgamated units which could apply mass production methods seems altogether impossible. At this level, multinationals can do little more than supply fertilisers or tractors.

Where the multinationals may have a useful role is in the field of protein production. First, since the human need for protein is chemical, they can develop new forms of protein synthesis. For instance, on a small scale the oil companies now produce protein as a petroleum by-product. Firms like Monsanto have developed in Hong Kong soft-drinks based on the locally popular soya beans, and will hopefully extend their market to other areas of South East Asia. International Flavors and Fragrances Inc. is developing ways of making palatable a fish meal protein concentrate. Second, such companies have enough experience to devise ways of making marketable the protein they do develop. In the case of Monsanto, this means developing soft-drinks. For International Flavors this means disguising the fish taste which will be repugnant in areas of the world like Africa and Latin America.

The Food and Agricultural Organisation report goes on to highlight a danger which has not yet had enough attention and which makes nonsense of many of the prestige, capital intensive projects which have been developed in L.D.C.'s. All evidence suggests that agriculture will become less dependent on manpower; yet there is absolutely no sign that enough jobs are being created in other spheres to absorb the extra population, let alone those whom increased agricultural efficiency will render unemployable. They point out that Asia already faces serious under-employment in the rural areas of developing nations, especially during certain months of the year. Their analysis shows that nearly half the additional people born between 1962 and 1985 will have to be absorbed by agriculture and they see no signs that this agricultural population will start to decline until well into the 21st century.

At this point the report's authors approach despair:

> In fact the main cause for concern over population growth rates in Asia stems not from the immediate prospects for the food supply, but from the long term implications for reduced efficiency as a result of shrinking farm size, lower farm income per capita, the relative shortage of urban employment, and all the tremendous economic and social pressures inherent in trying to cram still more people into the agricultural economy of the region.

They go on to potential political implications:

> It may be that the greatest threat to the technological revolution which could solve the food problem—at least for the foreseeable future—lies in the social disorganisation which could result from the ever-increasing millions dependent on a living from the agricultural economy.

Faced with problems of such magnitude, the multinationals can do little but contribute to the general flow of aid. Their most promising role may well be to supply industrial employment even in cultures which are not the most technologically advanced. Economists stress that the L.D.C.'s have not yet begun to exploit systematically their one abundant resource—cheap labour. Partly this is because the developed nations have a bad record of protecting industries like textiles which cannot otherwise survive in competition with cheap-labour countries like India and Taiwan. Partly governments have stimulated industries but lacked the world-wide marketing knowledge to ensure production of the right goods at the right quality and price. Finally, attempts have been made to set up a complete industry, when the alternative—producing a range of components for some company's world-wide operations—made better economic sense.

Baranson,[1] who studied the auto industry in Latin America, argued strongly not only that such industries should redesign their models to take more advantage of their low labour costs, but also that they should cooperate with the auto multinationals to develop models or components which can be integrated into a global range. Thus, labour intensive items like bus bodies or forgings could be produced in L.D.C.'s, creating not only employment but, just as important, guaranteed export earnings. On a more ambitious level, certain vehicles could be produced there—say, lorries or tractors where the technological skill needed is not so high as a passenger car requires.

Such plans require one of the multinational strengths most needed by L.D.C.'s—their ability to guarantee markets for components and products which are planned as part of their range. The multinationals will see the immediate disadvantages of using inefficient labour forces and managements, but they will gain from the political good will which cooperating with governments to supply employment and guaranteed export earnings should bring.

Intermediate technology

The F.A.O. report suggests that job creation is one of the L.D.C.'s highest priorities. But in facing this need, the level of

[1] Baranson, Jack, *op. cit.*

117

technology being introduced begins to matter. The examples just discussed of auto multinationals' placing certain labour-intensive operations in L.D.C.'s illustrate the process of adjusting advanced manufacturing processes to the needs of the L.D.C.'s. Another possibility is to export technologies to the L.D.C.'s which are obsolete in the most developed nations, but which suit the needs of less industrialised economies which need jobs. Whereas in the most industrialised nations planners tend to think of the number of jobs they can save in a given project, in L.D.C.'s they may think of the maximum number of jobs they can create for a given capital input (bearing in mind, of course, that there will be some lower limit beyond which adding labour may destroy the project).

The first reason for developing a technology less advanced than it could be is that, where the labour force has little industrial tradition, frequent mistakes will render expensive equipment inoperative and repairs may take longer than in developing nations. Karl Landegger, one of the most interesting entrepreneurs active in the L.D.C.'s, tells of Indian boilermen blowing up $300,000 worth of equipment by turning valves the wrong way. Given this possibility, the approach of Philips n.v. (discussed in Chapter II), in consciously designing production processes to the skill levels of the available managers and work force is most sensible. Similarly, Colgate-Palmolive, the giant U.S. household products group, has introduced a hand-operated washing machine because they were selling detergents to women still washing clothes in streams and tubs. They therefore marketed the hand-operated machine in Mexico at $3 apiece. Everyone involved in the project, including the U.S. development authorities, seemed enthusiastic and there was talk of $4 sewing machines and $10 refrigerators.

One group of economists, experienced in Asia and Africa, founded the Intermediate Technology Development Group. They started by assembling a catalogue, 'Tools for Progress', which listed simple low-cost processes and tools available in Britain but suitable for local manufacture under license, using mainly local materials and skills. They list machines like the Blake sewing machine for stitching a shoe's sole to its upper leather, a method first introduced in 1859 but since made obsolete in Britain by vulcanising or injection moulding. However, this machine, and similarly obsolete devices suitable for ceramics and baking, is still superior to traditional methods used in many developing countries. One British firm which had made simple horse-drawn units to which ploughs, seed drills and other agricultural appliances could be attached found their old blueprints could be used to start manufacturing in Pakistan.

Some political leaders suspect that their nations are deliberately exploited by imperial power when such old-fashioned devices are introduced. They argue that the L.D.C.'s which concentrate on outmoded technologies will never catch up with the advanced technologies. Two points must be made here. First, intermediate technology helps to solve the main problems facing the L.D.C.'s Not only does labour-intensive technology help to create jobs, a major long-range need; it also takes advantage of one of the few areas in which the L.D.C.'s have a global advantage, low-paid labour.

The question of how, if ever, the L.D.C.'s are to play an important part in the advanced technologies is secondary. Such contributions are unlikely except in the very long run to provide significant employment opportunities in the L.D.C.'s. But this question touches national sensitivities; the advanced nations must therefore make concessions if they are to remain useful advisers in other, more crucial, areas. What concessions should be made?

The location of multinational and research activities becomes less and less important as transportation technology improves. Tomorrow's advanced industries will increasingly depend on work done in university research laboratories. One can therefore argue that any serious attempt to raise the technological level of L.D.C.'s must start with the creation of research-oriented centres of excellence in each of the less-developed continents. The model would be Novosibirsk, the Russians' academic city built in Siberia specifically to help its development. Although much of the work done there has little direct application for Siberia, incidental geological surveys discovered new supplies of minerals which have more than paid for the original cost of the city.

These academic cities should first be set up in cooperation with leading universities which could locate a certain proportion of their research activities in them. The various aid-giving agencies could make up the extra costs involved in running worthwhile research from a considerable distance. The research projects should be selected after consultation with the leading multinationals, to guarantee that the research would aid industrial projects to be sited round the main academic city in each region. In other words, the aim of such cities would be to produce a viable industrial activity based on *avant-garde* research in certain fields. There would be no conscious attempt to produce goods marketable in the L.D.C.'s themselves; products would be aimed at the advanced technological economics.

For any of these academic cities to work, there would have to be considerable help from aid-giving bodies like the World Bank, the host nations, the universities and the international business community. Without the cooperation of any one of these institutions, the schemes would fail. In particular, multi-nationals, not generally noted for their selfless interest in L.D.C.'s, would have to make concessions based more on a vision of their social obligations to the world rather than on a strict balance-sheet mentality. Are the multinationals ever likely to identify themselves with a social role?

The project managers

Although most multinational companies prefer to ignore the developing world, it is an extremely promising market for those companies wishing to make some effort. The managing director of a Norwegian civil engineering firm, Norconsult A/S, put it this way:

> The United Nations invests every year over $150 million in its development programme. The World Bank finances annually projects amounting to about $1,200 million. The regional development banks are approaching a total capital investment equal to 50% of the World Bank. All these figures are increasing. ... Furthermore, equal amounts are available from the receiving countries as their share towards the costs of solving the projects involved.

These figures indicate a market of around $4 billion, which is obviously worthwhile. The companies most likely to master the market are those who see their role as project managers for nations lacking the expertise to bring off such projects by themselves.

Such an approach is opposite that of many American multi-nationals which stress the absolute necessity for 100% control over any overseas activities they create. Thus General Motors is not alone in refusing to invest in any project in which it lacks total control. This stance has been possible as long as national governments were weak and the international competition non-existent. However, increasingly sophisticated governments have been playing the established multinationals off against international newcomers from nations like Italy and Japan. In this market in which governments have been slowly gaining the upper hand, the companies who are going to do best are those which take a 'low profile' stance, keeping clear of political involvements and stressing their partnership with the local nations. Increasingly, the '100% control at all costs' approach is doomed because governments know they can get better terms and can only resent what seems to be multinational arrogance. Multinationals may maintain genuine world leadership of skills and knowledge; but when the multinational's dominance rests mainly on ineffective competition, such a rigid policy can only be counterproductive.

On the whole civil engineering concerns have first learned the rewards to be gained from working closely with the inter-national aid bodies and local governments. A typical example is Norconsult A/S of Oslo, which was founded in 1956 as much to export know-how as engineers. Now with a staff of 1,000 engineers, architects and economists, they have built up a turnover of $40 million by working on projects for the United Nations, the World Bank, the African Development Bank, the Asian Development Bank and the Inter-American Develop-ment Bank. They tackle problems ranging through conventional engineering, water supplies, sewage disposal, hydroelectric projects, road and traffic planning, aerial surveys and mapping, architecture and community planning. They see their job as bringing the best knowledge of the advanced world to bear on the problems of the developing world.

What such companies can bring to the developing world is the best management techniques available. Their value may not be in actually building roads, dams, etc., so much as in advising governments on the full implications of potential decisions. For instance, Lockheed International was granted a contract in 1967 by the A.I.D.'s Office of Capital Development and Finance to carry out a 3-year survey of Sudan's transportation system. In its course they were to prepare a 12-year plan, detailing the contributions various proposals could make to Sudanese economic growth. They were to use the full gamut of decision-making techniques, Matrices, P.E.R.T.-type constructions, computer models, etc. In similar planning, defence contractors turned their managerial skills to the problems facing California's legal and refuse disposal systems. The problems may differ, but they can all be attacked through the managerial skills of the best multinationals. In fact, this managerial advice is crucial since the best technology in the world can be vitiated by the lack of necessary supporting decisions. Where shortages of capital, especially foreign currency, may be desperate, advice on the cost effectiveness of various decisions can have a crucial effect throughout the rest of the project; i.e., well thought out advice to the top policy makers may pay for itself many times over in the more effective use of available funds.

However, it is not just in civil engineering projects that using the multinational as a project manager makes sense. Increasingly there is a market for firms or individuals who specialise in variations of 'turn-key' projects, i.e. who take complete responsibility for designing and then completely manufacturing plants. Such a person is Karl Landegger who has specialised in pulp processing plants for the developing world. After moving into paper-making machinery in the early 1950's he realised that while most developing countries lacked foreign exchange for the paper they needed, it was futile to sell them paper-making machinery by itself, since they often lacked the expertise to use it even when they could buy it. He therefore proceeded by first doing a feasibility study, then by arranging finance (often in conjunction with U.S. aid authorities), and finally by building the mill and training the supervisors and managers who would have to run it when he left.

His career reveals the disadvantages of working in the developing world. His first big contract in Colombia was cancelled when the Rojas regime was overthrown. Similarly, after seizing power, Castro reneged on the old Cuban regime's bills for a paper mill. However, many of Landegger's contracts have been with aid-giving bodies. The U.S. Government, for instance, put up two thirds of the cost of a Tunisian pulp mill, and part of the money for projects in Egypt and South Vietnam. French banks, with guarantees from a French Government agency, helped finance a mill in India, while the World Bank through its International Finance Corporation helped in Ethiopia. In the early 1960's Landegger moved into Eastern Europe, which he claims is more attractive a market than much of the Third World in one way—no one asks for bribes.

Obviously the developing world is a difficult market, but Landegger shows what can be done with it, providing one works closely with the aid-giving bodies to provide these nations' real needs. The financial risks can be pretty well discounted through investment guarantee programmes run by bodies like A.I.D. In return, Landegger has offered many nations a new, self-run industry, involving machinery specially developed to make pulp from local raw materials like kenaf, sisal, bagasse and elephant grass.

Landegger is in many ways a conventional entrepreneur. The move from selling the advanced countries paper-making machines to selling the developing world such machines is merely a fairly obvious development of an existing business. In a more interesting recent trend, increasing numbers of manufacturing firms are helping developing countries set up industries which, in the long run, will compete with their own. For instance, in complex 'counterpurchasing deals', the British aircraft industry has taken steps which will eventually lead to the creation of a Rumanian aircraft and an Italian aero-engine industry. To help Rumania buy some passenger liners, British Aircraft Corporation persuaded a much smaller British company called Britten-Norman to assemble 260 of their executive aircraft, the 'Islander', in Rumania. The parts will come from Britain and the final aircraft will be sold world-wide by Britten-Norman, but the Rumanians will gain both the foreign currency to help pay for their major passenger liners from British Aircraft Corporation and also the skills in assembling small aircraft—skills which they can build upon in the future by assembling more of their own parts and eventually designing aeronautical components themselves. Similarly, when it was decided that Rolls-Royce would supply the engines for the Multi-Role Combat Aircraft (M.R.C.A.), planned by British, West German and Italian air forces for the 1970's, Rolls-Royce agreed to sub-contract part of the engine work to an Italian partner, thus allowing Italy to build up experience in this field.

Fiat

Fiat, the Italian auto manufacturer, is a 'low profile' multi-national whose world growth has depended as much on its acceptability to suspicious regimes as on its technical expertise. In particular, Fiat has expanded its interest in Communist Europe from a joint venture in Yugoslavia, set up at the height of that nation's isolation from the world communist movement in the early 1950's, to building a Soviet car plant which will virtually create a modern, consumer-oriented passenger car industry from scratch. Fiat has gradually worked out a policy for developing nations from which both the firm and the host country benefit; the host countries receive export earnings which would have been impossible without Fiat's aid, and Fiat makes profits. Since the Soviet deal, Fiat has almost been able to choose between interested governments in planning to construct new car industries elsewhere.

Within Europe, Fiat is running neck and neck with Volkswagen. In European market shares Fiat is well in the lead (18·9% estimated in early 1969, against VW's 10·6%; Ford's 11·6% and General Motors' 11·1%), but once Volkswagen's world sales, particularly in the U.S., are included, there is less difference. A temporarily blocked merger with Citroën, the first major inter-European merger since the creation of the European Economic Community in the 1950's, has now installed Fiat firmly as the number one European auto-maker. The company's chairman, Signor Giovanni Agnelli, a vigorous pan-European and grandson to the company's founder, disproves the theory that dominant business families eventually decline because the offspring take the money but lose interest in company activities. The company, resting firmly on around 70% of the rapidly growing Italian market, markets a wide range of well-styled, sporty models. Most commentators accept it as the strongest European competitor to the American majors.

In fact, it is Fiat's Italian connections which have made it so successful in international dealings. For one thing, having to operate in the Italian economy, especially in the under-developed South, has taught them never to underestimate the hazards of developing nations. They have learned that it is often necessary to provide much of the infrastructure (roads, financing institutions, etc.) before an auto plant can succeed. Even in the industrial North of Italy, they helped build autostradi such as the one from Milan to Turin or the tunnel under the St Bernard Pass in order to help speed communications with France and Switzerland. Unlike American businessmen who have grown up taking things like adequate telephone systems or well-trained lower management for granted, Fiat has faced at first-hand the problem of building plants for labour with only agricultural experience.

In some ways, the lack of a major imperial past has helped, as has the fact that Italy has not been a leader in pacts like N.A.T.O. This means that nations which would worry about accepting help from Americans, British, or Germans, find Italian partners more agreeable; they offer less threat of political or financial domination. Thus the Italians can play a role similar to that of the Chinese in parts of Africa; states highly protective of their independence find such countries, which are not too worried about getting support in the United Nations in return for help, relatively congenial partners. Thus when President Kaunda of Zambia partially nationalised British and American copper interests in 1969, it was not entirely surprising that he also announced negotiations with Fiat about a new car assembly plant; with E.N.I., the Italian State Oil corporation, about an oil refinery; and with Agip, another major Italian government-owned organisation, about participation in an oil marketing corporation to compete with existing, mostly British, firms. Similarly, Fiat's deals with Yugoslavia and the U.S.S.R. would have been less easy for American, German, or British firms.

In the past, Fiat had no conscious policy about foreign operations, tending in some cases to drift into operations without even buying a financial stake. For instance, during the Peron regime in Argentina, they were invited to set up an auto-manufacturing plant in a factory in Cordoba with 10,000 workers and no real demand for the aero engines it was then making under license from Rolls-Royce. The invitation did not come entirely by accident since a steady flow of Italian migrants meant there were strong links between the two nations. In fact, President Peron had actually spent four or five years in a military academy in Turin, Fiat's home town. Fiat agreed to help, but persuaded them to settle for tractors at first (it was not until the late 1950's that a plant was set up in Buenos Aires to produce cars). They bought no financial interest in the tractor plant, which was built for the Ministry of Aviation. Only much later, when there was a danger that the Cordoba plant might be used to assemble competitors, did Fiat take a major financial stake in it. Similarly, in the late 1940's, they set up a factory in Barcelona (S.E.A.T.), in which they placed no capital. However, as the 1950's went by, the increasing product and component interchange between Spain, Italy and Argentina made it anomalous to rely on parts from a Spanish plant over which they had no financial control. So after some negotiating, they bought about 30% of S.E.A.T.

In 1954, Fiat became involved through General Racovic with Crvena Zastava ('Red Star'), a Yugoslav enterprise. Racovic, an engineer and general, had had friendly relations with Fiat for some time and was also friendly with President Tito. One of the enterprises he was running was an ex-munitions plant converted into an auto-assembly plant. Using Fiat's help to start with, he pushed only the smallest Fiat models such as the '600', which in 1969 was being produced in Yugoslavia at 60,000 units per annum, and the '1300' (30,000 in 1969). Since then, Yugoslavs have increased their manufacturing capability until they are totally manufacturing two models, one of which, the '750', is no longer produced in Italy. Other models are imported from Italy; but this trade is balanced by the fact that the Yugoslavs make some components, such as door panels for the '600', for the whole Fiat operation.

In 1969, it was announced that with more help from Fiat, Crvena Zastava was expanding still further. Plans were to enlarge to 183,000 units a year and to develop international capability. Fiat was to provide 12 of the $100 million needed for the expansion, international agencies $16 million, with the rest coming from Yugoslavia. Part of this money would be spent to produce parts for similar, Fiat-based operations in Poland and Colombia, and for the Fiat-constructed plant in Togliatti-grad when that is finally opened some time in 1970. Crvena Zastava and Fiat were also reportedly involved in joint talks with the Indian Government about setting up a 50,000 unit per annum plant to manufacture a 'people's car'. Obviously the Fiat-aided Yugoslavs have developed an increasingly viable auto industry.

Fiat's biggest coup so far has been winning the contract to construct a 600,000-car plant in Togliattigrad (named after the veteran Italian communist leader). This contract is for a 'turn-key' job. When they hand over the plant to the Russians, the basic models will be manufactured entirely in the Soviet Union and Fiat will have no managerial, policy-making or financial control over the enterprise. The Fiat management has led in the designing, with some Soviet participation; all equipment has been ordered by Fiat, drawing on its experience, while the construction is in Soviet hands. Fiat is thus building Russia an auto plant including all today's best auto manufacturing practices. The plant is designed to be a mile long, thus avoiding uneconomical assembly lines which are forced to double back on themselves; conveyor lines will total 94 miles in length, and five trains will be needed each day to take the output away. The models are to be three versions of the '124', with engines specially modified to Russian petrol and conditions.

Russian thinking seems clear. Facing an enormous pent-up demand for consumer goods, they decided existing Russian know-how could usefully be complemented by the best design and production technology of the non-communist world. Reportedly, there is a waiting list for these cars of at least one million people, enough to occupy the plant for its first three to four years.

For Fiat, the benefits may be more debatable. There were considerable delays in the construction (caused by the difficulty of organising Italian designers, suppliers from much of the Western world, and Russian constructors, and the company concedes it will not make a profit on the $900 million deal.

However, Fiat will obviously stand to benefit if the models prove successful and the Russians decide to call again on the company's design experience. More important, the publicity surrounding the operation has suddenly alerted nations which were once conscious only of Ford and General Motors that other car firms exist with whom they may strike highly satisfactory deals. In fact, so many governments have approached Fiat that the company has had to work out a general policy about setting up activities in developing nations.

In practice, their first reaction is to discourage governments thinking enthusiastically of buying an auto factory, just as they would a cement factory or some other reasonably self-contained industry. Since it is very rare for even a major western auto manufacturer to make more than about 40–45% of his car's total components, the total success of such a venture rests heavily on the efficiency of supporting industries. Fiat argues vehemently that nations should start by assembling imported components, to get a clearer idea of the problems. Fiat realises that it is setting up industries which will at some stage want to compete for markets. But the Fiat management obviously has decided that it will pay them in the long run to help these infant industries.

Obvious moves can be made such as hiving off a certain amount of Italian production to the developing industry. Since S.E.A.T.'s Barcelona plant had the necessary press shop, the body-stamping for the '600' was contracted out to them after the demand slackened in Italy. Similarly, the Italian company buys door panels and carpets from its Yugoslav associate. More interestingly, cooperation and interchange is thus encouraged between Fiat's associates round the world. Yugoslavia sends rear axles without brakes to Poland and receives brakes and body parts for the '125' model. S.E.A.T. is sending '600' parts to Argentina, Chile and Peru, though the aim is to make them gradually less dependent on parts from Europe.

By 1969, therefore, Fiat, based strongly on the fast-growing Italian market, became the market leader in Europe—a position which will be strengthened as the links with Citroën are cemented. It dominates through S.E.A.T. in Spain (275,000 Fiat cars produced there in 1968), through connections in

Yugoslavia and Argentina, and is building up its strength in the rest of Latin America. It is potentially a force to be reckoned with in the development of the Russian auto industry, and is being courted heavily by leading developing nations like India. Politically sensitive, it has been helping its associate companies to find export markets, even when this has entailed bartering dates, cotton and meat.

Obviously in comparison with the American giants, Fiat is still very small, its world-wide sales being well under one tenth of General Motors; but much of General Motors' success rests on dominating the American market. Outside the U.S., it will face far harder competition, now that companies like Fiat are around. There is strong indication that growth in an age of increasing economic nationalism will not depend on marketing or production skills but on political shrewdness. Fiat, at least, appears to have this quality.

The multinationals' demands

The usual international businessman looks on the Third World as an investment area where the normal commercial risks are increased by the risk of war, nationalisation and political upheaval; where the non-industrial national culture encourages very low productivity; and where corruption is rife. They can point to nasty cases where firms have gone under as a result of Third World fiascos. For instance, A. B. Svenska Skolastfabriken, a reasonably small Swedish shoe-machinery manufacturer, built turn-key shoe factories in less-developed nations. They invested $1·25 million in a project in conjunction with the West Nigerian Development Corporation, a government-sponsored agency which invested $150,000 and was due to produce a further $200,000 when the plant was commissioned, to be used as working capital. Because this money was never forthcoming, the plant could not open and the Swedish company went bankrupt; it had depended on receiving $250,000 at the plant's completion, partly from the development corporation, partly from the Nigerian shoe company's funds. In the absence of any government guarantees of such investments, the company had to fail.

Many companies will fear that their investment will be

nationalised. In 1968 and 1969 Peru nationalised the property of Jersey Standard's Canadian subsidiary, International Petroleum Co. Ltd., Chile nationalised Anaconda's Chuquicamata and El Salvador copper mines, Zambia took a share in the copper firms, Anglo-American Corporation and the Roan Selection Trust, and in the Shell-British Petroleum oil marketing organisation. Again, reluctant companies can point to the 50-or-so political coups which took place in the Less-Developed Countries during the 1960's.

These woeful tales would be convincing if rates of return on investment in L.D.C.'s were lower than similar returns in developed nations. The British figures, however, show that in the years 1960–5, British direct investment in developing nations continually gave higher returns than similar investments in the developed nations, though the gap was narrowing. (See Table 5.)

TABLE 5[1]

United Kingdom rates of return on direct investment overseas (%)

	1960	1961	1962	1963	1964	1965
Developing	10·2	8·9	8·5	8·7	8·9	8·8
Developed	7·0	6·5	7·1	7·8	8·2	8·1

[1] *Board of Trade Journal*, 26th January 1968.

The closing of the gap probably reflects the increased pressure put on the petroleum and mining companies over recent decades. Robinson (1968), while confirming from an American viewpoint this difference in rates of return, puts the case much more graphically. The multinational's choice, he claims, is between a 90% probability of getting a 12% return on an investment in West Germany and a 50% probability of getting a 20% return in India.

In fact, many of the risks feared by the multinational investor can be reduced. First, simple schemes whereby national authorities, or even international agencies, guarantee such investments against non-commercial risks can ensure that firms do not go out of business or suffer significant financial loss through, for instance, having a subsidiary nationalised. Countries giving such guarantees include the U.S., Germany, Japan, Australia, Denmark, Norway, the Netherlands and Switzerland. Not one of these countries claims to have suffered a serious loss as a result of such a scheme. If some international board including representatives of developing countries were set up to take over the insurance of such risks, such developing nations might well be more cautious, since irresponsible actions would have to be defended before a number of national representatives. The World Bank at one stage prepared draft articles of agreement for an international investment insurance agency, but the proposals have remained on the drawing board. Certainly, if private investment is really to play a full role in helping the L.D.C.'s, then adequate insurance is essential. In the long run, such schemes would preferably be run on a multilateral basis; at the moment, such disputes usually end with confrontations between two governments, a potentially more explosive situation than if the expropriating country argues its case to a largely uninvolved panel.

The second way in which disputes between firm and nation could be settled more constructively would be through international arbitration. Using gunboats and marines to counter the expropriation of multinational affiliates is a far from satisfactory way to settle such disputes. Equally unsatisfactory is a powerful government's straight economic pressure. Thus the provisions of the notorious (and gloriously named) Hickenlooper amendment, requiring suspension of American aid and sugar quota benefits to any government expropriating American-owned property without taking 'appropriate' steps (i.e. compensation or arbitration) to discharge its obligations under international law, remind us that ultimately such disputes can resolve themselves into naked struggles for political and economic power. What is needed is steadily growing caselaw in the arbitration of such disputes. Multinational planning would benefit from knowing the rough consequences of involvement in given situations. The L.D.C.'s themselves would benefit from having such disputes resolved by reason rather than force, providing of course, that such arbitration does not consistently favour the firms.

One such arbitration body, an arm of the World Bank called

the International Centre for Settlement of Investment Disputes, deals with investment disputes between governments and nationals of other states. By 1969, 60 nations had signed the convention which set this up. A similar body also exists under the auspices of the International Chamber of Commerce. Originally stemming from the I.C.C.'s unofficial involvement in commercial disputes during the 1920's, this Court of Arbitration now handles the cases which do not fit the World Bank's definition of an investment dispute. By 1969, this court seems to have won the trust of a significant number of nations and major firms. For instance, France and Algeria have written into their agreements about Algerian oil that disputes should be referred to the I.C.C. body. Increasingly, they find that the communist nations make similar demands in their contracts with western firms and governments.

While such international arbitration is essential, one can not expect quick or spectacular results. After all, the success of arbitration bodies depends on their winning the trust and respect of all—in this case, of multinational companies as well as nations large and small, rich and poor, communist and non-communist. This is why those who run such bodies insist on choosing with care the people serving on their courts. Thus an I.C.C. arbitration court might consist of an ex-U.S. supreme court justice, a French ex-cabinet minister, a university law professor. If such personalities are acceptable to both sides in a dispute, multinationals know they will not suffer from totally unreasonable governmental behaviour in the L.D.C.'s.

Conclusions

Considerable potential benefits await those L.D.C.'s which can come to a working arrangement with the multinationals. Conversely, many multinationals must come to terms with the developing world in order themselves to survive in an increasingly competitive world. Despite the fears of economic nationalists, this process should be encouraged. The major argument against accepting such aid is that it involves a developing nation's political subjugation. However, we shall see that the balance of power between nation and multinational is increasingly weighted toward the nations which want to exercise control.

The best reason for accepting aid from multinationals is that such investment involves technical and managerial know-how. Moreover, since a prime need of the L.D.C.'s is a viable manufacturing export capability, the multinationals, through their world-wide activities, are increasingly able to blend the activities of plants in the developing world into their global schema. Even when nations want to do more than simply provide components or models for a multinational's total range, the most capable countries can still use multinationals to develop manufacturing skills upon which national efforts can build.

If the developing nations can indeed usefully benefit from closer relationships with the multinationals, then it is time more effort was spent in persuading the companies to play this greater role. There are obvious steps to take, such as developing insurance and arbitration institutions, but it is also time for U.N.C.T.A.D., the United Nations body most concerned with the Third World's industrialisation, to study the records of the leading privately owned corporations. For instance, U.N.C.T.A.D. now regularly records the proportion of each major nation's Gross National Product which is devoted to aiding the developing world. Now that the largest corporations have turnovers on par with the G.N.P.'s of nations like Sweden, it is time for a similar exercise with them. They might start by determining what proportion of each major corporation's activities is located in the developing world. Then they could begin to pressure corporations which quite obviously have restricted their interest to the developed world, and could watch corporations which may be subtly changing the proportions of their activities. The next stage might involve setting targets for the manufacturing companies to devote a given proportion of their activities to the developing world.

Some such analysis of the major industrial corporations is important; although there are developing nations which would prefer not to accept much private investment, there are also other nations which want such investment badly but are incapable of obtaining the best of what such corporations have to offer. Such targets would not really harm the corporations either. The best ones already analyse nations to determine which ones are most likely to prove stable investment bases.

They would not find it difficult to pick those developing nations which most satisfy their criteria. Moreover, some firms which have not done much of this kind of investment yet, may well realise that the important potential markets in the Third World would justify accepting political conditions they would otherwise reject out of hand.

CHAPTER VIII

The Poker Game; Multinationals versus Governments

Gillette can borrow more easily than the government of Portugal. (*Fortune*, April 1968.)
General Motors has a greater revenue than any state in the Union and the fifty biggest corporations in the U.S. have greater revenues than the fifty states . . . future students of the twentieth century will find the history of a firm like General Motors a great deal more important than the history of a nation like Switzerland. (Jay, 1967.)

The multinationals' power

The larger multinationals control economic resources equal to those controlled by the governments of small- to medium-sized countries.

TABLE 6

The Gross National Products of various countries compared with the sales turnover of some larger multinationals. Year 1967. In billions of dollars

Countries		Multinationals
Spain	26·6	
Sweden	23·9	
Netherlands	22·8	
	20·0	General Motors
Belgium	19·7	
Switzerland	15·9	
	13·3	Standard Oil (New Jersey)
Denmark	12·2	
Austria	10·6	

TABLE 6—(*continued*)

Turkey	10·6	
	10·5	Ford
	8·4	Royal Dutch-Shell
Norway	8·3	
	7·7	General Electric
Greece	7·1	
	6·2	Chrysler
	5·7	Mobil Oil
	5·6	Unilever
	5·3	International Business Machines
	5·1	Texaco
Portugal	4·6	

SOURCES: *Fortune* and *Main Economic Indicators* (O.E.C.D.).

Obviously these comparisons should be taken with a pinch of salt. In one way, they understate the relative power of the multinationals: the budget over which a government has direct control will be only a small proportion of the country's G.N.P. On the other hand, multinational employees are counted in hundreds of thousands rather than millions. General Motors, for instance, employs 757,231 people (1968 figures). If one assumes that each of these employees averages two to three dependents, and if one assumes that around half of the cars assembled are made of components brought in from outside suppliers, then he can argue that around 3–5 million people are directly dependent on decisions made by the General Motors management. In that sense, General Motors lacks the direct power held by the governments of major cities with 8 million or more people (London, New York or Tokyo).

Second, the multinationals have not grown any faster than the smaller countries they are compared with. General Motors started the decade with sales which put it ahead of the G.N.P.'s of Sweden, Belgium, Spain and the Netherlands; it was overtaken by three of them by 1967 and will probably be surpassed by the fourth, Belgium, by the early 1970's. Austria, Denmark and Turkey have steadily been moving up on Standard Oil (New Jersey), the world's second largest company. Portugal has, over the decade, gone ahead of Gulf, Western Electric and U.S. Steel. The one exception is I.B.M., which since the mid-1950's has increased in size by about seven times, while Japan, the fastest growing nation, has increased a mere five times. What is more, I.B.M.'s pace of growth actually increased in the late 1960's. During this time it moved from 48th position in the *Fortune* list of the top 500 U.S. firms to 6th in 1968, overtaking the G.N.P.'s of nations like Eire and Portugal on the way. By the early 1970's, it will certainly overtake Greece and Norway. By 1975, it should be seriously challenging General Motors for position as the world's largest corporation and should have passed Turkey, Austria, Denmark and Switzerland along the way. By 1980, anti-trust authorities willing, it will leave Belgium, the Netherlands, Sweden, Spain behind; Canada and Italy will be the next targets. By 1985, if one extrapolates the relevant growth rates between 1955 and 1967, I.B.M.'s turnover could equal the Japanese G.N.P.

There are, of course, reasons why I.B.M.'s growth-rate could start declining, even if there is no such sign at the moment. At some stage, competitors should start making inroads on I.B.M.'s market share; the computer market should shift from the manufacture of the central hardware to stronger emphasis on the soft-ware market in which programmes and equipment are tailored to the specific needs of customers; I.B.M.'s competitors may be able to grow in such changed markets; government protection round the world may lead to favoured local companies operating in protected markets. Nevertheless, although one can list situations which may start working against I.B.M., there is still no evidence of anything like this emerging. I.B.M.'s growth has depended strongly so far on the U.S. market which has by no means stopped growing. The computer market is now all set to grow fastest in the relatively advanced, non-American countries. World-wide I.B.M. is just as well established as in the American market. Politically, the company is one of the most sophisticated of U.S.-owned multinationals; and it would be surprising if it ever ran into serious problems by treading clumsily on the corns of the more sensitive economic nationalists around the globe. Even the company's most dangerous enemy, the U.S. anti-trust authorities, are increasingly powerless since it is doubtful if they could do more than, say, insist that the international division becomes

137

independent of the U.S. parent. Even in that case, one would have units which would be significantly large. All in all, the future for I.B.M. looks awe-inspiring.

Multinationals and the freedom to locate

The greatest threat to nation-states does not lie in the sheer size of the multinationals. Despite the lurid pasts of some, the typical manufacturing multinational keeps its head pretty low concerning local politics in its host nations. The area in which governments may consciously or unconsciously affect multinationals is in attracting their investment in the first place. The nation which does not worry that a chaotic economy, or a markedly xenophobic policy, will encourage little interest by potential multinational investors will not risk their pressure to change policies. However, as long as a nation values the inward investment from multinationals, then some trimming of policies may be expected.

Not enough is known about the factors that go into the investment decisions of the major multinationals. Obviously economics will dictate quite a lot, but just how much are value judgments about the quality of national leadership, etc., fed into the equation? Imperial Chemical Industries' overseas coordination director in 1966 pointed out that a manufacturing firm has far greater freedom in locating subsidiaries than does a tea or rubber planter. He discussed the need for splitting countries up into four categories, depending on the likelihood of certain risks (war, nationalisation, chaotic economy, price control, freezing of freedom to remit dividends, etc.) occurring in the next twenty years. He then suggested a typical strategy: "Your investment plan would be to have a *minimum* of 80% of your investment in the countries you regarded as really safe; and 20% or less in the three groups (out of four) with varying 'risk lives'." Helping the developing world must increase the amount of investment going to those nations with relatively high 'risk lives'.

Du Pont is investigating an even more ambitious approach to this problem. For each country, they isolate 15 or 20 interest groups on the assumption that government policies result from the interplay of economic forces with the relative power of these key groups. They then draw up models to predict which groups will have the most influence in any situation which interests Du Pont. Many other multinationals make similar efforts. Thus Monsanto has a three-man staff advising its international division, which feeds up information ranging from usual published sources to regular reports from special Monsanto 'correspondents' located normally in the countries in which Monsanto operates. Again, they specifically produce an investment climate rating of the countries in which the company is interested.

One institution which advises multinationals comments that for senior information analysts, "military intelligence experience appears to be a good background". The classic case of the company with intelligence connections was United Fruit Company. Horowitz (1965) describes the events in Guatemala leading up to the overthrow of the constitutionally elected government in 1954. United Fruit held a dominant position in Guatemala's economy. In 1948 bananas represented 41% of the country's exports. In return, the company's activities were virtually untaxed. Business profits were untaxed, except for those resulting from the sale of consumer goods in company stores. In 1950, Jacobo Arbenz, a reforming military man and landowner, was elected president. In 1952 he enacted a programme of land reform—in particular, expropriating idle land owned by United Fruit. The U.S. Government was heavily involved in the dispute that followed. Given the circumstances, this comes as no surprise. John Foster Dulles, the U.S. Secretary of State, was both a stockholder and a long-time company lawyer for United Fruit and had even advised the company during the drafting of key contracts with the Ubico dictatorship in Guatemala during the 1930's. To make matters more complicated, Allen Dulles, John Foster's brother and director of the C.I.A. during the 1954 coup, had actually been United Fruit's president at one time. The coup was not wholly concerned with the United Fruit case, since Arbenz was accused of going to Czechoslovakia for arms (Arbenz replied that the U.S., whom they had approached first, would not sell any to Guatemala). However, the basic reason for the coup was that actions like the land reform measure appeared too leftist—especially to those with United Fruit interests. And so a right-wing Guatemalan colonel marched in, and the U.S. ambassador dictated Arbenz's successor.

The United Fruit case may be exceptional, though it is hard to tell since companies do not advertise their connections with intelligence agencies. From the outside, one can see that intelligence agencies could find multinationals very useful; their global activities could provide a useful cover for gathering information. From the company viewpoint, the situation is more complex. Intelligence connections would obviously help the company when dealing with potentially hostile governments. If the intelligence agencies are willing to engineer coups to keep out anti-business politicians, then the advantages are even clearer. On the other hand, one could lose much when such crude power ploys increasingly appear indefensible in the eyes of world opinion. Certainly, multinationals competing for communist markets would be exceptionally stupid to involve themselves in any major spying. Businessmen obviously do get involved in intelligence work, but the ones who get caught (like the Briton, Greville Wynne) seem to be relatively unimportant in the business world.

This area is grossly understudied. The classic firms with intelligence links, like United Fruit, are relics of the bad old days of open 'dollar imperialism'. We need to know more about how the manufacturing newcomers to the world scene are conducting themselves. If they do tend to use military intelligence veterans to run their information analysis sections, how much information swapping takes place? Just as important, what type of intelligence personnel go into industry? Does their presence explain why some multinationals seem to lack sensitivity when dealing with the developing world?

What worries governments is that multinationals are increasingly able to act on the basis of such information analyses. On a relatively harmless level, Dow Chemical and Union Carbide have followed a different strategy in Latin America because Dow gambled that economic integration would be a long-term haul at best, and therefore has put up small protected plants in each country. Union Carbide bet on integration coming fast and therefore built large capacity plants in the major Latin American countries with capacity to supply the future integrated markets. On a more serious level, De Gaulle's intransigent policies toward foreigners in the mid-1960's led Ford Motor to switch an investment from Thionville to Belgium, while Phillips Petroleum similarly switched to Benelux from a proposed site in Bordeaux. The ex-Belgian Congo supplies an example of commercial actions resulting from a straight political decision. Despite all pressures from the United Nations and the Belgian Government, Union Minière payed their taxes to Tshombe, and not to the central Congolese Government. Other companies have found themselves in the same quandary, notably those whose oil fields were in rebel territory when the secessionist state of Biafra broke away from Nigeria.

On the whole, the bargaining power of oil and mining multinationals is declining. If a government owns potential oil fields it can play off prospective bidders against each other. On the other hand, a manufacturing multinational can choose between supplying a national market from within that market or from outside. This means that the multinational can bargain back, sometimes quite effectively. In the late 1960's the British Government devised a scheme for building two aluminium smelters which, given regional subsidies and some reductions in the price of power, should just about become economical compared with the existing smelters in Scandinavia. This import saving scheme favoured British Aluminium and Rio Tinto. But one of the companies which had been left out, Alcan, announced plans to build another smelter in Eire, which is covered by a free trade treaty with Britain. With no available counter pressures, the British Government gave way and Alcan now has a plant under construction at Tynemouth, North-umberland. For better or for worse, Britain is to have three aluminium smelters when all informed opinion agreed that the British market could economically support only two. Further, the people of Eire were used as a pawn in negotiations they were powerless to influence. Can any nation guarantee that they will never find themselves in a similarly powerless position?

Further limitations are imposed on national governments by the fact that their own companies are going multinational. It is very difficult to be tough on subsidiaries of foreign-owned multinationals and still find one's own multinationals treated as

141

welcome intruders. For instance, when the U.S. anti-trust authorities tried to block the British Petroleum bid for Sohio, the competitive U.S. petroleum companies were among those most concerned. They stood to lose European privileges if harsh treatment of B.P. created a wave of economic chauvinism there. Similarly, no major nation could expropriate the subsidiary of a foreign-owned multinational now without placing their own multinationals in danger of reciprocal treatment. Further more, it is increasingly difficult to nationalise any industry without causing severe unrest in other countries, although railroad and steel industries have been exceptions since they have not usually had significant activities outside their national boundaries. But if the British nationalised their chemical industry today, what would happen to Imperial Chemical Industries' integrated plants in the Netherlands and Germany, which rely on flows of feedstock from a British ethylene plant? If Italy nationalised Fiat, what would they do with its shareholdings in Citroën? And nationalisation of an I.B.M. subsidiary would only saddle a government with a worthless plant. After all, I.B.M. computer components are only of use to other I.B.M. plants in other nations.

Policies of nearby nations impose a major constraint on any government. With tariff barriers falling it does not often matter whether some plants are located two to three hundred miles away. De Gaulle discovered some of the perils of moving unconventionally regarding investment policies, as would any nation which deviated strongly from its neighbours on taxation or nationalisation. One suspects that the multinationals will increasingly be able to pick off nations which are notably left of their neighbours. On the other hand, companies which are too enthusiastically investing within notably reactionary nations may find their positions growing untenable. Swedish companies have been forced to drop dam projects in Rhodesia. Political activists in the U.S. have already begun to harass the headquarters of multinationals involved in South Africa, Greece, Mozambique and other countries which are anathema to the left-wing. One potential consequence of the multinationals' centralisation is that they are more vulnerable to political pressure aimed at their activities elsewhere in the world.

Finally, the pressure which multinationals can put on

countries is only one result of a general trend toward a world economy in which countries are increasingly linked by economic ties. In the words of Kindleberger,[1]

> The way to maximise independence is to close the economy and move to autarky. A country loses independence through trade as well as investment, through borrowing abroad in debt form, through welcoming tourists, owning direct investments and market securities in its own turn, as well as subscribing to the International Monetary Fund, the Organisation for Economic Co-operation and Development, the General Agreement and so forth, not to mention the network of political links to the rest of the world. To talk of national independence as an absolute and to work to maximise it, fails to put the issues in perspective.

Petroleum and economic nationalism

Oilmen believe that oil is always discovered in inaccessible and desolate locations. This means that historically, they have dealt with and often dominated some of the world's smallest or weakest governments. In the 1950's and 1960's, however, the producer governments have gradually been gaining the upper hand over the oil multinationals, until an oilman can say without too much exaggeration that the smallest government is stronger than the biggest company.

Governments have needed the refining companies in the past because they lacked the capital and know-how to prospect for oil, or to develop the fields discovered and then market the product satisfactorily. The oil companies therefore seemed benefactors, and no-one looked too closely at the incredible concessions some of them won. They secured their interests by buying up those politicians and leaders who would help them most, so that the people in the best position to query their activities were effectively silenced.

The most publicised attempt to fight the majors only showed how much national governments depended on their cooperation. In 1951, Iran's Prime Minister Mossadegh, on a wave of nationalistic opposition to Britain's past imperialism, nationalised Anglo-Iranian, the British company which was exploiting Iran's oil fields. During the two years in which the dispute

[1] Kindleberger, Charles P., *op. cit.*, 1969.

dragged on, Anglo-Iranian blocked the sale of Iran's crude or refined products throughout the world. The major oil companies refused to handle Iran's products for fear they might find themselves in a similar position elsewhere in the world. A couple of Italian and Japanese companies which purchased a small amount of oil from the Iranian Government were sued and scared off. Iran's oil sales plummeted from 640,000 barrels a day in 1950 to 20,000 in 1952; even after the two sides made their peace in 1953, production did not again reach 600,000 barrels a day until 1957. Total sales in 1952 and 1953 produced government revenue equivalent to a single day's royalties under the old regime. In the meantime, Anglo-Iranian (now calling itself British Petroleum) built up production from the nearby Arab states of Iraq and Kuwait, thus losing relatively little, especially after receiving compensation from the British Government and the other oil majors. The latter formed a consortium which came in with the newly named British Petroleum to operate its former business in Iran after a compromise solution in 1953.

Not all such expropriations have been disastrous. Petroleos Mexicanos, the sixth largest petroleum organisation on the basis of sales, and the only Latin American corporation with sales round $1 billion, was created by nationalising American, British, Dutch and Canadian oil companies in 1938. At the time there was considerable outcry, with the British severing diplomatic relations with Mexico for several years. It was assumed that the new nationalised industry could not survive due to lack of trained personnel; and for the first seven years its position was precarious. Since 1945, however, it has steadily grown until it now employs 56,000. Pemex, as the company is called, has now diversified into petrochemicals, runs a fleet of 22 tankers and around 200 other vessels, pumps oil from the continental shelf in the Gulf of Mexico, and has constructed many pipelines to aid natural gas sales. Other Latin American governments now look to Pemex for advice. Peru's Minister of Development flew to Mexico to seek technical aid when the Peruvian Government expropriated American oil interests in 1969. What the Mexicans did yesterday, perhaps the Peruvians can do tomorrow.

These two cases suggest that national governments have

always been free to try such extreme measures, but that the hostility of the world's petroleum industry would guarantee a very hard time indeed while the new nationalised concern was finding its feet. Except in the most unusual cases, such attempts to run alone were doomed to failure. Major expropriations, however, are only part of the picture. Just as significant is the activity on a humbler level.

The development of O.P.E.C.

In the early years, oil companies working in Venezuela got their concessions for a flat sum. Slowly, after 1918, they were required to pay the government a percentage of the final market prices for Venezuelan oil; and by 1938 the government was receiving 13% of the total declared value of oil ($44 million, or 35% of the government's tax revenues). In 1943, the government felt strong enough to start charging the companies a small amount of income tax, and by 1948, persuaded them to accept a 50–50 agreement whereby the profits from Venezuelan oil should be halved with the government. Since then, the government 'cut' has been pushed up further. Under President Betancourt the profits going to the government were raised to 52% in 1957, to 65% in 1958 and 69% in 1959. Later regimes pushed this up still further to 72% in 1966. In 1969, the government was demanding government participation at the operational level—the so-called 'service contracts'.

Obviously the oil companies have not liked these concessions but have had to bow before the Venezuelan bargaining position. For most of this century it has been one of the top two oil-producing nations and, more important, the major one in the Western hemisphere. Understandably, the oil majors have competed for access to such an important source of crude oil; and Venezuelan Governments, however weak they might have been otherwise, have always had the power to revoke concessions or to show favouritism in granting new ones. For instance, in the 1969 negotiations about government participation in running company activities, the government's strongest weapon was its concessions. The service contracts were to operate in new concessions around South Lake, Maracaibo. At first, only one of the newly established international companies on the oil scene, Occidental, would accept these terms. However, once it became clear that the Gulf of Venezuela would be the next area offered, oil majors like Shell and Mobil decided to cooperate after all.

As it happens, the tax policies of America and Britain, whereby oil companies can deduct taxes paid on their foreign operations from their domestic tax bill, helped reconcile them to the switch from paying royalties (which count as a cost and therefore are not deductible) to paying taxes on profits. Increasingly, the figures on which these 'profits' are calculated have become distorted.

In 1960, the oil majors decided that since world oil prices were falling, they should pay less in taxes to the producer governments. They therefore announced a cut in the 'posted' prices—the formal price on which the profit calculations were based. Disturbed producing nations formed O.P.E.C. (the Organisation of Petroleum Exporting Countries) to act as a government pressure group against the oil companies. With headquarters in Geneva, they have produced a lot of detailed work on the behaviour of oil companies. Although they have been unsuccessful in getting posted prices raised to the 1960 level, they have succeeded in keeping them static since, despite the fact that there is less and less relationship between the price the companies eventually sell the oil for and the posted price on which their tax liabilities to the producer governments are calculated. Because world prices have continued downward, the companies are paying an increasing proportion of their profits to the producing countries. But they compensate for such losses by manipulating the transfer prices they charge between their producing and refining activities and then by running their refining operations for very low profits in developed markets like Europe.

O.P.E.C. tries to make sure that the oil-producing nations place roughly equal demands on the oil companies. Their chief success has been to persuade Libya to tax its companies more. Libya in the early 1960's was a danger not only to the other oil-producing nations but also to the established oil multinationals. A number of relatively small American companies—Continental, Marathon and Amerada—by winning concessions in Libya had stumbled on to one of the world's largest sources of oil. This source, moreover, was usefully close to Europe, while the established majors were tied to oil reserves on the far side of the Suez Canal. To establish quickly a share of the European market, the Libyan companies launched a price-slashing campaign against the existing majors. To make matters harder, Libya was taxing her companies more leniently than the other oil-producing countries, thus allowing the newcomers considerable lee-way in their price-slashing campaigns. For instance, by 1965, the Libyan Government was still 17 years behind Venezuela in demanding only 50% of company profits. Under heavy O.P.E.C. pressure, Libya finally in 1965 pressed its companies to 'convert' their concession agreements to new O.P.E.C. terms. Those which refused would get no new concessions to explore; but those which agreed received a government pledge not to scrutinise tax returns going back to 1961.

Since 1950 the squeeze on the oil majors (or the seven sisters as Enrico Mattei called them) has been dramatic. In 1952, these seven—Standard Oil (New Jersey), Royal Dutch-Shell, British Petroleum, Texaco, Socal, Gulf and Mobil—claimed 90% of the oil production, 72% of the refining, and 75% of the product sales outside the U.S. and the communist countries. By 1965 their proportion of oil production was down to 75% and their product sales to 60%. No doubt this trend will continue as the competition increases. Such competition explains why the oil majors have been forced to make concessions on such a scale. Companies which once monopolised oil production in various nations now find a pack of international newcomers snapping at their heels. The three companies making somewhat protected Libyan profits have moved into world exploration, using aggressive marketing techniques which have not been happily received by the petroleum establishment.

Just as interesting has been the incursion of a number of companies based in nations with no traditions in the international oil industry. For instance, the Arabian Oil Company, owned by Japanese consumer businessmen, suddenly turned up in the Middle East. In 1957 they signed a deal with Saudi Arabia to take over concessions in the offshore waters of the Neutral Zone and in 1958 made a similar deal with Kuwait. To gain these concessions, they agreed to terms which made their competitors shudder. First, they agreed to pay a hitherto unprecedented 57% of their profits in tax, and second, they agreed to let the governments purchase at par 10% of their shares after discovery of oil in commercial quantities. Neither of these agreements would have been happily made by an established company. Similarly, a Spanish company has moved into Kuwait; the Italian E.N.I. into Iran and Saudi Arabia; the French E.R.A.P. into offshore Iran and Iraq. The only major country not hunting for oil at this point is West Germany, though Germans have plans to move in this direction.

The oil majors are thus being squeezed heavily. Between 1961 and 1966 European oil companies' profits fell by 25%, while payments to producer governments rose by 11%. In 1966–7, the return on capital outside North America and Venezuela dropped for the first time below that inside these countries. Oil company payments to the eight principal producing countries—the 6 Arab States, Iran and Venezuela—have risen from nearly $2 billion in 1957 to over $4 billion ten years later. This increase should continue, since the oil companies are currently on the run. Iraq, for instance, withdrew from the Iraq Petroleum Co. (I.P.C.) all concessions that it was not actually using or exploring, leaving it with a mere 1% of its original concessions. Saudi Arabia broke the stranglehold of four U.S. companies by giving concessions to U.S. independents like Sinclair and Natomas, which is operating with a Pakistani group. Iran has successfully pushed up the royalty and profit payments due to her from the consortium operating her oil interests, up to a straight $1 billion for 1969–70.

And yet, this particular poker game may well get more complex. O.P.E.C. is an exception to the rule that agreements between the countries producing commodities and raw materials rarely work. It is working so far because the world market is expanding fast enough for every nation to increase production each year. Moreover, the number of key producing countries has been relatively small. This situation has changed as a result of world-wide exploration which has turned up new fields in Nigeria, Libya, Alaska and Indonesia. It was very noticeable, for instance, that whereas the closing of the Suez Canal in 1956 led to petrol rationing in a number of European countries, the similar closure since 1967 has been no more than a minor nuisance. The Middle East fields can now be supplemented from other sources.

This may mean that the oil-producing countries will find the oil majors less willing to accept their more radical future demands. In particular, trouble may loom as each nation tries to increase its oil exports each year. Iran's 1969 demand for $1 billion in revenues from its oil consortium, for instance, represented a 16% increase over its revenues in 1968. And the Shah has demanded similar rises in annual income for the years 1968 to 1973. Iran aims to persuade the oil companies that she has better claims to such sums than the Arab States nearby. She points out that her oil kept flowing during the Arab-Israeli six-day war in 1967, and that her 27 million people need the money far more than do the sparsely populated sheikhdoms of Kuwait and Abu Dhabi. Oil revenues per person in 1969 were $25 for Iran, $1,200 for Kuwait and $4,500 for Abu Dhabi. Iran has been arguing effectively that necessary social change could only be promulgated at the expense of oil producers in other countries. Up to 1969, such demands have ended with compromises in which the oil consortium has loaned Iran the necessary money against future royalties, without absolutely guaranteeing that it will raise oil production from Iran by the desired amount. In the 1970's, this sort of proposition is likely to lead to some dissension. Certain oil companies may decide to relinquish some of their holdings in the more demanding nations, preferring to shop around for oil from cheaper sources. Second, the oil-producing nations may well quarrel when it becomes apparent that the strongest demands some are making can only be satisfied at the cost of others' production. If the volume of proved reserves moves sharply ahead of demand (if only for a limited time), then the oil majors could withdraw completely from some countries, and drive down the price of crude oil by playing the remaining countries off against each other.

This suggestion is not totally implausible since 'downstream' operations (i.e. shipping, refining and marketing) are becoming an increasingly capital-consuming part of the business. In 1968, for instance, three quarters of the petroleum industry's capital expenditure outside the U.S. was spent outside the oil fields. Any newcomers who decided to take their place in oil production would find themselves having to go through the majors' distribution network unless they had really powerful financial resources. In a time of overproduction, the newcomers (and the governments relying on them) could be tightly squeezed. In some ways at the moment, the oil companies actually protect oil-producing nations from the full blast of naked competition with their counterparts.

On the other side, the producing countries are becoming more and more sophisticated in their knowledge and experience. For instance, in 1969 King Idris of Libya was overthrown by a military junta. The new prime minister, Dr Mahmoud Maghribi, was a former Esso lawyer who had been jailed for bringing about an oil embargo in 1967. The new minister of petroleum, who immediately pressed claims against the oil companies, was a petroleum engineer from Colorado University who had joined the Oasis oil consortium, and also had been jailed for his part in the 1967 oil embargo. Helping the ministry was a young Libyan economist who was seconded from one of the oil companies. In their demands on the oil companies, the Libyans argued from reports prepared by economic and marketing executives who had been sent to Europe by the old regime to assess the actual realised prices of Arab oil. The oil companies were therefore no longer arguing against ill-informed amateurs who could be bribed, threatened or coerced, but against militant nationalists who knew the oil industry from the inside, using information from fully professional surveys. Increasingly, as the producer nations push for greater national participation in the activities of the global oil giants, this pool of professional nationalists will grow.

The days are over in which the oil majors can trample over their opposition. In the late 1960's the power distribution between countries and companies was more and more finely balanced. The pendulum which has been swinging towards the countries all through the 1950's and 1960's may, if anything, start swinging slowly the other way as new petroleum deposits are brought on stream. In the game of bluff and counterbluff between the two contestants, a climax may be near.

The copper industry

As far as the multinationals are concerned, the copper industry has gone the way of petroleum. The producer countries have allied themselves against the giant corporations which have controlled their economies. In this case, Chile started the movement by 'Chileanising' the huge Kennecott El Teniente copper mine. Fifty-one per cent of the control was forcibly sold to the Chilean Government, who agreed to pay for this share over 20 years. In 1969, Chile's lead was followed by an almost identical move in which the Roan Selection Trust (majority shareholding, American) and the South African-owned Anglo-American Corporation were forced to sell 51 % of their operations to the Zambian Government, again on deferred payment terms. Thanks to judicious partial nationalisation, the non-communist copper industry rests firmly in the hands of three governments—Chile, Zambia and the Congo.

Noticeably, these steps have been with some cooperation from the former privately-owned copper producers. The president of Kennecott's metal-mining division told *Fortune* that the partnership with Chile's government had worked well and had led to a noticeable relaxation in labour tensions.

"I am convinced", he said, "that joint ventures are the most promising approach for American enterprise abroad. . . . [In] the long run, this is not only one way for American corporations to operate profitably abroad, but for many it may be the only way."[1]

In the case of Zambia, the Roan Selection Trust had offered President Kaunda participation in their activities in 1964, when he took control after winning Zambian independence from British colonial rule. With left-wing pressure and Chile's example to guide him (there is some evidence that Chile quite actively encouraged him), Kaunda convinced the companies that a half share of something is far better than a full share of nothing, so they went along with his plans without too many objections.

These companies are obviously wise. Mining is an industry which is particularly vulnerable to nationalist attack. Not only are the mining companies physically removing the soil of the nation but they are often also using foreign managers while employing a large number of citizens, thus guaranteeing that labour problems wear a national complexion. To some extent, this is different from oil which, although an extractive industry,

1 *Fortune*, October 1969, p. 64.

is a technologically more complex one, using less labour than copper mining. It is not surprising therefore to find mining firms like Rio Tinto-Zinc and Kaiser Aluminum, which have made it their policy to seek local partners wherever possible round the world. Kaiser deliberately limits itself to a 25–30% interest in foreign ventures. For this, it gets a voice in management, some earnings and, above all, a relatively quiet life as far as political controversy is concerned. The British-owned Rio Tinto-Zinc is a bit more requiring, normally expecting to hold a majority shareholding in projects it is involved in; but, apart from this, it is normally only too happy to sell shares to the local business community.

Latin America—the drive for independence

Latin America will provide the most stringent tests of multinational strategy. This continent, historically the prime target for private investment in less-developed nations, is currently riding a wave of economic nationalism which makes the future for private, foreign-owned companies look very questionable indeed. First, most of such investment in the past has come from the U.S., a country which is now an investor's liability while the Latin Americans assert their independence of their northern neighbour. European and Japanese firms are challenging U.S. supremacy by offering more flexible terms than some of the longer-established American ones. Moreover, the traditional alliance of the military, the landed property owners, and the Catholic Church has slowly started to break down. In a number of countries, the military appears attracted to the popular nationalism hitherto best represented by the Peron regime in Argentina after the Second World War. The church is also affecting social issues because many priests at the local level are advocating social change. This breakdown of the coalition which has protected private investors in the past spells trouble for the multinationals. Only the most intelligent and flexible will survive, and they will survive only with government permission.

Latin America's prime complaint is that its exports have been growing slower than the world growth of trade, and that what increases they have made are nullified by an expanding volume of payments to the developed world as interest on aid loans, profit repatriation, etc. From 1961–7 the continent's basic trade balance was consistently in the black, but was pulled into deficit by payments which led to deficits ranging from $433 million in 1963 to $1,568 million in 1967. Latin Americans feel wronged because much of this outflow results from the unrealistically high interest rates of official aid or of the U.S. multinationals, repatriation in 1967 of all but 2–3% of the profits they made there. Similarly, as long as the Latin American economies rely so heavily on basic crops like coffee, they remain very sensitive to slight changes in world prices. For instance, a one cent decline in the price of coffee in the U.S. costs Colombia $8·7 million, Central America $8 million and Brazil $24 million. In this sort of situation, it is not surprising that hot tempers and ill-feeling turn against the agents of the developed world.

The initial expression of this hostility comes in attacks on the motives of the United States. Governor Rockefeller's 1969 Latin American tour illustrated not only how close to the surface this Anti-Americanism lies, but also how easily U.S. owned companies can become prime targets for retaliation. Officially backed by President Nixon, the tour suffered the indignity of being invited to stay away from several countries because governments could not guarantee its safety. Thirteen 'Minimax' supermarkets in Buenos Aires, owned by the Rockefeller-controlled International Basic Economy Corporation, were burned by protestors, as was the administrative building of General Motors in Uruguay. Similar forms of urban terrorism have led to the assassination in Guatemala over two years (1967–9) of an ambassador and three U.S. military attaches. In Brazil, the U.S. ambassador, Mr C. Burke Elbrick, was kidnapped and only released after left-wing political prisoners were freed in Mexico.

What must be even more worrying to the established American business community is that the military, once the staunchest supporter of the right-wing status quo, seems to be moving toward 'populist' policies. Within a week of taking power in Peru, General Juan Velasco nationalised the La Brea and Parinas oil fields of International Petroleum Company Ltd., which is ultimately controlled by Standard Oil of New Jersey. Soon after, Peru and Chile nationalised the long-distance phone company controlled by I.T.T. Then with Ecuador, Peru retaliated against moves to invoke the Hickenlooper amendment by impounding U.S.-owned tuna boats infringing on their territorial waters, which they claim up to 200 miles from their coastline. Finally, this military government introduced one of the most extensive land reform schemes yet seen outside Cuba, including the expropriation of land owned by the U.S. firm, W. R. Grace Inc.

Increased pressure on U.S. interests by the governments of Colombia and Ecuador followed Peru's moves. Then in October 1969, the military leader in Bolivia, General Ovando Candia, nationalised the assets of Bolivian Gulf Oil, opened full diplomatic relations with Rumania, received a Russian envoy, and made conciliatory gestures toward Cuba. Oddly enough, General Ovando himself had helped to hound down Che Guevara, until Guevara was finally killed in Bolivia. Though Ovando actually admitted that he thought nationalising Bolivian Gulf was not in Bolivia's best interest, the times are radical enough in Latin America to force military leaders to respond.

The gradual leftward drift of the military is likely to be speeded by the emerging social conscience of the Catholic Church, whose leaders in Latin America have often fervently supported the status quo. A sign of the times is the occupation of the National Cathedral in Santiago by over 200 priests, nuns and laymen at the time the Pope visited Bogota, to protest against this traditional unholy alliance between the military, the rich and the church. In practically every Latin American nation, it is possible to find increased activity by near-Marxist Catholic priests who have chosen to go out into the villages and practice their social ideals. In Colombia there is now a new martyr, a priest who was killed when leading an anti-government group. This grass-roots concern has been slowly reflected by actions on the part of the Catholic hierarchy. The 1968 conference of the Latin American bishops in the Colombian city of Medellin ended with 'social pronouncements' which have given the radical priests considerable heart. In particular, such priests follow the doctrine of 'Conscientización' which stresses the need for encouraging the indigents to make demands for themselves. This militancy has led church leaders to take

154

political stances unthinkable during the 1950's. During Castro's rise in Cuba, or the Peron regime in Argentina, the church enthusiastically backed the status quo. But by 1969, the church was the prime source of opposition to the regime of the Bavarian-born General Alfredo Stroessner in Paraguay, a country Stroessner has policed heavily throughout his long tenure of office. Coalitions between the church and students led to deporting Jesuit leaders, closing a church weekly newspaper, and physically attacking processions of nuns and priests. The local church authorities retaliated by excommunicating some of the regime's officials and by refusing to hold a mass which Stroessner was to attend. All the evidence points to increasingly routine clerical militancy. Certainly, the multinational companies, allied as they are to developed nations and the capitalist system, can no longer expect the church to protect them as it has in the past.

Even at the highest continental level, evidence of the Latin American desire to be independent of the U.S.A. appears. Traditionally, the problems of the hemisphere have been discussed in the United Nations Economic Commission for Latin America, and the Organization of American States. On both of these, the United States has been represented by large, visible delegations. The result has been the *ad hoc* growth of C.E.C.L.A. (Comite Especial Coordinador Latino-Americano), the special Latin-American coordinating committee. This committee was set up as a pressure group for the nations of Latin America in any negotiations potentially leading to more aid, etc. Originally formed just before the New Delhi conference of U.N.C.T.A.D. (The United Nations Conference on Trade, Aid and Development), it produced an 'economic bill of rights' at a special conference of foreign ministers at Viña del Mar in June 1969. The bill included 35 points including the needs for less protectionism by developed nations, for more and cheaper flows of capital, for the reduction of transport costs; and the committee delivered these directly to President Nixon.

What should we make of all this? First, one can worry about the exact strategy, which looks as though it will be followed by the majority of Latin American governments in the immediate future. In many ways, these governments seem heavily influenced by the success story of Japan, which has grown fast without taking any significant direct American investment. However, Japanese success rests as much as anything on high calibre governmental and industrial leadership, a work force which is reasonably well educated, and a domestic market which is large by world standards. Latin America so far has not begun to show that kind of political or industrial expertise necessary to match Japan. Moreover, one of the effects of the continent's surge of economic nationalism is an emphasis on developing steel mills, auto plants, oil industries—the kind of prestige projects which can be disastrous. The Japanese, though strong in these industries, meticulously developed industries in which they could win world mastery.

In the emotional atmosphere which is developing, the U.S.-owned multinationals are going to be heavily tested. Firms which rely on total control of their Latin American subsidiaries, choose to raise their money within Latin America itself, and repatriate the bulk of their profits out of the continent can look forward to an exceptionally bleak time. Firms like Ford and General Motors already lost bids for an auto plant in Colombia, because, unlike France's Renault, they were not willing to accept a 50% government shareholding in the venture. Even within the American ranks, it is possible to point to companies which are following differing policies. For instance, Standard Oil (New Jersey) took a relatively restrained line when Peru nationalised International Petroleum Corporation. Gulf Oil took a far harder line by publicly calling on the U.S. Government to suspend aid to Bolivia when Bolivia hit their subsidiary, and promptly drew up plans to get Bolivian oil blacked in international markets. Although one can sympathise with the Gulf management, since it is doubtless infuriating to have their legal assets snatched away from them, it is extremely doubtful if this reach-for-the-gun type of reaction will ever help. If anything, the tactics are counter-productive; governments elsewhere on the continent will no doubt notice that Gulf is still acting as a classic 'imperialist', trying to use its global power against countries with which it is in dispute. In any case, relative newcomers on the oil scene like Armand Hammer's Occidental Oil are quite happily offering bargains which make hardliners amongst the oil community irrelevant.

Hammer, who will cheerfully tell government negotiators about the time he dealt with Lenin, has offered Venezuela package deals which include helping the government develop its nickel and silver mines and establishing petrochemical plants. Other newcomers to the Latin American scene like the European and Japanese companies tend to be extremely compliant in accepting government or local participation in ventures. Volkswagen, for instance, sold 20% of its plant in Brazil to local shareholders when it set up there in 1957. The precaution has paid off impressively.

Multinationals must adjust to an international environment which many of them will find distasteful and dangerous. Some of the more uncompromising may well choose to retire into the developed markets where competition may be keen, but where the business environment is not likely to be endangered by changes in government. In the short run they may be wise to do this. In the long run, they will be opting out of the growth areas. On another level, they are also opting out of a duty to use their skills and resources to help close the gap between the advanced and developing economies. Ranged against them will be a number of challengers who will accept the political risks and compromises inherent in dealing with the developing world. They will realise that the developing nations need technology, capital, experienced advice but that they will be increasingly sensitive about companies which want to run the whole show themselves. However attuned to nationalistic feelings, they may still find themselves being nationalised, but in this kind of situation they will rely on reasonably gentle pressure, preferring insurance compensation to open bullying of the relevant authorities. They will still be basically motivated by the search for profit, but they will have reasonably well developed codes about what proportion of their profits should be earned from different parts of the world, and will be aware of their obligations not to make things too difficult for governments by remitting profits out of the developing world in large quantities. They will learn that the survivors in the developing world will be those who best fit in with the priorities imposed by governments and international aid agencies. They are no longer the sole arbiters of what is good for a country.

CHAPTER IX

The Developed Nations' Responses

A government's first reaction to the power of multinationals is to think of protecting the nation's most important industries from the predatory foreigners by measures like banning foreign investment, or controlling it with an eagle eye. Tempting as this strategy may be to some politicians, it is unrealistic for developed nations since current thinking advocates greater freedom of capital movements. Slowly, for instance, tariff barriers are being dismantled through both common markets and devices like the Kennedy Round, which lowered tariffs heavily between the U.S. and Europe. Current thinking accepts the principle that capital should be free to invest anywhere it chooses. Provisions on these lines are written into the European Common Market statutes; and bodies like the Organisation for Economic Co-operation and Development (O.E.C.D.) are also pledged to move in this direction. Although it is still possible to restrict capital movements (the U.S. mandatory controls of 1968 are a major example), it is becoming harder and harder to do so. In giving up this control, however, governments lose an effective method of curbing the undue influence of multinational companies. Given total freedom to invest where they like, the multinationals will be able to ignore countries they find inhospitable. Some nations are still trying to fight the tide.

Japan

Looked at from any direction the Japanese case is fascinating. While fostering an economy which has been growing at least 10% per annum, roughly twice as fast as any rival economies, she has deliberately excluded all but the merest trickle of direct foreign investment. This ploy makes her seem a model to governments in the developing world who would like to repeat the Japanese success story, especially without accepting compromising foreign control of their economy. However, Japan's record resists over-simple generalisations. Moreover, Japan's policy is due to be heavily modified under very severe international pressure. A policy of economic autarky can cause severe diplomatic complications.

From the time the Meiji overthrew the Tokugawa Shogunate in 1868, the Japanese government has been deeply concerned to take the best from the developed world without compromising Japanese susceptibilities. In this, they merely followed the aims of the Meiji charter oath which instructed them to 'seek knowledge far and wide' in order to create a modern state. Even before 1939, the Japanese government sought foreign capital on behalf of the industrial sector, by borrowing and re-lending through intermediary institutions like the Industrial Bank of Japan or the Yokohama Specie Bank. Through these bodies the government was able to protect the relatively weak industrial sector from being swamped by foreign financial power. On the other hand, these firms are over-suspicious of foreign investors in a later age in which direct contact is no longer avoidable. During this period some foreign firms have invested directly in Japan, notably the oil majors and electrical firms. Thus, in 1969 Shell is the largest foreign investor, with well-established competitors like Caltex, Tidewater, Esso and Mobil.

After 1945, such investments were put under greater scrutiny, with foreign investors tolerated only if they could contribute to self-sufficiency and a healthy balance of payments. As a result, very few other companies got in, I.B.M. and Coca-Cola being the two main exceptions which were allowed to set up 100% subsidiaries. At the same time, the government was encouraging Japanese industry to seek licensing and technical agreements with the best foreign companies, did market research itself to decide the future growth areas and backed local 'high technology' companies with financial aid if their resources were overextended. As part of the government involvement in Japanese industry, the official export inspection system aims to catch shoddy goods before they damage the new Japanese advanced technological image abroad. Similarly, J.E.T.R.O., the 90% government-owned external trade organisation, does basic market analysis of promising economies for the benefit of Japanese industry as a whole, and carries out specific on-the-spot surveys at a moderate cost for any single Japanese firm. As a result of these policies, Japan's growth has involved considerable technical help from foreigners via licenses, etc., but a minimal direct investment, which had a total asset value of only $868 million (Ford has invested almost double that amount in Britain since 1953). During the 1960's, such direct investment averaged around $50 million a year, which is a negligible figure for an economy the size of Japan's.

In 1964, to demonstrate her economic 'coming-of-age', Japan joined the O.E.C.D. One O.E.C.D. term requires member governments to liberalise inward and outward capital movements. Quite legitimately, Japan used its privilege to lodge reservations against the liberalisation of inward investment, arguing that in many ways it still had an underdeveloped economy. Indeed Japan can argue that she possesses a dual economy similar to, say, Italy's, in which world beating high-technology firms are the tip of an iceberg whose base is a large, non-industrialised population (in 1967, 19% of the Japanese population were still employed in agriculture or forestry), very many small, low-wage, uncompetitive enterprises, and a social structure which is only capable of slow transformation into an internationally-oriented economy. Ever since 1964, however, she has been under severe pressure to allow in much more foreign investment.

This pressure has come mostly from the U.S., though most developed countries agree. In particular, powerful lobbies like the auto interests argue that it is unfair to allow Japanese imports into the American market in ever-increasing numbers while U.S. firms may not compete fully in the rapidly expanding Japanese market. The Japanese argue that they need time to merge some of Toyota and Nissan's five smaller competitors and that anyway, the industry's ratio of exports to total production is a mere 12%, versus 30% for the British, French and Italian industries, and 50% for the German. This argument has not convinced many people; so, somewhat reluctantly, the authorities have twice since 1967 removed a number of industries from the restricted list.

The results have been amusing rather than significant.

Admittedly, 200 out of a total of 600 industries were liberalised, but these have mostly been in areas which only the foolhardy would enter. For instance, foreign companies were allowed in to build 200,000 ton tankers when one sensibly would go to Japan only to build 300,000 tonners or more. But the larger ships were still forbidden to foreign capital. Similarly, foreigners were allowed in to build motor-bikes (against Honda and Suzuki?), or to manage driving schools (which require a highly detailed knowledge of the local market). But important sectors like cars, cosmetics, supermarkets, petrochemicals and sophisticated machine tools still remained protected from foreign entrants.

Since pressure on the government increased toward the end of the 1960's, significant concessions will come. For one thing, Japanese big business realised that they wanted a share of Alaskan pulp mills and Canadian or Australian mineral deposits, and that a protectionist policy in Japan could lead to retaliation against them elsewhere. Secondly, the devaluation of the Deutschemark left the Yen under-valued; and a nation which is making persistent balance of payments gains does not argue convincingly that its economy needs protecting. However, there are real grounds for worrying about what will happen after a reasonable amount of liberalisation.

For one thing, the Japanese business environment is genuinely different from that of most advanced nations. Traditionally it includes employment for life with one firm, promotion by seniority, payment by annual bonuses, heavy expenditure on fringe benefits, an understanding tolerance of the struggling, small, supplying firms. Zealous foreigners might easily fail to observe many of these practices which are second nature in Japan.

Secondly, the xenophobia of the local business community may grow as foreigners bring in alien business practices. Toyota, for instance, passed a regulation saying that no foreigner should ever sit on its board; and regulations in the Stock Exchange were tightened so that foreigners could not gain more than 20% of the shares of any Japanese company. Even more distressing is the reaction of people outside the business community, where anti-capitalist, particularly anti-American, prejudice is strong. The Zengakuren (the All-

Japanese Federation of Student Self-government Associations) is the coordinating body of left-wing students who between 1965–9 have disrupted over 100 of the 845 Japanese universities. Admittedly split into twenty or so factions, they have been strong enough to close eighteen of these universities almost permanently. Moreover, they unite in condemning war (Vietnam in particular), Imperialism, the bourgeoisie, the U.S. way of life, etc. Taking to the streets, they have influenced the discussions between the Japanese and U.S. governments on the future of Okinawa, one of America's most important bases in South East Asia. From 1970 onwards, the Japanese-U.S. security treaty will guarantee tension because it becomes revocable by either side after one year's notice. In this kind of situation, only the daring firms will choose to invest directly, rather than rely on patent and license agreements which have insulated foreign interests from the full attention of the local community. Even though the 100 million strong market is highly attractive, the political consequences of such an investment could be serious.

And yet, foreign firms obviously are eager to take advantage of the lowering barriers. Through 1968, the U.S. Government pressured Japan to lower tariffs protecting the auto industry three years early. Again, there was heavy pressure for an enlargement of the annual quotas on engine imports. Both Ford and Borg-Warner formed joint ventures with Japanese firms to manufacture automatic transmissions, a technology which the Japanese have not yet mastered. In 1969, Chrysler astounded everyone by reaching an agreement with Mitsubishi Heavy Industries whereby Chrysler would take a 35% share in a joint Company. Chrysler was to import Japanese cars into the U.S., while the possibility was left open that future Valiants might be assembled in Japan. M.I.T.I. (the Ministry of International Trade and Industry), which has overall responsibility for preparing the Japanese economy for world competition, was, according to one report, 'greatly shocked' that a Japanese group should join with foreigners before the auto industry could be restructured on a purely Japanese basis. The Ministry therefore blocked the move and warned interested foreigners that when they were finally permitted to invest in Japan, they would not be allowed to join with established auto manufacturers but would have to link with component manufacturers or else start a venture from scratch. Reputedly, the Ministry was not the only group worried about this move. Ford and General Motors could not be happy that Chrysler had been willing to accept a mere 35% of the proposed venture, thus making their task that much harder when they bargained themselves in the future. In fact, Ford had already undermined the case of Borg-Warner, which had argued strenuously that it should have 51% control over a planned joint venture with a Japanese firm. Ford was willing to accept the more normal 50% in its venture in automatic transmissions with Toyo Kogyo and Nissan.

Only a brave man will predict when the Japanese auto industry will finally be opened to the foreigners, but it increasingly looks as though 1972 will be the last year the authorities can hold out. Even so, investment conditions will still be stringent. Liaisons between existing Japanese auto manufacturers and foreign competitors will be actively opposed. In any case, the Japanese authorities can hinder foreigners by non-statutory means such as delaying bureaucratic decisions, etc. It is likely that even when the foreigners are allowed in, they can still expect considerable resistance from government ministries within the letter of the law.

In fact, the early 1970's promise to be a very lively period for incoming investors. Tempers are already somewhat short. Some firms want to hit back at their Japanese competitors on their home ground, but one doubts if the local business community is actually ready to accept full-blooded competition from foreign intruders, especially when some firms are bound to make mistakes in the field of labour relations and fringe benefits. Moreover, the increasing trade between Japan and Red China (up from $84 million in 1962 to $557 million in 1967) has encouraged the growth of a number of firms which, in the interests of trade, are happy showing their leftist sympathies. Some of these 'friendly firms' already contribute to left-wing student groups as a simple way of maintaining their Maoist credentials. They will be in an excellent position to take advantage of any blunders by the newcomers. All in all, the situation will be inflammatory and only the most careful firms will flourish.

163

Not all Japanese reactions are purely negative. After all, keeping out foreign investment makes sense only if steps are being taken to prepare the local industry for the final concessions. On this score, the Japanese record is fairly good. Their practice of spurring industry into areas of maximum growth potential is convincing. In 1970, for instance, the government is giving major support to the creation of a technology development centre in which 200 researchers (eventually 1,000) will work on the creation of sophisticated computer applications packages, an area in which the Japanese have little experience. Given the declining importance of the central computer compared with the sums to be spent on specially tailored 'software', this is a wise move to develop Japanese expertise in the most rapidly growing section of the computer market. Similarly, for over ten years the government has been trying deliberately to build a Japanese oil industry in order to reduce their dependence on the existing oil majors which in 1969 were still providing 80% of Japanese oil. In 1960 they had some success with the Khafji oil find by the Arabian Oil Company. By the later 1960's, Japanese interests were prospecting for oil in Abu Dhabi, Alaska, New Guinea, Canada, Sumatra and Kalimanti. However, the Japanese authorities are still willing to work with the established firms where local expertise has not been adequate. In the oil search just offshore Japan, Shell and Mitsubishi form one combine, while Standard Oil Indiana and Idemitsu form another.

The record is less impressive in the official stimulation of mergers. Like many governments we shall discuss later, Japan feels that by international standards many of her firms are too small. In crucial areas like the auto industry, however, the authorities find it difficult to persuade Toyota's and Nissan's five smaller competitors to merge. Fuji Heavy Industries has joined Nissan, but other companies like Mitsubishi have preferred to play with the idea of linking with foreign companies ranging from Chrysler to Fiat. The major merger so far has been in Steel: the Nippon Steel Corporation has been formed out of Yawata Iron and Steel and Fuji Iron and Steel, both the offspring of a pre-war *Zaibatsu* (industrial empire) unscrambled after 1945. This is, admittedly, one area where fear of international competition is not particularly credible;

but the merger has been allowed, despite anti-trust authorities' opposition. This tension between internationally viable mergers and the anti-trust authorities is faced by a number of nations. Most of them will normally approve such linkings without much resistance, providing comparisons with international competitors are brought in. For when necessary, national monopolies can always be checked by encouraging those foreign competitors if the local businessmen abuse their power.

The Japanese policy towards multinationals is, therefore, a strange mixture of blatant xenophobia and a genuine fear of allowing foreign investment in all at once. Unlike some countries, Japan is putting to good use the time she is buying herself through protectionist policies, by actively strengthening her own industry. To the multinationals, Japan is both a tempting market and also an attractive base for approaching South East Asia, where countries like Taiwan, Singapore and Southern Korea show strong growth rates. Political problems may prove to be the stumbling block. The Japanese Government could benefit from spelling out in detail exactly what kind of business behaviour is expected of firms that come in, particularly in areas like industrial relations where the industrial culture of Japan is reasonably unique. The multinationals would be clever to keep their activities in a deliberately low key. However much they may want to control their Japanese ventures, they would do well to work through Japanese partners and use Japanese management as much as possible. While these fears may be exaggerated, still leaving the Japanese a maximum of independence in joint ventures would seem wise. Over-enthusiastic, half-considered investments could prove disastrous.

Canada and the sleeping elephant

Like Japan, Canada is fascinating to analyse, though it is atypical in a different way. Her economy is greatly dependent on foreign (particularly U.S.) investment. And though a number of major controversies have risen from this domination, nothing much is being done either to protect the economy from the incoming investors, or to strengthen Canadian firms so that they can compete.

In 1963, foreigners owned 54% of Canadian manufacturing —nearly 100% of the auto industry, 64% of oil, and still more of mining and smelting. By the end of 1964 the book value of foreign investment in Canada was $27 billion. Since 80% of these owners are from the U.S., Canadians have become increasingly worried about the status, image and cohesion of Canada as a nation. American takeovers of Canadian firms have exacerbated this concern, and the development of Alaskan oil with all the dangers of polluting Canada has not improved the situation. As Premier Trudeau once explained to the U.S., "Living next to you is in some ways like sleeping with an elephant. No matter how friendly or even tempered is the beast . . . one is affected by every twitch and grunt."

Over the years, various Canadian governments have introduced minor measures to help preserve some aspects of Canadian independence. Between 1958 and 1960, legislation dictated that companies in radio, television or cable industries should have at least half their directors, and well over half their shareholders, coming from Canada.

1963 saw a somewhat nationalistic budget which taxed interest paid to non-Canadian lenders at a 10% rate if the company was more than 25% Canadian owned, but at 15% if less than 25%. This deliberate attempt to force foreign firms to sell off some of their stock has been successful to some extent; firms like Union Carbide and Reader's Digest diluted their control by selling off shares. After the U.S. First National City Bank acquired the Canadian Mercantile Bank in 1963, the Bank Act was amended to limit the foreign ownership of any Canadian Bank to 10% of the equity for each individual or corporation, with total foreign ownership limited to 25%.

The major flaw in such measures is that they merely scratch at the surface of the problem, and in one case, may actually be harmful. Encouraging foreign subsidiaries to sell off 25% of their shareholdings to Canadians does not in any way put any important power into Canadian hands. It could well be that this money, so tied up in subsidiaries which would usually have been set up in Canada anyway, could have been better used in other sectors of the Canadian economy, possibly to back those Canadian firms most likely to fight the U.S.-owned

166

multinationals. Finally, some evidence suggests that subsidiaries less than 100% controlled by their American parents export less than those which are wholly U.S. owned. In such a case this measure may actually harm the Canadian economy by encouraging U.S. manufacturers to export from home factories what they might have exported from Canada.

Neither of two major studies recently carried out in Canada has shown that Canada has actually been economically harmed by freely accepting U.S. investment. In *The Foreign Ownership of Canadian Industry* (1966), A. E. Safarian concludes that with some protective tariffs,

> . . . Canada was better off economically having access to direct investment rather than doing without it.

Similarly, the 1967 government Task Force set up under M. H. Watkins on the economic and political aspects of foreign industrial ownership concluded that, weighing the economic benefits against the political costs, action was needed only to mitigate some of the worst burdens.

Some of the Task Force's recommendations are fairly negative. For instance, probably too much attention was given to the danger that U.S. trading-with-the-enemy provisions may restrain the export performance of U.S.-owned, Canadian subsidiaries. It also pointed to the danger of allowing the U.S. anti-trust authorities control over Canadian activities and suggested that it should be illegal for firms resident in Canada to comply with foreign anti-trust laws, or even to move commercial records at the order of a foreign court. Though there is some justification for this recommendation, the basic problem is slowly getting better now that the O.E.C.D. member countries have agreed to consult each other in cases where the actions of one's courts implicate another. The Task Force further suggested establishing a set of mandatory guidelines to good corporate behaviour for Canadian subsidiaries of foreign-owned companies. Basically, these call for subsidiaries to be run in the interests of the Canadian economy; for listing the export markets, pricing, procurement and investment policies, the Canadianisation of management, the publication of adequate information and the opportunity for equity investment by the Canadian public. Further, they suggest creating a

167

government agency to survey the operations of multinational companies in Canada.

None of this can be seriously faulted, though equity investment by Canadians in subsidiaries and the Canadianisation of management are measures chiefly designed to give the semblance of control when, in practice, the multinationals will probably lose no real decision-making power in making such concessions. More important was the call for a Canadian Development Corporation which should have power and money to help strengthen local Canadian firms. Many of the problems connected with subsidiaries owned by foreigners can be circumvented, providing the nation has powerful nationally-owned firms which refuse to take orders from other nations. In this respect, despite Canada's relatively high economic ranking, her largest industrial company is Alcan Aluminium, only the 48th largest non-U.S. industrial company in the world. Furthermore, Canada has only 4 such companies in the top 100, which puts her behind the U.K. (22), Japan (18), West Germany (17), France (15), Italy (5) and Switzerland (5). There is a clear need for a Development Corporation charged with stimulating mergers and backing those Canadian businessmen who will run Canadian enterprises with the efficiency and independence required. Such bodies in other nations have worked well (see the section on the Industrial Reorganisation Corporation in Britain pp. 177–80). The only caution is that this Development Corporation should be a positive, not a defensive, institution. Thus it is important that it should not become heavily involved in protecting declining or near-defunct Canadian firms from politically embarassing foreign takeover bids. Rather, it should concentrate on building up the growth firms in Canada so that they become fully competitive on the international market.

Ultimately, Canada's response to multinationals boils down to a straight question of the political future for an economy so closely meshed with another that decisions taken in one country have to be complemented by similar decisions in the other.

Increasingly, the economies of the U.S.A. and Canada are managed as one. When the Johnson administration clamped down on the outflow of capital through direct investment in 1968, the Canadian economy had to be exempted. In return,

Canada announced voluntary guidelines for Canadian businesses, modelled on the U.S. mandatory provisions. Similarly, Canadian securities are exempt from the U.S. Interest Equalisation Tax, designed to lessen the U.S. citizen's desire for foreign holdings. The respective government departments in charge of economic and financial affairs cooperate closely in order to avoid disruption. Already there has been the automotive trade agreement which has created a quasi-free trading market in automobiles and their parts. By the early 1970's similar deals may have occurred in the fields of petroleum products and airline routes. In this kind of situation, the Canadian Government's control over the economy will depend less on its skill in manipulating the traditional economic and financial tools than on its ability to bargain with Washington. Thus the Canadian Government becomes an appendage to the U.S. Government with about the strength of the California legislature. The major difference is that an American president can lose elections if he ignores a state like California, whereas he gets no votes in Ottawa. Moreover, as economic integration between the two economies increases, the Canadian Government has less and less leverage with U.S. decision makers because it has less retaliatory powers.

This dilemma is by no means unique. After all, any nation entering into a free trade pact with other nations will eventually find itself in this position. The major difference is that the disparity in size between the U.S. and Canada is so large that there is a real danger Canadian views will be swamped by those of the United States. Economically this does not matter so long as the U.S. authorities run reasonably sane policies. Otherwise, the average Canadian citizen has benefited from this integration and the pull toward parity of wages between the two nations. Tension is likely only if this economic integration leads to serious pressure on Canadian governments to conform in social issues or in foreign affairs. This is no immediate problem since full integration is still a long way away. But in the long run, pressures about social policies must arise since running twin economies will be difficult if there are major differences in taxation levels. If one country taxes lightly, then nationals from the other country will apply for jobs over the border, or will at least argue for getting better pay. Either way, individuals

169

and firms are likely to pressure the governments to establish similar conditions.

These differences could be serious if one country emphasises prestige defence and space projects more than the other, or urban renewal less. If the U.S. continues to fight wars in Asia and send space probes to Mars, either the U.S. tax rates on corporations or individuals will rise, or else domestic spending will decline. If Canada chooses a relatively pacific role in order to devote greater resources to improving the quality of domestic life, she might begin to appear a more attractive place to live and work in. In this case, the U.S. Government could find itself under strong domestic pressure to tone down her ambitions and adopt the Canadian type role. On the other hand, if the U.S. Government decided to make a major assault on urban poverty, keeping tax rates relatively high in order to finance the costs, U.S. industry might start locating in Canada.

In this sort of situation, heavy pressure might be put on the Canadians to raise their tax levels.

Although it is easy to dream up scenarios in which economic integration would lead to clashes between the two national governments, they should probably not be taken too seriously. Such clashes would occur only if national priorities became seriously different between the two nations, and whether this would happen is a moot point. Certainly, during the 1960's the U.S. seemed more willing to play an active world role while Canada preferred to withdraw from foreign entanglements wherever possible. If this reflects a genuine difference in national priorities, then there could be problems ahead. The logic of the present situation is that Canada could benefit quite heavily from free trade agreements providing she is willing to bargain hard. She is likely to be able to offer a business environment which is marginally attractive to North American firms, either by keeping her taxes lower or by spending highly on various social improvements which make Canada an attractive place to work or invest in. Ultimately, if Canada is too successful, the U.S. could argue that by spending the money needed to protect the continent from the communists, she is subsidising the Canadians who should, therefore, refrain from taking advantage of the situation.

Although this discussion of future relations between the U.S.

and Canada is necessarily somewhat hypothetical, it teaches several lessons. First, economic integration will eventually lead to similar orders of priorities since integrated economies cannot run under widely different taxation levels. When one nation subjects its firms and citizens to relatively high taxes or to a relatively backward social infrastructure (spending on roads, schools, health declines), there will be tension until the other nation modifies its policies in the direction of the first, or vice versa.

Two final questions remain. First, is this process automatic, however dependent on the subsidiaries of multinationals a nation may be? The answer must be that the existence of multinationals per se is irrelevant. Even if all world commerce was carried out by importing and exporting alone (i.e., with no overseas subsidiaries), governments which put a high priority on providing jobs for their nationals, at steadily growing rates, would find themselves with just as severe constraints. Too heavy taxation levels make firms unable to reinvest enough to stay competitive; too many small firms make achieving maximum economy impossible; too savage treatment of executives (by nationalising a large part of their industrial structure) severely hinders competition with more unhampered firms of other nations. Consequently, anxieties about a nation's national identity probably cannot be dissipated by actively discouraging the activities of multinationals, which are merely part of a far larger process. Instead, the wisest governments should learn how to take the best that such companies can offer.

The second question concerns the overall strategy of governments which, like Canada, are acutely aware of the gradual decline in their freedom to formulate independent policies. A government concerned with preserving its national identity should study the developing decision centres most likely to cover its particular country. While Canada is stuck with Washington whether she likes it or not, the Europeans, being more evenly matched, are evolving institutions whose final importance has yet to be realised.

Once this is clear, then governments will be judged historically by their efficiency in fighting their causes in these decision centres. Thus, to go back to Canada, any action taken by the Canadian Government about multinational subsidiaries in

Canada is ultimately irrelevant (though being tough on foreign firms may help to unite Canada internally). History will judge Canadian governments by how effectively they manipulate their relative strengths and weaknesses to get the most out of Washington—not by how vigorously they swim against the tide of underlying events.

Europe

The situation in Europe is in some ways more complex and in other ways simpler than Canada's. The same forces are at work but, whereas Canadian and U.S. cultures are not widely different, European nations range from right-wing catholic military dictatorships to left-wing protestant social democracies. Further, linguistic differences will make any moves toward European integration both difficult and controversial. On the other hand, at least the European nations are reasonably well balanced with no one nation dominating the continent as the U.S. dominates North America. In any moves toward integration, even the smaller nations will be able to preserve some form of independence.

During the 1960's, Europe received the most attention from U.S.-owned multinationals, even though the rate of investment slowed down toward the end of the decade, both as a reaction to the preceding boom and as a result of the clamp down on capital flows from both the U.S. and the U.K. In 1967 Europe received just under 40% of the plant and equipment expenditure by affiliates of U.S.-owned firms, while Canada took 23%. But these expenditures have not been evenly spread within Europe (see Table 2). The United Kingdom usually receives the bulk of such U.S. investment, basically, one suspects, because of the common language and the financial institutions built up to service British commercial activities round the old British Empire. Since the formation of the European Economic Community, continental Europe has grown more attractive to U.S. investors, but countries like West Germany, France and Switzerland still trail far behind the U.K. as a base for U.S. investment.

Political integration in Europe has been a potent factor in arousing the interest of multinational companies. The evolution of the E.E.C. and E.F.T.A. created an atmosphere conducive to rapid multinational growth. Whereas less than 60% of U.S. direct investment in the U.K. was placed there since 1960, more than 70% of such investment in the E.E.C. has been introduced since that date. Obviously the formation of the E.E.C. has sufficiently persuaded multinational investors to risk the linguistic and cultural barriers that had restrained them in the past. Although there is a chicken-and-egg argument here (did the political integration come because of economic integration or vice versa?), the formation of the two major European trading blocs clearly gave multinationals a much more flexible environment in which to work; and by the late 1960's, the political problems rising from the multinationals' response forced significant moves toward further integration.

As one would expect, not all European nations have reacted to the problems created by multinationals in the same way. Countries like France have taken an emotive hostile line, while others like West Germany have barely conceded that any problem existed at all. Most other countries fell somewhere in between; but, significantly, they seem increasingly aware of the tensions created by blind acceptance of inward investment.

France

By no accident was it a Frenchman, Servan-Schreiber, who produced the most emotionally convincing argument against passively accepting investment from the U.S. multinationals. Particularly under De Gaulle, France followed a line which at times was openly hostile toward such companies. Some industrial areas boast a long history of discrimination against certain foreigners. Since 1928, a discriminatory oil policy uses a licensing system favouring state-connected French companies by requiring oil firms to import at least half of their crude from franc-zone sources; this has worked against some of the majors like British Petroleum which own no franc-zone crude oil. In the thaw from 1958 to 1962, the 1958 devaluation and restoration of franc convertibility were accompanied by the lifting of the more severe controls affecting capital movements and the operations of foreign-owned companies. In fact, French planners positively encouraged foreign investment in areas like food-processing, where French industry needed outside assistance. The growth of gold and foreign exchange holdings from nearly nothing to around $3 billion in 1962 was much assisted by an influx of foreign investment in response to what promised to be a reasonably stable and friendly investment climate.

There then followed a period in which some consequences of this generosity became apparent. In 1962 General Motors and Remington Rand executed their famous sackings. In 1963 Chrysler gained a majority holding in the car firm Simca. Finally, an acute cash shortage led Machines Bull, France's largest electronics and computer manufacturer, into the arms of the U.S. firm General Electric, which took a 50% holding after attempts to find a national or European solution proved futile.

Whatever the rationale behind these events, a stricter policy toward foreign investment was initiated; by 1964 applications to make direct investments in France were routinely shelved or blocked. Some relaxation subsequently occurred, probably after General Motors' threat to switch a planned plant to Belgium, and after Ford located a plant there which could easily have gone to France. Also, in this period of official hostility a number of investors actually pulled out of their commitments and liquidated their French holdings. In 1962 these liquidations of direct investments amounted to 784·4 million French francs; by 1966, this figure had risen to 1,515 millions, about half the total of direct foreign investment received by France that year (3,099)—a total already below its 1964 peak.

In January 1967, new provisions laid down the ground rules for future foreign investment. French subsidiaries of foreign-owned firms must declare their investment plans in advance, whether these involved the simple acquisition of French firms or 'green field' projects. The Treasury has the power either to approve whether the finance comes totally from abroad or to force firms to shelve disapproved plans. Apart from this and some restrictions on borrowing, funds may be transferred freely when they take the form of dividends, royalties, management fees, etc. On the whole, the Treasury has applied this policy quite liberally except for takeover situations. However, this wide scope for official discretion could make some multi-national investors a bit wary. During 1969, the E.E.C. Commission objected to the way this procedure seemed to discriminate against firms based on other member countries, despite the fact that the Rome Treaty provided for the free movement of capital within the six member countries, regardless of the nationality of the firm's owners. The French argue that the multinational company's power to swamp national economies is something which has grown since the drafting of the Treaty and has not been reflected in subsequent Community rulings either. In particular the argument concerns the treatment of multinationals which have subsidiaries in another E.E.C. country but which are owned by countries outside the Six. By the Treaty of Rome, these companies should receive treatment equal to the purely E.E.C. firms. Although the French were willing to give automatic consent to the purely E.E.C. firms, they were in the early days of the Pompidou administration exceedingly reluctant to allow the subsidiaries of U.S.-owned multinationals similar freedom.

The general picture

During the 1960's other nations have gradually tightened their control over incoming investment, but no nation has taken so hostile a line as France. The new British policy involves being slightly tougher on would-be purchasers of British companies. The Netherlands and Belgium, long-standing competitors for foreign investment, have taken steps to protect their national firms from being snapped up. Even West Germany, which has left multinational companies almost totally free, intervened when American and French interests were about to buy the largest independent German oil company, Gelsenberg. In fact, since it emphasises the lead in size and technology which the U.S. multinationals have over their European competitors, this takeover situation most often evokes a negative control on multinational investment.

Industrial restructuring

Many European firms first reacted to this challenge by moving toward some form of multinationality. Some German firms realised that putting up plants in their major foreign markets could buy good will by showing Germans fully committed to production outside Germany. Fiat tried to take control of Citroën. Compagnie Française des Pétroles tried for

175

Gelsenberg. Chemical manufacturers I.C.I., long dependent on the British and Commonwealth market, decided in 1960 to invest heavily in continental Europe; they backed this in 1966 with a new division, I.C.I. Europa, located in Brussels, at least in part to show that I.C.I.'s European interests were not just an offshoot of its British activities. A number of companies like B.A.S.F., Bayer, British Petroleum and K.Z.O. moved more aggressively into the American market by bidding for U.S. companies or by setting up plants.

This movement had not gone very far by the end of the 1960's. Most of the action had occurred purely within individual nations and some firms which had tried to acquire companies in other European nations had been blocked just as firmly as if they had been Americans (notably Fiat, Compagnie Française des Pétroles, and S.K.F., the Swedish ball-bearing firm which tried to strengthen its position in Britain). Given these limitations, the movement towards industrial mergers gathered speed throughout the 1960's, producing units beginning to approach a size viable for international competition. One should not under-estimate the psychological barriers which have traditionally stopped such mergers. Given a continent where cartel arrangements, price-fixing, etc. have been rife, and where the anti-trust movement has been weak, smallish, family-controlled firms have flourished. It sometimes escapes American eyes, in particular, that only seven out of the twenty largest German firms are public in the fullest sense of the word—with shareholdings sufficiently spread so that family cliques cannot pass effective control from generation to generation. In Italy one finds dominant business families like Pirelli, Fiat and Olivetti controlling not just their own companies, but through cross-shareholdings and directorships, also a large part of Italian industry. Sweden, too, has its Wallenburg dynasty.

In such circumstances, it is no wonder that the bloody take-over battle common to Anglo-Saxons is a relative rarity in much of Europe. In fact, one can isolate, in a number of nations, battles which served to notify cosy financial circles that global competition means the extermination of inefficiently run firms. In Britain, there was the I.C.I. bid for fellow fibre manufacturer Courtaulds in 1961; in France there was the unexpected bid by glass manufacturer Boussois-Souchon-

Neuvessel (B.S.N.) in 1969 for its giant competitor Saint-Gobain, which set the financial community at each others' throats.

The Industrial Reorganisation Corporation

The British have led Europe by positively stimulating mergers as an act of government policy. The chosen weapon has been the Industrial Reorganisation Corporation (I.R.C.) which was set up in 1966 with the specific task of aiding the concentration and rationalisation needed to make British industry not only more efficient but internationally competitive. In many ways the I.R.C. acts like an officially sponsored merchant bank, investing some government money in situations where it feels the investment will persuade companies to merge. By 1969, its total investment came to 155 million dollars; but money is not normally its crucial tool. It specialises in long, confidential analyses of specific industries in which it feels that the average firm is too small to provide the research or servicing facilities needed if the industry remains competitive against foreign multinationals. Having formed some idea of the strengths and weaknesses of the firms and personalities involved, it then tries persuading firms to merge or to hive off activities to other companies. At this point, when personal suspicions or traditional rivalries block solutions which look good from a national viewpoint, its ability to offer money in the form of equity holdings or straight loans may be crucial for overcoming psychological barriers. Most investments made in these circumstances involve some I.R.C. representation on Boards of Directors; they are seen as short-term investment which should earn commercial rates of interest and should be liquidated quickly so that the funds are again available. By 1969 it was running profitably and paying dividends for its relevant government department.

In its first year or so, the I.R.C. concentrated on those major industries which were in worst shape. The British market leader in autos, British Motor Corporation, while losing money and market shares, had virtually no new models on the drawing board. The I.R.C. triggered a bid from Leyland Motors, a considerably smaller truck manufacturer which had a very impressive export record. The resulting company, British

177

Leyland Motor Corporation, looks far healthier than its predecessor. The I.R.C. played a more active role in the heavy electrical engineering field when it found there considerable over-capacity and some rank bad management. Somewhat controversially, the I.R.C. took sides in an initial takeover battle in which General Electric Company (no relation to the U.S. firm, G.E.) successfully bid for Associated Electrical Industries, a company with many friends in the financial community but with a decidedly dubious profit record. By taking sides openly, the I.R.C. made enemies; but the logic of the final solution, General Electric Co-English Electric, is not seriously questioned since the firm is directed by one of the industry's most talented managers, Arnold Weinstock. Similarly, in computers, the I.R.C. helped form the British computer firm, International Computers Ltd., from the computer interests of English Electric, Plessey and International Computers and Tabulators. In lesser industries such as compressors, scientific instruments, pumps, trawlers, the I.R.C. has also been active.

Obviously the activities of a body like the I.R.C. are controversial, especially when it gets involved in contested takeover bids. In one case, it spent $15·5 million supporting one scientific instrument firm's attempt to control a similar company, and ward off a rival bid from the Rank Organisation, a cinema and (via links with Xerox) reprographic company. I.R.C. felt for various reasons that the market support for the Rank Organisation's bid was misleading and would be damaging in the long run. Since it is difficult to evaluate this type of argument, one must assess instead the extent to which one trusts I.R.C. judgement. First, there are no strong reasons to assume that the normal workings of the market must always be right. They can be influenced by the amount of cash a firm has available at a given moment, the relative price of its shares, and temporary fluctuations in its profits. One can therefore accept that a government sponsored body like the I.R.C., charged to take a long-term view of future industries, may judge as shrewdly the merits of specific bids as the conventional market mechanism. Naturally safeguards are necessary. The most efficient is to limit the organisation's supply of cash from government sources and to make plain that it must make a profit from its activities.

Under such conditions, the I.R.C. cannot stay in business long if it is influenced often by non-objective factors. Certainly, most observers give the I.R.C. considerable credit for rationalising a number of major industries quickly and relatively painlessly.

Perhaps the most interesting point about the I.R.C. is its apparent tendency to seek solutions in an increasingly multinational context. In one case in 1969, it specifically backed an American firm, Studebaker, in forming a joint company with a British firm in the pump-making field. In one of its first operations it was involved in the bargaining when Chrysler finally took a majority shareholding in the ailing British auto company Rootes. But the I.R.C. has also acted to prevent foreign firms from taking over British companies. In particular, it backed a series of mergers designed to stop the Swedish ball-bearing firm, S.K.F., from extending its hold on the British firm Ransome and Marles. The I.R.C. justified this apparent chauvinism through its stated goal to help British industry improve its export potential. Apart from Sweden, the only European country with a strong surplus in its ball-bearings trade was West Germany, where an independent company, Kugelfischer F.A.G., contributed much of this surplus. In I.R.C. words,

"IRC was also aware that SKF, a strongly based international group, acting in the interests of its own efficiency and profitability, might well find it advantageous to rationalise its production facilities, locate its research and development, buy its raw materials and machine tools and direct its marketing policy in ways which would not necessarily benefit the U.K. economy"[1]

Two questions remain. First, are mergers within one nation the best answer to international competition? If they are not, what will best stimulate the necessary links between companies in different nations? For instance, though it is clear that in the short run the merger of British computer industries into I.C.L. was the best solution immediately available, I.B.M. managers argue that Europe could have produced stronger international competition by merging the German, Siemens, with I.C.L., while leaving English Electric-Lec Marconi free to develop

[1] I.R.C. statement. *Economist*, 24th May 1969.

links with America's R.C.A. The reasoning is that much of the early period of I.C.L.'s existence was spent reconciling the incompatible technologies of its two main constituents. The alternative arrangement would have linked British, German and American firms according to their technological compatibility, thus producing stronger international competition for I.B.M. than the purely British solution.

The I.R.C. is also increasingly sceptical that size provides the best solution in an uncompetitive industry. If, for example, the management of that industry is generally incompetent and technically backward, creating one large firm might actually make things worse. Instead it might well pay to develop links with foreign firms which have the required skills. Thus the I.R.C. concludes that some industries might be stronger for union with German firms, providing the British firms are not totally swamped.

If such transnational links are desirable, how are they best stimulated? We will see later how few genuine transnational mergers have formed in Europe. After a few technical reasons are acknowledged, psychological barriers seem the strongest explanation. Most people know that mergers must come, but none is particularly eager to participate in them. Just as the I.R.C. was designed to break down this kind of situation within Britain, a similar body is obviously needed on a European scale. A new organisation must be created, and the I.R.C.'s managing director, Mr Charles Villiers, suggested in 1969 that the European Commission should set it up. It should have a reasonable supply of money, should act in a commercial fashion, and should earn commercial rates of return on its funds. He continued, "The new body would not be effective if organised as a bureaucracy and it should apply to its work the characteristics of a banque d'affaires, whose client is the interest of European industry."

The merger boom

Even without such a body, however, European industry is going through a merger boom. In Britain mergers have led to British Leyland, International Computers Ltd. and General Electric-English Electric. West Germany's largest steel company, August Thyssen-Hütte, linked with Hoag, while the

Hoesch steel firm merged with the Dortmund Hoerder Union to produce Germany's second biggest steel company. In the oil industry, eight German refiners have set up a joint refining company, Deminex, to search for badly needed crude oil. In Italy, Montecatini-Edison, Europe's second largest chemical and textile firm, was formed by merger. French mergers restructured the auto industry (Citroën and Berliet), and electrical engineering, where Thomson-Brandt was formed by a merger in 1966 and then took in the Compagnie de Telegraphie sans Fils in 1967. In the Netherlands, the chemical manufacturers A.K.U. and K.Z.O. merged to form about the 25th largest company outside the United States.

Firms which have linked across national boundaries are found less frequently. Some have done this by taking 50% interests in a foreign company, as Philips did with Ignis, or the French mail order company, La Redoute, did in 1969 with Milan's Vestro. But the number of transnational European mergers is rising. The Anglo-Dutch companies, Royal Dutch-Shell and Unilever, have long coordinated companies owned and controlled from two different nations. In the latest boom, two photographic companies, the German Agfa and the Belgian Gevaert came together somewhat messily to form Agfa-Gevaert. National feelings of the two managements have strained exchanges of personnel. As a compromise, they have divided the firm's activities, locating some in the Belgian plants, some in the German. For fiscal reasons, moreover, the firm ended up with four company 'shells', all necessary if Agfa-Gevaert was to be recognised as a fiscal and legal entity by the relevant countries. For three or four years, the complications in this case daunted many European firms, but gradually reservations have dropped away. The Italian Fiat bid for French Citroën would have succeeded except for government interference. In 1969, Vereinigte Flugtechnische Werke (V.F.W.), a German aircraft manufacturer, and the surprisingly successful Dutch manufacturer, Fokker, announced their merger, each taking 50% of the resultant organisation. Germany's largest chemical firm, Hoescht, with a large minority holding in the French pharmaceutical firm Roussel-Uclaf, also started bidding for a share in the British paint manufacturer, Berger Jenson and Nicholson. Finally the British brewing industry expanded into

Europe when Allied Breweries took control of d'Oranjeboom, the third largest beer producer in the Netherlands. Other British brewers expanded into Belgium and France. Perhaps more typical are the consortia of different nationalities springing up in such industries as nuclear power and aviation. Thus one project, the Multi-Role Combat Aircraft (M.R.C.A.) which the British, German and Italian governments are producing to fit their own defence requirements in the 1970's, has spawned at least three such consortia: Avionics-Systems Engineering G.M.B.H. to produce the avionics, Panavia Aircraft to produce the main body, and a third group to produce the engines. Each of these groups has German, British and Italian members and obviously signals alliances which may blossom into more formal multinational links sometime in the future.

Active as the European scene may be, even mergers may not create firms equal in size and capabilities to their U.S. competitors. For one thing, the inter-European takeover or merger is still rare, most countries settling for joint ventures in given fields, rather than more formal links between the parent companies. In any case, even from American experience it is clear that many mergers fail because the benefits expected from rationalisation and streamlining never appear. In Europe one would expect a much higher disaster rate, since one is dealing there with work forces and managements speaking different languages and operating in different cultures. The Agfa-Gevaert case, for example, is one in which top management must continually be aware that both halves of the company must get their share of the action. Pruning out the less competent managers may well prove necessary if competition increases, but could be impossible if it left significantly more managers of one nationality than the other. In many ways the situation reminds us of that within the largest British auto firm during the 1950's and the early 1960's. Formed by the merger of two proudly independent auto manufacturers, Austin and Morris, the resultant British Motor Corporation never performed the tough job of rationalising the company structure, partly because of the decision-makers' loyalties to their old firms. When the resulting American competition disastrously cut into B.M.C.'s market share, the company had to be rescued by Leyland Motors. The same danger exists for most European mergers because national pride and old company loyalties obstruct the rationalised decision-making needed for long-term survival.

The barriers to transnational mergers

Barriers to transnational mergers include a number of factors. After two full-scale continental wars in fifty years, national suspicions remain strong. And many managements are as yet unaware of the changes necessary for survival on a national, let alone international, level. One would expect governmental resistance to foreign suitors to diminish as time goes on. But fiscal barriers dissolve less easily. Even within the E.E.C., firms find they cannot offset the losses of a subsidiary in one country against the profits made in another; goods flowing within the firm but across national borders are liable to turn-over-based, value added taxes which would not apply if the firm was transferring the same goods within the same country. Again, mergers often become liquidations, in which assets are first sold, then transferred to a new owner after the 'proceeds' have been taxed at normal rates. It is therefore almost impossible to transfer ownership without heavy taxes, an occurrence very unlike practices in the U.S. and Great Britain. Further diffi-culties arise from the German institution of codetermination, whereby labour representatives sit on the board of directors, a practice which does not appeal to most industrialists elsewhere.

Finally, accounting procedures in much of Europe are a game rather than an exercise in assembling useful information. Americans are often staggered by European accounting, and even Britain, with fairly thorough rules of disclosure, has witnessed such *causes célèbres* as the 1969 Leasco bid for Per-gamon Press. The normally astute Leasco suddenly discovered that a harmless situation changed when accounting assumptions on which book-keeping rested also changed. The accounts of many companies merely reflect conditions in the headquarter's country. Some companies use tax havens as a base for con-solidating their non-domestic interests since they can produce meaningless consolidation figures there which worry nobody. Often large private companies are obligated to report nothing, and in France companies the size of publishers Librarie

Hachette, the Nestlé subsidiary, and Avions Marcel Dassault, give no public figures. Michelin, long noted for intense secretiveness, admits to a turnover of only a derisory $12 million. The Italian situation is as bad, and one reason some multinationals met disaster there is that they were misled by figures presented to them. Until European companies begin to overhaul their company legislation, this situation can only impede European integration. Adequate financial information is a necessary precondition for successful mergers.

Removing the barriers

On paper, one simple way of removing some of the problems facing multinationals in Europe would be to create a 'European' company, enjoying uniform legal and fiscal treatment throughout Europe. In practice, this achievement has not been easy. The E.E.C. Commission appeared to back a group of legal experts who suggested that uniform legal, tax and fiscal provisions should prevail for all those companies above a given size which opted for European status. Ignoring the problem of how non-E.E.C. countries fit into this picture, the plan is a non-starter. Either the laws relating to the European company are less harsh than those of individual nations, in which case firms will opt for it to escape their obligations; or else they will be more harsh and no one will be interested. For instance the Germans had visions (probably justified) of German firms rushing to register as 'European' to escape their codetermination commitments in Germany. In any case, the proposals raised the question of who would collect the taxes and how the money would be divided. France, for one, saw that this could lead to the strengthening of the E.E.C.'s political institutions, and therefore blocked these suggestions. Instead, the Six formally signed a convention of mutal recognition of firms, companies and legal persons—an innocuous piece of paper allowing firms registered in one E.E.C. country to get fair treatment in all the others. Since it took four years to produce this, it is obvious that no large steps toward harmonising company law on a European-wide basis are likely in the near future.

In the immediate future the most promising approach seems to lie in harmonising those technical regulations which can effectively bar economic integration. Every country develops a host of technical regulations like safety rules for cars or laws about electrical appliances which can be used to block the import of unwanted goods. For a while the French were able to hold off the all-conquering Italian refrigerator manufacturers by insisting on electrical standards which discriminated against them. Similarly, companies exporting cars to the U.S. market have found the demands for anti-pollution and safety devices a severe strain on their resources. Although the Detroit giants were not particularly happy either, their enormous financial strength meant they could meet the conditions more easily. The pharmaceutical industry is a good case where national markets have been almost sealed off from each other by national laws. In the E.E.C. 80% of the market is sold through the 25,000 different branded products, but conditions are so tough that few brands can be sold in more than one country. The manufacturers have therefore been forced to set up plants in each nation instead of concentrating their European production in a few places. The E.E.C. Commission calling for a genuine common market in this industry was very suspicious of governments' motives: "It is extremely difficult to distinguish where economic interest ends and concern for the protection of people's health begins."[1]

The European Commission is trying to generate some momentum in this area. With pharmaceuticals it is trying to take member nations to the Court of Justice to encourage swift action. In other fields like foodstuffs and electrical appliances, action is long overdue. More recently safety regulations in cars have become an issue, since most nations are happily drafting mutually contradictory legislation. What is more, in 1969, the six E.E.C. nations could not even agree to suspend national legislation in such fields until the matter had been dealt with on a European-wide basis.

The most promising development comes in patents where the system has been breaking down as multinational companies register discoveries in patent offices round the world. In May 1969, a seventeen-nation group in Brussels discussed proposals for a European patent convention. A working group of experts from six countries was created to draw up a report on the legal

[1] *Financial Times*, 2nd October 1969.

aspects of European patents, and the aim would seem to be to establish a European patents office which would grant patents for the whole of the E.E.C., and also have its rulings accepted by non-E.E.C. members. Although measures like this will not revolutionise conditions for European multinationals, they will at least help to take some of the soul-destroying paper work out of going multinational.

Conclusions

This description of European reactions to the rise of the multinationals is somewhat pessimistic. European industry remains relatively small and inefficient, though management standards are rising. Efforts of individual nations too often stay on a national basis. One or two firms have started merging with other European companies, but most industrial activity is limited to informal alliances, not fully integrated operations across national boundaries. National governments which should be leading this process still think in narrow chauvinistic terms. However, slowly spreading government-sponsored industrial projects conceived on a continent-wide basis will prepare the ground. Aeronautical projects like the Anglo-French Jaguar Strike Trainers and the Concorde airliner suggest that international projects can be made to work quite smoothly. Subsequent projects like the Anglo-German-Italian M.R.C.A. are being used to develop aircraft industries in both Germany and Italy. Similar schemes are discussed in the computer field and are being tried by the Dutch, British and Germans in a centrifuge-based uranium-enrichment process.

Behind this industrial cooperation must come also political integration. The North-East corner of France along the Belgian border, for example, is potentially very attractive for industrial investors since it is in the heart of the golden triangle—enclosed by London, Paris and the Ruhr. But this region now relies on declining coal and textile industries. Despite incentives offered, new investment prefers Belgium, which is equally well placed. The Belgians offer bigger investment grants; Belgian land can be bought at around 6–8 francs a square metre, against the 18 francs required just across the border in Lille; though the Belgian wage-rates are higher, fringe benefits are less so that the investor in Belgium suffers no disadvantages there either; finally, the years in which the French economy has been run for the benefit of Paris have left such declining areas as this bereft of infrastructure. This case in which all investment goes over the Belgian border is what economic integration is all about. Once countries abandon traditional protectionist devices, areas such as this can only be saved if they can match what is offered on the other side of the border. As industries become even more footloose, marked differences in terms offered to industry can affect hundreds of miles. Thus governments can only move to coordinate policies and thus avoid cutting each other's throats through offering financially ruinous terms.

Finally, we come to one of Europe's biggest paradoxes—Italy. This country was in the late 1960's running a consistent surplus on its current account, and yet was sometimes close to devaluation. In 1968, the current account balance was $2 billion, reflecting the boom conditions in the auto and consumer durable industries. At the same time, industry's good work was being undone by a massive exodus of capital. Swiss banks just over the border in towns like Lugano were being swamped with Italian banknotes from Italian citizens. This capital flight reflects the very grave mistrust the average Italian has of his country's creaking official administrative procedure. At the top level, parliament's unstable alliances between dissimilar parties refuse to cooperate with the communist party, though it includes about a quarter of the delegates. When decisions are made, the Civil Service often finds itself unable to carry them out expeditiously. Over 500 days may elapse before projects approved for the depressed South of Italy actually get started. There are even instances in which large sums of money designated by parliament to be spent within a given time go unspent because administration is so slow—the problem of 'residui passivi'.

Because of this top level confusion, many social problems are being ignored. In particular, two to three hundred thousand Italians move from the depressed South to the industrialised North each year. They crowd into shanty towns which have grown up round the major cities like Turin. The established political process has done little to alleviate their conditions, so that their protest has increasingly taken to the streets and the

187

factory floor. This militancy has led to right-wing reaction and even talks of military coups. Many Italians, both rich and relatively poor, wonder how long the industrial boom can survive what look like worsening political tensions.

In the past, such fears would have little impact on the outside world. Today, even the small man can help preserve his financial position by driving with all the banknotes he can lay his hands on over the border to Switzerland, which is only too happy to accept them. Lugano has 30 banks, one for every 1,000 of its population—a ridiculous ratio. But the Italian clientele keeps them going, and some are even Italian owned. In a peak month of speculation in 1969, some 145 million dollars in banknotes were smuggled out of Italy, a job made simple by the easily smuggled 100,000-lire banknotes worth some 160 dollars each.

The Italian story has two main implications. First, to halt such speculation, governments can only remove the psychological and objective causes of the fear which prompts it. With increased tourism, mobility of labour (many Italians work in German industry), and spreading motorway complexes, speculators are finding life easier each year. Second, such speculation also embarrasses other nearby countries. Few other European nations would like to see the lire devalued, since it is obvious that Italy's industry is already perfectly competitive in many areas. All that is wrong is that the Italian political process is scandalously outmoded and could prove a liability to the rest of Europe. So far few governments can tell others how to run their internal business. Possibly the intercontinental pressure put on West Germany whenever the neo-Nazis show any signs of electoral success comes closest. Italy is, nevertheless, a classic case in which internal shortcomings are beginning to embarrass others. Already some have suggested that she take steps to invigorate her stock exchanges which are virtually non-existent as instruments for attracting investment in equities. The largest bourse, in Milan, has less than 120 shares quoted and only 20 of these are considered to have any growth potential. In many cases, most of the Italian successes are not quoted on the bourses at all, still being in private hands. Other firms which were once publicly owned, like Montecatini-Edison, have fallen into government ownership, much to the horror of small shareholders. In the long run Italy is sure to find itself increasingly pressured from international bodies to reform its political system.

National independence is being challenged by the freedom with which capital, products, and people can move from one country to another. Unless a government can completely block its border, it must be influenced by the actions of those in neighbouring countries. The multinational strengthens this influence since its success depends on seeking out those areas in which it can operate with the best returns. A continent like Europe has to cooperate when faced with this power. If the countries do not cooperate, each must offer heavier and heavier incentives to incoming investment. At the same time, if their own firms preserve their independence, European governments must provide environments allowing those firms to become multinational themselves. Whether they like it or not, European governments have to resign themselves to the death of simple, nationalistic policies. Some of them, like France, have still not fully accepted the logic of this situation. In the long run they will have to become internationalists, if not out of any deep conviction, then because the multinationals have adopted a philosophy in which each nation is as important as the other, what really matters to them are the terms offered them to invest, the quality of the market, etc.

Motivated increasingly by objective evaluations of what each country has to offer, the multinationals can severely discomfort nations which get too strongly out of line with their neighbours. The days when the advanced nations could run their economies without reference to each other are over.

CHAPTER X

The Future

Businessmen in the Free World are building an international economy, an economy which transcends old borders and old ideologies . . . the international corporations and world commerce are the most effective supranational relationships the world has and they survive and flourish in a political and legal world designed in an earlier era. Much of what the International Chamber of Commerce does is to try to find palliatives for an archaic world order.[1]

One day soon, what's good for General Motors may be great for West Germany and South Africa but lousy for America.[2]

Anonymous businessman about working for giant companies:

It's like being a mushroom. First they keep you in the dark for months; then they throw dung on you; then they can you.[3]

We live in a world in which decisions taken today can have their full impact years afterwards. The sooner one identifies what may happen if no action is taken, the sooner one can try to get the policy-making decision moving. In the field of multinational companies this is particularly important since the people best placed to do the necessary analysis—the multinational managers—are not doing it. Professor Vernon of Harvard Business School, one of the world authorities on multinational companies, was quoted as saying:

One area where progress comes specially hard is in getting men in multinational business enterprises to think out loud where their relationships may be heading . . . many businessmen simply will not discuss the issue out loud. Some feel that being a good guest

---

[1] Watson, Arthur K., 1969, President of the I.C.C.; Chairman of the Board, I.B.M. World Trade Corporation.

[2] Jay, Anthony, *op. cit.*

[3] Source: Industrial Folklore.

or being socially responsible in foreign countries will take care of the issue. Few will seriously entertain the possibility that there may be really painful dilemmas posed by the rise of multinational enterprise—ones which cannot be solved by the simple application of goodwill and mutual understanding, and which may lead to major changes in the relationship between such enterprises and the nation state.[1]

This chapter attempts to widen the debate from the negative one of 'how do we fight off foreign companies?' to the positive examination of what is likely to happen in the future if we pursue current policies.

Perlmutter predicts that the bulk of the non-communist world's trade will be dominated in 1988 by 300 large companies of which 200 will probably be American. I think he probably underestimates the impact of economic nationalism and over-estimates the dominance of American firms. However, the outlines of his general picture are correct. The firms of 1988 will be comparable to small- or medium-sized nations; I.B.M. will almost certainly have a sales turnover in excess of $100 billion and could well—anti-trust authorities willing—have a turnover larger than the G.N.P.'s of any nation other than the U.S.A. Most of these firms' activities will be in developed nations and in those like Mexico, Spain, Yugoslavia, the Phillipines, etc., which expect massive development in the near future. Some firms, though probably not many, will follow a conscious strategy of investing in developing nations, relying as much on their political as their commercial skill. Top executives will still tend to be nationals of whatever country the firm originally sprang from, and White Anglo-Saxon Protestants will still dominate the establishment; while conservative individuals, they will tend to think internationally. They may well feel misused as economic nationalists in developing nations harass them. Also provoking and experiencing unrest will be the generations of young people who are increasingly sceptical of the profit motive in its more blatant forms, and who will demonstrate vigorously against these firms whenever they are involved in any scandals round the world. The firms themselves will retain fairly authoritarian, undemocratic structures, though their internal power distribution will become more

---

[1] Quoted by Parker, 1968.

complex as national demands are superimposed on the normal conflicts one finds within firms. Finally, bodies like the International Chamber of Commerce (I.C.C.) will develop into a form of businessmen's United Nations where issues relevant to the international business community will be discussed.

Profit motive, social conscience, racial problems and the Third World

Multinationals will become more involved with the developing world for two separate reasons. First, some multinationals will have to move into the developing world in order to survive, just as I.B.M.'s competitors were forced into Europe. As commercial success comes to mean higher and higher expenditures on research and marketing, some firms lacking the resources to survive in straight competition may take their chances in the politically complex world of the developing nations. They will not find this market easy, especially as economic nationalism develops still further. The companies meeting the challenge of the developing world will be the politically sophisticated which manage to convince the governments they deal with that maximum profit is not their sole motive. The second pattern of company involvement will emerge as pressure builds on large multinationals to invest a given proportion of their assets in the developing world. Since these companies are as big as nations, they will be expected to share some of the obligations that advanced countries have— the duty to provide aid to poor nations being one.

The day when a company need recognise a duty only to its shareholders is slowly ending. In order to survive, or in order to fight off the moral pressure put on them, company headquarters must accept a duty to invest in countries where investment risks are bad, or where freedom to remit profits is limited. Die-hard 'free enterprise' advocates will not like such moves, but they will be necessary if multinationals are to have a stake in the future. As it happens, several U.S. firms are now obeying a social conscience in their employment-training programmes for minority groups. Sceptics may question their motives, but what private enterprise has tried to do to alleviate the plight of the coloured worker would still make some of the more swashbuckling entrepreneurs of the early twentieth century rotate in their graves.

During the 1930's, an attempted scheme for training the 'disadvantaged' (mainly white) disappeared into oblivion. The 1954 Supreme Court ruling on desegregation was taken at first to have mainly political implications, so industrialists felt they should merely hire their token Negroes and avoid blatant discrimination. By the end of the 1950's it was clear that some positive action was needed from industry; in 1961 the White House called the leaders of U.S. business together, argued the case for raising the proportion of Negroes employed by the leading companies, and left the businessmen to get on with devising a scheme. The result was Plans for Progress, a businessmen's organisation, mandated and financed by the government, with a professional staff seconded at full pay for one-year periods from the sponsoring businesses. At the start, 91 companies employing 3·6 million, 5% being non-white, subscribed to the campaign. By 1969, 446 firms employing 9·7 million were involved. In particular, 10·4% of their labour force (1,007,757 in all) were non-whites. Obviously, the business community did produce results.

By 1967, the problem was more complex. Companies were employing their full quota of non-whites, but the ghettoes were still left with a large floating population of 'unemployables'. Without special action from the business community, these people would remain unemployed for the rest of their lives, a drain on the welfare system and of greater importance, likely to rear children who in turn would share their bad education, difficulty in getting jobs, and consequent destitution. President Johnson therefore called another meeting at the White House in which he asked business to employ 500,000 hard-core unemployed within three years. Each employer present promised to allocate about 1% of his vacancies to such cases, if the government paid the cost of necessary extra training. The meeting resulted in the formation of the National Alliance of Businessmen.

Henry Ford II became chairman, and Ford Motor Company sent one Vice-President full time to Washington. Chief executives of major firms were also appointed chairmen in 50 large cities. Each chairman delegated one of his top staff full time to the organisation of the local effort. They concentrated on getting employment for school dropouts, the unemployed aged under 22 or over 45, the physically handicapped, and those lacking training, with obsolete skills or a criminal record. The results were impressive. Within six months 12,000 private firms hired a total of 84,000 unemployables, 61,000 of whom stayed on the job (i.e., nearly three quarters). After a year, 15,000 firms had employed 178,000, of whom 102,000 stayed on. Obviously, one can question these figures. For one thing, the profile of the unemployable is fairly loosely drawn, so that some of these would have found work in a booming economy anyway. What is impressive, though, is that two thirds of the firms involved refused to take government money for their activities.

Simultaneously, many business leaders have supported activities aimed at improving urban environment. In the aftermath of the 1967 ghetto rioting in Newark and Detroit, a group of national leaders including Andrew Heiskell, the chairman of Time Inc., Walter Reuther of the U.A.W., John Lindsay, the Mayor of New York and Civil Rights leader Bayard Rustin, decided the time had come for a consortium to link the private sector, labour, the communities and the church. Their efforts resulted in the National Urban Coalition which named as President John Gardner, President Johnson's Secretary of Health, Education and Welfare. By 1969, similar coalitions existed in 44 cities round the nation. In New York, institutions like McGraw-Hill, Union Carbide, Consolidated Edison, the New York Stock Exchange and the Bowery Savings Bank all played important roles. Typically, the Urban League sponsored 16 street academies to help high school dropouts get back into the educational system. In Detroit, a similar body, the New Detroit Committee, raised 10 million dollars to spend in schemes like one which builds or rebuilds 'low to moderate' cost housing units for the Negro community. Local banks help supply mortgages and the scheme uses black developers and contractors wherever possible. Grants to another body in Detroit have spun off a black bank, the First Independence National Bank of Detroit, which Ford has promised to patronise with deposits.

Obviously, some firms are more active in this field than others. Among those with particularly notable records would be Ford, McGraw-Hill, Chase Manhattan Bank, Litton Industries, Equitable Life Assurance and General Electric.

By no means has private industry's involvement with the Negro community been consistently successful, but at least companies have been wrestling with problems somewhat like those of developing nations. Both the successes and failures are instructive.

The first lesson is that enthusiasm is not enough. Projects in the ghetto, just like any other projects, must be planned carefully with a market in mind. The tale of Watts Manufacturing Co., a subsidiary of Aerojet-General one of the Californian aerospace companies, illustrates this necessity. The idea for the company came from a distinguished chairman who had been born in Watts and was moved by the 1965 Watts riots. In 1966, Watts Manufacturing was created with a president and general manager (a Negro father-and-son team). Only after incorporation did they begin to think what the company might produce. They started with a military contract making tents for Vietnam and then diversified and expanded into wood pallets, containers, furniture and metal products. Soon they had 500 workers, but training was more expensive than anticipated (they had a turnover of 45% per annum), and untrained workers made mistakes with alien products. Moreover, government contracts were not always renewed, so they had to cut back their labour force to 300 in early 1969. Without any secure markets, the future looked bleak and losses ran into hundreds of thousands of dollars. Similar troubles were suffered in Boston when E.G. & G., a $112 million electronics company, tried setting up a labour intensive operation in the Negro slum of Roxbury. They decided to try making simple metal products and chose a manager who was skilled in training but knew little about metal products. They won a $575,000 training subsidy from Washington, but hoped-for government contracts never materialised, so they were training operatives with nothing to produce.

The companies which have done best in the ghetto have been those which have integrated the output of the new plants with company operations. Thus North American Rockwell runs a 'vestibule' operation in Los Angeles, N.A.R.T.R.A.N.S., in which the training operation is run basically as a plant in its own right. It supplies the parent company with seven types of products and services, four of which were covering their costs by 1969. I.B.M. established a plant in the centre of Bedford-Stuyvesant, a coloured area in Brooklyn. Planned as carefully as any other I.B.M. project, this enterprise produced components for the 360 computer range. Thus the plant enjoyed a guaranteed market. They chose as head of the operation a Swiss immigrant who had lived in Brooklyn. The five-man management team consisted of two whites and three blacks, all specialists who had worked an average of 10 years with I.B.M. To guard against overselling the scheme, they initially promised 100 jobs by the end of 1968, but actually produced 200. Of these workers, 83 had not finished high school, 112 were unemployed, and 40 had records of arrest. While absenteeism runs up to twice the average I.B.M. rate, the plan runs smoothly otherwise, even producing employees with promotion potential. Ultimate costs are higher than they might be because of the transport, sales, and property taxes of a city location. Second, sufficient land is difficult to find. In fact, the plant was not located in Harlem simply because a large enough site couldn't be found. And even using the largest available building in Bedford-Stuyvesant, they can create only 300 jobs in a community of 200,000.

Of course, some genuine commercial fall-out has occurred for companies involved in such schemes, since there is now a market for things like training packages for the disadvantaged. A firm with its own training scheme can easily adapt it for general use elsewhere. Thus firms like Corn Products, I.T.T., Bell & Howell, and Westinghouse—to name four—have diversified into this field. Other companies are even more ambitious. In the mid-1960's some Californian aerospace companies carried out projects for Los Angeles in which they turned their skills of systems analysis, developed for the aerospace industry, to the problems facing the city. They produced reports on topics like garbage disposal (an increasingly vital problem), the legal system, and water supplies, and came up with pioneering reports, though with the usual flaws of pioneering studies. I.B.M. now has a Civil Projects Division as a full branch of its U.S. operations. Basically, this division exists to see how I.B.M. can help in fields like water resources, traffic, urban development, police work, education, air and water pollution. Apparently, this division's activities may be extended to include the problems of the Third World. As an I.B.M. manager put it, the firm is in the problem solving business, and what bigger problem can one get?

It is far too soon to tell just how genuinely private enterprise will concern itself with social problems. After all, present enthusiasm could well follow to oblivion that enthusiasm for aid to the developing world which was genuinely strong during the late 1950's and early 1960's. Some firms, for instance, find it increasingly difficult to restrain their indignation when black activists fail to appreciate their efforts. In fact, some major companies have almost pulled out of several schemes because the recipients are not 'grateful'. On the other hand, firms have strong commercial reasons for getting involved. As governments (not just in the U.S.) realise how much effort is necessary to prevent urban environments from wrecking the people who live in them, markets grow. As governments switch the bias of their spending away from defence and toward health, education, etc., companies producing equipment good enough to be bought by the relevant institutions will prosper. However, there are problems involved with this market. Above all, in emotionally sensitive areas like social services, there will problably be heavy interference with the companies' freedom to set prices. One area due to grow rapidly is C.A.I. (computer-aided instruction) in which schools will buy computers, terminals and learning programmes, making an eventual market of at least $250 million. Two firms, I.B.M. and R.C.A., will probably dominate the field. Already Britishers worry that British schools will be forced to use commercially developed programmes to go with American-designed equipment. Moreover, the size of the companies involved is likely to raise questions about how much they should be allowed to profit from the educational needs of children. As with pharmaceuticals, one would expect a lot of government control in all countries. The companies may find themselves running their activities in such fields on a non-profit-making basis, as a form of social service to the community. Obviously, 'non-profit-making' would be meant in the broadest sense. Necessary research would require some profits, but it would be understood that no private shareholders would claim ultimate revenues, and that excess money after normal operational and research costs should be ploughed

197

back into the educational, or health fields, if necessary as an outright grant. In the past, the nearest we have come to such a system is the activities of charitable foundations set up by businessmen. But public pressure might force corporations into similar steps. The welfare services, for example, may increasingly find themselves dealing with a handful of multinational companies. But as long as the companies are run for profit, the relationship will always be uneasy. For education today, suppliers come in many shapes and sizes (chalk, blackboards, overhead projectors, textbooks are all provided by a reasonable number of competitive suppliers). Computer-Aided Instruction, by making education capital-intensive, will reduce the competition so much that there must be a considerable public revolt.

Once again, the lesson is clear. The multinationals will be moving in an environment demanding considerable political sensitivity and skill. But will they ever get involved seriously, as a matter of conviction, in the developing world? In the short run, no. Unlike the racial tension in the U.S. which actually can be seen to affect top management, the grievances of the developing world seem unjustified demands having little to do with the advanced world. If Indians starve in Bihar, only Indian national prestige and political stability is involved; but malnutrition in Harlem can mobilise Presidential action (sometimes), and create some social conscience even in American multinationals. For this limited step forward, observers of all political complexions must be grateful.

In the long run, the situation is more hopeful. For one thing, some companies will have to specialise in working with developing nations in order to survive. Italian companies like Fiat show that this strategy can be perfectly feasible. Second, any form of multinational involvement tends to lead to further involvement. After all, a company attracted to Brazil by the size of the market cannot forever stay aloof from Brazil's economic problems. In particular, as the local management of the subsidiaries becomes more experienced and indispensable, it can better pressure multinational headquarters for more favourable treatment for their nation. In the next section we will also see that international institutions representing world business may also impose global obligations on their members, much as the United Nations (whatever its failings) has obligated the richest countries to help the poorer ones.

So far we see that the problem of race in the U.S. and the problem of world economic development are in many ways similar. Both involve moral obligations for governments and companies which manipulate resources on a scale comparable to governments. Because the political system of the nation-state is well developed, the multinationals' social conscience will first be scaled to single nations. This has happened already in America. It is only a matter of time before company headquarters start discussing world obligations as seriously as they now discuss their roles in the ghettoes. Their motives may often be far from idealistic, their actions may often need watching with care, but, in the long run, they will make the effort. They will face the same problems as they face today in the ghettoes: the suspicion and hatred of the people they try to help; unskilled labour forces; badly rundown or non-existent infrastructures. The companies which thrive in the ghetto can also thrive in the developing world.

A Businessmen's United Nations?

The world is now filled with scores of international agencies all making decisions which affect businessmen in some way. G.A.T.T., U.N.C.T.A.D., I.B.R.D., F.A.O., E.C.O.S.O.C., U.N.I.D.O., O.E.C.D., O.A.S., I.M.F., B.I.S. all stand for agencies concerned with problems ranging from the freeing of capital movements through to those of the developing world. All make decisions which affect businessmen, and which businessmen often wish they could influence. These wishes reveal themselves in two ways. First, an increasing number of restricted meetings are held in which the business élite meet with government or international officials to think through given policy areas affecting them. Second, the body which comes nearest to deserving the title 'businessmen's United Nations', the International Chamber of Commerce, is taking a more and more active role in forming world investment, commercial and trading policies.

One industrial 'summit' meeting was held in Britain late in 1968. Called by the British employers federation, the C.B.I., a British and U.S. delegation met for three days to discuss their countries' balance of payments troubles as well as ways world trade might expand in the post-Kennedy Round era. The British were particularly interested in the behaviour of the multinationals' subsidiaries outside their home country. The two delegations included the chairmen of companies like Shell Transport and Trading, Caterpillar Tractor, I.C.L., Standard Oil (New Jersey), Courtaulds, Lockheed, British Steel Corporation, U.S. Steel—among others; vice-chairmen represented I.B.M., I.C.I., Bowater Paper, Unilever. Also present was the editor-in-chief of *Time*.

Other meetings are more international. In February, 1969, the United Nations arranged a summit meeting in Amsterdam on the problem of private foreign investment in the less-developed countries. On one hand were businessmen like David Rockefeller, Chairman of Chase Manhattan Bank, Sir Duncan Oppenheim, President of British American Tobacco, and Dr Pieter Kuhn, a director of Unilever. The governments and central bankers of some L.D.C.'s included Mr L. K. Jha, the governor of the Reserve Bank of India, Mr Ali Attiga, Libya's minister of planning, and Mr Tom Mboya, Kenya's late minister for economic and development planning. In the middle were officials and aides from various national agencies. All in all, fewer than fifty people attended.

Such meetings are increasingly common (and unreported in the press). Organising them most consistently is the International Chamber of Commerce, a body set up in 1919 in the era which produced the League of Nations and the International Labour Organisation. Up to the Second World War, it did little of note, but served as a forum for world traders. After 1945 and the growth of intergovernmental organisations, it set up a permanent consultative body to advise government representatives. Gradually, it has formed working arrangements with bodies like G.A.T.T., the World Bank, and the I.M.F., whereby the I.C.C. is formally consulted on their policies.

In 1969 the I.C.C. received the ultimate accolade when a special consultative committee was created in which an I.C.C. delegation would meet annually with the heads of the United Nations economic agencies (International Bank for Reconstruction and Development, International Monetary Fund, Food and Agricultural Organisation, the U.N. Conference on Trade, Aid and Development, the Development Programme, the Industrial Development Organisation, and the Economic and Social Council) as well as the director general of G.A.T.T. The I.C.C. thus has a formalised institution whereby it can exchange views or initiate dialogues with the relevant United Nations agencies. The international business community now has a say in the top councils of the world. As it happens, this step further formalises the business community's role in the world. There has been in the past a certain amount of personnel interchange from the various agencies to the I.C.C. For example, the consultative committee to the U.N. is chaired by Dr Marcus Wallenberg, a Swede who, as well as being former president of I.C.C., was also chairman of the business lobby to the O.E.C.D., the Business and Industry Advisory Committee. Similarly, the I.C.C. adviser on international trade policy is Jean Royer, a former deputy executive secretary of G.A.T.T.

To all but the initiated, this array of anonymous agencies is confusing. One fact, however, remains clear. The international business community is more active in world politics and its representatives are gaining more and more acceptance. But does the I.C.C. really represent the international business community? What kind of problems are they concerned with?

Basically, the I.C.C. is made up of national committees representing 42 countries. These committees normally cover the activities of trade associations, banking associations, more general businessmen's federations, chambers of shipping, etc. In another 30 nations, the I.C.C. has affiliated members who may be individual firms or individual associations of some sort. The main area where they are not represented is the communist world, though this may change. After all, many of the problems arising from international trade affect communist countries. By 1969, Bulgaria, Czechoslovakia, East Germany, Poland, Rumania and Yugoslavia had all been involved in arbitration arranged by the I.C.C. Hungary and Czechoslovakia's Chambers of Commerce both subscribe to an international code of advertising practice drawn up by the I.C.C. According to 1969 reports, the I.C.C. planned to continue a series of regular meetings with Chambers of Commerce from Eastern Europe to see where cooperation would benefit both sides. The most promising fields for discussion seem to be international arbitration, the I.C.C.'s code for advertising practice, the standardised procedure needed if goods are to be admitted temporarily to a country, and the proper documents for gaining credit during the trading process. Yugoslavia has an affiliated national committee, but more conservative communist nations will probably stay formally aloof for some years to come. For obvious reasons, the existing I.C.C. hierarchy are firm advocates of private enterprise, but are moving slowly away from the most extreme positions. Their policy statements on the developing world discuss the issue of local participation sanely and sympathetically. It is also clear that delegations from the less advanced nations are taking a more moderate line than some of their American colleagues. But, for the moment, communist countries will likely find the I.C.C. too capitalist in spirit and will probably limit themselves to exploratory talks and sending observers to I.C.C. conferences. On the other hand, the I.C.C. has gained reasonable acceptance amongst the developing world. Countries like India, Pakistan, Ceylon, Morocco, and most of those from Latin America are formally represented. Less formal representation comes from countries like Algeria, Burma, Iraq, Syria, Tanzania and Zambia—to cite ones which are most obviously concerned with the neo-imperialism threatened by international trade and investment.

If I.C.C. is not yet wholly representative of the international trading countries, it is also not fully representative of the multi-national companies. Looking through the biographies of businessmen involved in the numerous I.C.C. committees, one finds some glaring absentees. The major U.S. auto manufacturers seem under-represented, though a Ford executive is on the U.S. national committee. Likewise, the major U.S. chemical manufacturers are not yet active. On the other hand, long-established multinationals like Standard Oil (New Jersey) and I.B.M. are well represented. In fact, to an outsider, it looks as though I.B.M. is overly influential. For one thing, the Thomas J. Watson line 'World peace through world trade' tends to turn up at the top of I.C.C. publications. Then the I.C.C. president from 1967–9 was Arthur K. Watson, a Vice-Chairman of I.B.M. World Trade Corporation. Finally, leading I.B.M. executives from Argentina, Venezuela and Sweden are all active somewhere within the I.C.C. set-up. Other U.S. firms involved include Pan American Airways, General Electric, Merck & Co., whilst European multinationals like Unilever, Royal Dutch-Shell, Philips, I.C.I., Atlas Copce, Rhone-Poulenc, Saint-Gobain, Swissair, Sandoz, Hoffman-La Roche, Fiat, Pirelli, Olivetti, Montecatini-Edison, and A.E.G.-Telefunken are also active.

I.C.C. strategy seems to work on two levels. On one hand, it spawns a host of committees to standardise technical regulations in highly specialised fields. For instance, the development of containers has meant difficult work to standardise documentation, since a container may not only travel by road, rail, sea or air, during one journey, but may also be filled with goods belonging to more than one company. How then can documentation be simple enough to avoid delays at borders, etc., which start reducing the time savings containers otherwise make? The habit of leasing equipment, rather than buying outright, again creates problems, since different nations treat leased equipment in different ways. The spread of credit cards again demands uniform understanding round the world about how cardholders should be treated. In particular, the I.C.C. is campaigning to remove the host of non-tariff barriers which still distort trade even after tariffs have been reduced.

More ambitiously, the I.C.C. is working out a specific 'line' on issues such as ways to continue the expansion of international trade, and ways private investment can contribute to the development of the Third World. They hope by 1971 to have prepared a specific programme of action for the decade following the full tariff reductions agreed to in the Kennedy Round of the 1960's. They feel that this 'I.C.C. round' (as they hope to see it called) would give momentum to the drive which has slowed up since the signing of the Kennedy Round agreements, toward free movement of goods throughout the world. Basically, the industrialised countries would agree to dismantle all tariff and non-tariff barriers affecting manufactured goods within ten years of 1972. Obviously such a programme would include safeguards for countries particularly badly hit in the process. At the same time, the programme should foster exports from less-developed countries by extending all concessions to the manufactured goods of these countries, while still allowing them to protect their infant industries. Again, the application of tariff reductions to these developing countries should be carried out faster than the timetable for liberalisation between the advanced economies.

These proposals illustrate what is good about the I.C.C. Believing in free enterprise, it genuinely seems to oppose any form of protectionism. For instance, during President Johnson's administration, the deterioration of the U.S. balance of payments created feeling favouring some forms of protectionism within the U.S. Overtly, this took the shape of various guidelines for capital expenditure outside the U.S. The U.S. council of the I.C.C. worried sufficiently about this trend to help form the Emergency Committee for American Trade, which helped fight it. Again, the developing world seems to be playing a full part in the development process, liaising with the relevant agencies, making submissions of evidence, etc.

Clearly, the I.C.C. will develop further influence on the international scene. Although its underlying ideology may worry some people, it hopes to represent all those involved in international commerce, whether they come from developed or underdeveloped, communist or non-communist, countries. It obviously cannot ignore the justified complaints of the developing world when it has representatives from many of these countries playing important roles in the organisation.

Two final points need making. First, the I.C.C.'s philosophy of expanding world trade—a philosophy accepted by most well-meaning commentators—does have its side-effects. It will not really be enough in the long run to divide the world into two blocs—the developed which trades freely within itself, taking imports from the less-developed world without any barriers; and the less-developed bloc which will be allowed to protect its own interests. This will be far too simple a distinction, since within either of these blocs some countries will be more attractive than others, thus polarising each group. Within Europe the Mezzogiorno (South Italy) will probably be developed only by a European-wide regional policy, since Italy alone cannot offer enough incentives. It is a fact, perhaps unfortunate, that firms do not always follow the laws of the economic textbooks. With no practicable barriers separating advanced economies, firms will flock to the fashionable areas where other firms are locating. Thus American firms gravitate toward California; European firms toward the golden triangle of London, Paris and the Ruhr. These movements come at the expense of other areas in these continents, which lose out doubly since their best workers also emigrate to where the most work is. Traditional economics suggests that such polarisation should end when labour becomes scarce in the congested areas, or as their congestion grows. Bitter experience shows that nothing short of physically rationing the number of firms allowed to expand in the popular areas has any effect. An individual country can do something about such trends within its own borders, but the increasing freedom of trade and capital movements means they will escalate to a continental scale—where they can be countered only by concerted international policies. While supporting the basic I.C.C. philosophy about the importance of world trade, one must realise that such trade incurs costs. Obviously industry should be able to locate where it is most able to produce the maximum number of goods at the cheapest price; but, and this is a big qualification, if this freedom destroys local or national cultures then a balance must be struck. Industry should be subservient to social needs which may not be expressed solely through the market place.

The final point about the I.C.C. is that although it plays an active role in formulating the ground rules for private investment in the developing world, it has not yet seriously suggested that firms have a duty to contribute to this process. The world is still only just getting used to the idea of systematic aid to the developing world. Bodies like U.N.C.T.A.D., the most representative body of developing nations, are still new and somewhat chaotic (U.N.C.T.A.D.'s first conference was only in 1964). Such bodies are putting pressure on those institutions they are most used to, the governments of the advanced world. And yet the large firms are manipulating resources which give them the strength of some nations. For instance, it is ridiculous to monitor the aid performance of Switzerland, when aid agencies ignore General Motors which has a world sales turnover higher than the Swiss G.N.P. In many ways, multinationals can respond more easily to such pressures since they are relatively free from political checks and balances that governments must observe before making decisions. Providing they can make profits high enough to keep dividends moving upwards, their locations do not matter too much. U.N.C.T.A.D. therefore should start formulating a statement about what proportion of a multinational's assets should be located in the developing world. The details of this obvious demand could then be argued out in the I.C.C. What should the exact proportion be? Should companies tithe themselves—i.e., make contributions in proportion to their profits to, say, U.N. agencies which would then give the money out as a normal aid. I have heard executives from one firm briefly consider such a strategy. Alternatively, if firms invest a given proportion of their assets directly in the developing world, what should the ground rules be about dividend remission, the selling of equity to local interests, etc.?

A United Nations conference on the role of the multinational?

Some observers have gone further (notably Kindleberger,[1] 1969) and called for a conference on the role of the multinational corporation, to be held under U.N. auspices. As with all such conferences, a couple of years would be needed to prepare position papers. At the end of the conference, they would like to see the growth of an international agency like U.N.C.T.A.D. (a body not always very popular), which would collect all information about direct investment. It would also have some powers in the international anti-trust field, being able to prohibit investment which substantially reduced international competition, even if both countries had agreed to the investment. The body should also have powers to intervene in situations where two nations demand contradictory things from a firm and its subsidiary. This could happen, for instance, if a developing nation ordered a subsidiary to finance its activities in a way conflicting with guidelines from the parent country.

Such a call makes sense. At the moment, we badly lack information about the behaviour of private investment in the developing world, and collecting it would be useful for everyone concerned. Secondly, plenty of evidence shows that conflict between multinationals and individual countries is increasing. At the moment, such conflicts are dealt with on an *ad hoc* basis

[1] Kindleberger, Charles P., *op. cit.*, 1969.

which seems to work quite smoothly, by bodies like the arbitration courts of the World Bank and the I.C.C. But in the long run, a more publicly controllable system must develop—at the very least, the general guidelines for such bodies should be decided in public debate. Third, the need for some form of international anti-trust policy is clear. The balance between the giant multinationals and their smaller, national based competitors will be a delicate one. The multinationals might well be able to use profits earned elsewhere to support a price war which drives the national competitor out of business. Should such behaviour be monitored? If it should, then a general U.N. conference would help establish the principles at stake in such conflicts.

The more visionary commentators have sometimes gone one step further, suggesting that as multinationals spread round the world, their ownership and control should pass to the United Nations, itself. This 'U.N. syndrome' (as some jaundiced managers describe it) is obviously impracticable for anything but the very long term. First, the companies themselves have every reason to fight such moves. Managers will argue that, during disputes with governments, the active backing of their relevant home government is sometimes essential to what they see as their interests. The U.N. as the ultimate authority would be unlikely to intervene strongly in any dispute. Firms backed by the U.S.State Department would be very reluctant to lose its protection. Second, it is obvious that the U.N. itself is not ready for any such developments. For a body made up of so many different ideologies suddenly to accept control of the multinationals would involve a completely new thinking from many delegations.

If anything like this does happen, the moves toward it will be slow and gradual. It could happen like this. A U.N.-sponsored conference on multinationals should be possible by the end of the 1970's. Precedents suggest that it takes between 10 and 20 years for an issue to move from the stage when national governments perceive a problem, to the stage where global action is necessary. Although the aid programmes started in the late 1940's, it was not until the early 1960's that a U.N. body, U.N.C.T.A.D., was created to systematise the whole process. Again, pollution became a general, topical issue in

207

many countries in the early 1960's; but the first U.N. conference on the international implications of pollution is not due until 1971. If one assumes that the spate of writing on multinationals which has appeared since around 1966 is the beginning of a similar process, then he would expect U.N. action ten to fifteen years later. The momentum is there. The conflict in Latin America between nationalistic governments and the multinationals is evidence of the existing tension.

Once such a conference is called, then one would expect the creation of a U.N. agency to carry out global information-gathering and basic regulatory work. This body would probably have to become involved with anti-trust matters, since bodies like the I.C.C. could not be expected to develop such a policy, given their close links with the business community. From anti-trust policy to questions of ownership, etc., would be but a small step. The final stage would be some form of 'United Nationalisation' (!) in which the U.N. might actively take over control of some of the larger multinationals. This may sound extreme, but would really only be an international extension of a right which most national governments claim for themselves—the right to claim the assets of companies or industries which are particularly important to them. Two kinds of industries seem particularly susceptible to such takeovers. First, the transportation industries have always been vulnerable to nationalisation at the local level. On an international level, shipping and airlines are already subject to much international control. Through the 'conference' system, the shipping industry has successfully avoided any serious disruption to the world industry caused by new countries or firms flooding existing routes with more ships. The airlines fix prices all round the world, deliberately trying to avoid forcing some of the smaller national airlines out of business.

The basic problem of the airline industry is simple. It is above all an industry involving national pride. Every nation wants its own airline. Often it gets one by hiring planes from the giant carriers, painting its national colours on the fuselages, and claiming it as a national airline, even when the pilots are hired out by the giants as well. At the same time, it has become an industry where new competition is virtually impossible. The prices now quoted for the larger aircraft will guarantee that

208

only airlines with a world-wide route network and substantial supplies of capital will be able to buy them. At the lower end, the various medium-haul airbuses were selling in 1969 for around $17 million. The supersonic Concorde will come to $21 million or over. The Boeing Jumbo jet to around $25 million a plane, while the planned U.S. version of a supersonic passenger aircraft was budgeted to sell at $40 million. Since some of these planes also involve particularly expensive modifications to ground facilities (one U.S. airport opted out of receiving the 300-plus seaters since they would have had to spend $6 million to upgrade their facilities), it becomes plain that for most countries, a national airline is an unjustifiable expense.

However, even if they opt out of this expensive industry, their nationals will still fly, and it will seem unfair to them that the carriers should be profit-making bodies, whose success is mainly due to their being based in the most advanced economies at the time air travel started booming. Therefore, demands may grow for the long-distance carriers to be not just controlled, but also owned by an international body like a U.N. agency.

The second type of industry particularly vulnerable to 'internationalisation' could be one in which a single firm has become notably successful. I.B.M. furnishes the most likely example. As the dominant company in the world's most consistently growing industry, I.B.M. must persuade the world that its domination is beneficial to all concerned, or demands may grow to turn I.B.M. into an internationally-owned and controlled body forming the base of a global computer manufacturing utility.

In the long run, these problems will concern only the most visible multinational companies. What are the problems to be faced by the more typical firms?

How stable are the multinationals?

One of the arguments of this book has been that the very nature of the multinationals will have to change if they are to survive. The tradition of an authoritarian clique making fundamental decisions about company activities is no longer workable. Such a system can be run only so long as subordinates believe in the legitimacy of those at the top of the pyramid. To some extent, then, multinationals are by their nature self-destructive, since the introduction of nationalism into such organisations must turn them into alliances in which national interests (and one should not forget the interests of the various divisions) are pitted, one against the other. Because multinationals are moving in this direction, and because it is much harder to maintain rigid discipline over thousands of miles, we might well see a series of 'revolts' by subsidiaries against multinational headquarters.

Revolts within companies are by no means unknown, though fairly rare. Most are fairly simple cases of dissident directors winning the support of key financial interests behind the firm. Occasionally they have been more interesting. The legendary Howard Hughes (aerospace manufacturer, ex-Hollywood star-maker, property owner) has in fact been involved in major revolts at least twice. In the first case, 80 top scientists, engineers and managers walked out of Hughes Aircraft in 1953 because of basic policy disagreements with Hughes. Always hard to locate, Hughes delayed decisions and enforced whims like refusing to pave runways needed for airforce planes because he personally preferred the feel of landing on grass. Again, the management wanted to expand into electronics, while Hughes was only interested in government contract work. The dispute finally erupted into this mass walk-out. Later in the 1960's a similar battle was fought within Trans World Airlines (TWA), at that time also controlled by Hughes. The top management were increasingly disturbed that Hughes would not give them the chance to buy jets. They actually sued Hughes, arguing that his failure to give this remission was harming the company. Eventually the dispute was settled when Hughes sold his share-holdings in TWA (subsequently he used this money to buy heavily into Las Vegas). This case was particularly fascinating, since the top managers argued that a company's ultimate owners did not have the right to harm it by failing to make timely decisions.

One or two other cases have developed on a multinational level. The Varian Co. from California tried to take over Edwards High Vacuum, a British firm strong on vacuum freeze drying equipment. The board of Edwards High Vacuum agreed to the bid, but 12 senior executives and technicians threatened to resign on the grounds that they did not want to see the firm's technology taken out of Britain. Faced with this, Varian had to drop the bid. More complex was a revolt by the Italian subsidiary of Arthur G. McKee & Co., a Cleveland-based engineering firm. The company's Rome subsidiary, Compagnia Tecnica Industrie Petroli (C.T.I.P.), was its European foothold. It had been bought in 1966, while the Italian firm was in a shaky financial position after an unprofit-able contract in the United Arab Republic. With the American financial backing the Italian subsidiary flourished, signing up to build plants for firms like Gulf and B.P. In March, 1969, a newly appointed joint managing director met secretly with Technip, a government-owned French engineering firm. They signed a general agreement calling for a reshuffle of C.T.I.P.'s ownership among Technip, McKee and various Italian companies. McKee countered by getting the executive com-mittee to sack the person responsible for this, plus a couple of collaborators. Eight hundred and fifty employees then occupied C.T.I.P.'s Rome headquarters, brandishing banners with slogans like 'Let the profits go where the brains are.'

Of course, in their ultimate form, such revolts can have political roots. An oil major was building a refinery in Cuba round the time of Castro's revolution. For several years before this, observers in the company had noted that many of their Cuban technicians were football mad, often disappearing off to Czechoslovakia 'to watch the football.' When the revolution came, these technicians waited until the refinery was finished and all the components had been delivered and then occupied the office block on Castro's behalf.

Blatant revolts will probably be rare; after all, the courts will normally back up the property rights of the multinational, unless governments attack the company as well. On the other hand, the chances of revolt grow stronger as the companies employ higher proportions of local personnel in their foreign subsidiaries. A multinational which offends national suscepti-bilities, especially if the top management is visibly foreign, is likely to face acute nationalistic pressure from its subsidiary. Such a situation could prove serious for the company, since vital information might well be blocked or distorted by the subsidiary, thus making it even more difficult for the headquarters to control what is going on.

Anti-social multinationals?

I have usually assumed throughout this book that multinationals will be a reasonably benign force in the world, even though extreme vigilance will be necessary to curb some of the worse situations in the developing world. The problem of the company which abuses its power and corrupts governments is one which will continue to be with us for some time to come. How quickly it disappears depends first on the power of the governments to fight back. As this power increases, the firms most likely to survive will be the ones which cooperate with governments rather than fighting for everything. In Latin America, a firm like Standard Oil (New Jersey) takes a softer line with economic nationalists than Gulf Oil, which fights extremely hard when its strategic interests are threatened. If the Standard Oil approach gets the best results, then one would expect the more hardline companies eventually to soften their methods. At least, enlightened public opinion should get around to waging campaigns against companies whose overseas records are dishonourable.

What well may become more worrying is the growth of a number of companies which are actively dishonest, and who have gone multinational in order to escape supervision in closely-policed countries. The blitz against organised crime in the U.S. will lead to the shrewder operators settling down, say, in the Caribbean where the tourist industry is expanding fast, and where a number of small 'micro states' can be played off against each other. Since such companies pay little attention to public opinion anyway, they will be much harder to control than the traditional 'neo-colonialists' which owed their past profits to exploiting countries in the thrall of the old imperial powers. As opinion in these countries gradually renounces the worst type of exploitation, these traditional multinationals should become amenable to public pressure.

Of course it would be naïve to expect the fiercely individualistic characters around international business to become converted overnight. Many of them will still exploit every situation they can, and if the values of the more sensitive observers get trampled on, so much the worse. However, the high degree of education now required by the complexities of modern management, and the pressures of governments and managers all round the world, should ensure that the top men remain of reasonable good will. It would be unrealistic to expect them to volunteer concessions without being pressured, but they are probably more sensitive to informed criticism than ever before.

This book has presented the range of problems thrown up by the rise of the multinationals. We are slowly moving toward a world economy in which wage rates, prices, and interest rates become increasingly standardised. To some extent this is happening because governments are willing it to happen, but, more importantly, the dynamics of the multinational company are bringing it about whether governments will it or no. There is in fact a kind of vacuum in which such companies can find themselves outside any form of national control. Sometimes this matters, and this book has tried to identify these areas. Potentially, the multinational company is an overwhelming force for material progress in the world. The best of their products, we should accept; the political and social cost, we must not overlook.

BIBLIOGRAPHY

ADLER, JOHN H., ed. 1967. *Capital Movements and Economic Development*. Macmillan/St. Martins Press, London/New York.

ANSOFF, H. IGOR. 1969. *Business Strategy; selected readings*. Penguin, London.

BAIN, J. S. 1956. *Barriers to New Competition*. Harvard University Press.

BAIN, J. S. 1959. *Industrial Organization*. Wiley, New York.

BARANSON, JACK. 1968. 'Will there be an auto industry in the LDC's (Less Developed Countries) future?' *Columbia Journal of World Business*, Vol. 111, No. 3. May–June 1968, pp. 48–54.

BRADSHAW, MARIE T. 1969. 'U.S. exports to foreign affiliates of U.S. firms.' *Survey of Current Business*, May 1969, pp. 34–51.

BRASH, D. T. 1966. *American Investment in Australian Industry*. Australian National University Press.

BRENT, JOHN E. 1957. 'Case Study: I.B.M. World Trade Corporation: History, policy and organization.' International Management Association, special report.

BROOKS, JOHN. 1969. *Business Adventures*. Victor Gollancz, London, Weybright & Talley, New York.

BUCHAN, ALASTAIR, ed. 1969. *Europe's futures, Europe's choices; models of Western Europe in the 1970's*. Chatto & Windus, London.

CATHERWOOD, H. F. R. 1968. 'United States investment in Britain.' Paper obtainable from the National Economic Development Organisation, London.

CHANDLER, A. D. 1962. *Strategy and Structure*. Doubleday Anchor, New York.

CHORAFAS, D. N. 1968. *The Knowledge Revolution*. Allen & Unwin, London.

DEMAREE, ALLAN T. 1969. 'Business picks up the urban challenge.' *Fortune*, April 1969. pp. 103–5, 174–84.

DOUGLASS, WILLIAM. 1969. 'Business for the people.' *Management Today*, November, pp. 107–9, 180.

DUNNING, JOHN H. 1969. *The role of American investment in the British Economy*. P.E.P. broadsheet 507, London.

ERWIN, CLARENCE E. 1957. 'Case study: I.B.M. World Trade Corporation; Financial operations.' International Management Association, special report.

FALTERMAYER, E. K. 1963. 'It's a spryer Singer.' *Fortune*, Vol. 68, No. 6, pp. 145–8, 154–68 (reprinted in Ansoff, 1969).

FOOD & AGRICULTURAL ORGANISATION. 1969. *Indicative world plan for agricultural development*. F.A.O., Rome.

FREEMAN, CHRISTOPHER. 1965. 'Research and development in electronic capital goods.' National Institute for Economic Research, No. 34. Nov. 1965, pp. 40–9.

HARTSHORN, J. E. 1967. *Oil Companies and Governments*. Faber & Faber, London.

HELLER, ROBERT. 1968. 'The march of the multinationals.' *Management Today*, April 1968, pp. 98–103.

HOROWITZ, DAVID. 1969. *From Yalta to Vietnam*. Penguin. London.

HUFBAUER, G. C. & ADLER, F. M. 1968. *Overseas manufacturing investment and the balance of payments*. U.S. Treasury Department.

JAY, ANTHONY. 1967. *Management and Machiavelli; an Inquiry into the Politics of Corporate Life*. Hodder & Stoughton, London.

JENSEN, W. G. 1969. 'Two case studies of the role of American investment in the British economy: pharmaceuticals and electronics.' Appendix to Dunning, 1969.

KAHN, HERMAN & WIENER, A. 1968. *The year 2000: A Framework for Speculation on the Next 33 Years*. Crowell Collier.

KEEGAN, WARREN J. 1968. 'Acquisition of global business information.' *Columbia Journal of World Business*, Vol. 3, No. 2, Mar.-April, 1968, pp. 35–41.

KINDLEBERGER, CHARLES P. 1969. *American business abroad: six lectures on direct investment*. Yale University Press.

LAYTON, CHRISTOPHER. 1967. *Transatlantic Investment*. Atlantic Institute Press.

LAYTON, CHRISTOPHER. 1969. *European advanced technology; a programme for integration.* P.E.P./Allen & Unwin, London.

LEVINSON, CHARLES. 1969. 'Boardrooms selling Britain short.' Interview reported in *Guardian*, 26th May 1969. London.

LITVAK, I. A. & MAULE, C. J. 1968. 'Guidelines for the multinational corporation.' *Columbia Journal of World Business*, Vol. 3, No. 4, July–Aug. 1968, pp. 35–42.

LUMSDEN, ANDREW. 1968. 'Massey-Ferguson's billion dollar battle.' *Management Today*, October 1968, pp. 66–73, 146.

OGLESBY, CARL. 1968. 'The new Roman wolf.' *Interplay*, November 1968, pp. 30–8.

OKITA, SABURO & MIKI, TAKEO. 1967. 'Treatment of foreign capital—a case study for Japan.' Printed in Adler, ed., 1967.

PARKER, PETER. 1968. 'Multinational company; the significance of international management.' British Institute of Management Conference, London.

PEARSON COMMISSION. 1969. *Partners in Development.* Pall Mall Press, London.

PENROSE, EDITH & ODELL, P. R. 1968. *The Large International Firm in Developing Countries; the International Petroleum Industry.* Allen & Unwin.

PERLMUTTER, H. V. 1965. 'L'entreprise internationale—trois conceptions.' *Revue économique et sociale*, 23, No. 2, May 1965, pp. 151–65.

POLK, JUDD. 1968. 'The new world economy.' *Columbia Journal of World Business*, Vol. 3, No. 1, Jan.–Feb., pp. 7–15.

POLK, JUDD. 1968. 'NAFTA: sovereignty; infra, extra, supra.' *Columbia Journal of World Business*, Vol. 3, No. 5, Sept.–Oct. 1968, pp. 15–25.

REDDAWAY, W. B. 1967. *Effects of U.K. direct investment overseas; interim report.* Cambridge University Press.

REDDAWAY, W. B. 1968. *Effects of U.K. direct investment overseas: final report.* Cambridge University Press.

ROBERTS, E. & WAINER, H. A. 1968. Article on Route 128. *Science Journal*, December 1968.

ROBINSON, RICHARD D. 1967. *International Management.* Holt, Rinehart & Winston, New York/London.

ROBINSON, RICHARD D. 1968. 'The global firm-to-be; who needs equity?' *Columbia Journal of World Business*, Vol. 3, No. 1, Jan.–Feb. 1968, pp. 23–8.

ROLFE, SIDNEY. 1968. 'Updating Adam Smith.' *Interplay*, Nov. 1968, pp. 15–19.

ROLFE, SIDNEY. 1969. *The International Corporation*. International Chamber of Commerce, Paris.

ROSE, SANFORD. 1968. 'The rewarding strategies of multi-nationalism.' *Fortune*, 15th Sept. 1968, pp. 100–5, 180–2.

SAFARIAN, A. E. 1966. *Foreign Ownership of Canadian Industry*. McGraw-Hill.

SERVAN-SCHREIBER, JEAN-JACQUES. 1968. *The American Challenge*. Hamish Hamilton, London, Atheneum Publishers, New York.

SHONFIELD, ANDREW. 1969. 'Business in the twenty-first century.' *Daedalus*, Vol. 98, No. 1, Winter 1969.

SWANN, D. & McLACHLAN, D. L. 1967. *Concentration or Competition; a European dilemma?* Chatham House/P.E.P., London.

THAYER, GEORGE. 1969. *The War Business*. Weidenfeld and Nicolson, London.

VERNON, RAYMOND. 1968. *Manager in the International Economy*. Prentice-Hall.

VERNON, RAYMOND. 1969. 'The role of U.S. investment abroad.' *Daedalus*, Vol. 98, No. 1, Winter 1969.

WATKINS, M. H. *et al.* 1968. (Canadian Task Force report.) *Foreign ownership and the structure of Canadian industry*. Ottawa, Queens Printer.

WISE, T. A. 1966. I.B.M.'s $5,000,000,000 gamble.' *Fortune*, September 1966, pp. 118–23, 224–8.

WISE, T. A. 1966. 'The rocky road to the market place.' *Fortune*, October 1966, pp. 138–43, 201–12.

ZENOFF, DAVID B. & ZWICK, JACK. 1969. *International Financial Management*. Prentice-Hall.

ZINKIN, MAURICE. 1968. 'Multinational companies.' *Moorgate & Wall Street*, Fall 1968.

INDEX

Abernathy, Rev. Ralph, 100
A. B. SVENSKA SKOLASTFABRIKEN, 129
ADELA INVESTMENT COMPANY, 114
Adler, F. M. (Hufbauer-Adler Report, 1968), 68
A.E.G.-TELEFUNKEN, 203
AEROJET-GENERAL, 195
AFRICAN DEVELOPMENT BANK, 121
Agency for International Development (A.I.D.), 122–3
AGFA-GEVAERT, 181–2
AGIP, 125
Agnelli, Giovanni, 11, 124
A.K.U., 2, 181
ALCAN ALUMINIUM, 141, 168
ALLIED BREWERIES, 182
Amalgamated Engineering Federation (A.E.F.), 102
AMERADA PETROLEUM, 146
AMERICAN CYANAMID, 41
AMERICAN VISCOSE (subsidiary of COURTAULDS), 54
ANACONDA, 130
ANGLO-AMERICAN CORPORATION, 130, 151
ANGLO-IRANIAN (now BRITISH PETROLEUM), 143–4
Anti-Trust, 49–55, 165
  and I.B.M., 137–8
  in U.S., 15
ARABIAN OIL COMPANY, 147, 164
Arbenz, Jacobo, 139–40
Argentina
  and FIAT, 126
  economics of auto production, 110

ASEA, 48
ASIAN DEVELOPMENT BANK, 121
Assembly Policies—see Less-Developed Countries
ASSOCIATED ELECTRICAL INDUSTRIES (A.E.I.), 56, 178
ATLANTIC RICHFIELD, 53
ATLAS COPCE, 203
Attiga, Ali, 200
AUGUST THYSSEN-HÜTTE, 180
Australia
  assembly policy (auto industry), 109–10
  U.S. investment in, 7–8
AVIONICS-SYSTEMS ENGINEERING G.M.B.H., 182
AVIONS MARCEL DASSAULT, 184

BADISCHE ANILIN UND SODA FABRIK (B.A.S.F.), 30, 52, 55, 176
Bahamas
  gambling and the Mafia, 79
  tax haven, 77
Bain, J. S., 32
Baranson, Jack, 110, 117
BARREIROS DIESEL S.A., 28
Barreiros, Don Eduardo, 28
BAYER, 50, 176
BEECHAMS, 31, 52
BELL AND HOWELL, 196
BERGER, JENSON AND NICHOLSON, 181
BERLIET, 29, 46, 181
Betancourt, President, 145
BILLERUD, 93
B.M.W., 29
BOEING, 53

219

DATE DUE
